BEATING
BURNOUT

BEATING BURNOUT

Balanced Living for Busy People

HOW TO BEAT BURNOUT
BEFORE BURNOUT

Two Bestselling Works Complete in One Volume

Frank Minirth, M.D. • Paul Meier, M.D.
Don Hawkins, Th.M. • Chris Thurman, Ph.D.
Richard Flournoy, Ph.D.

INSPIRATIONAL PRESS

NEW YORK

First Inspirational Press edition published in 1997.

Inspirational Press
A division of Budget Book Service, Inc.
386 Park Avenue South
New York, NY 10016

Inspirational Press is a registered trademark of Budget Book Service, Inc.

Published by arrangement with The Moody Bible Institute of Chicago.

Library of Congress Catalog Card Number: 96-79818

ISBN: 0-88486-162-7

Printed in the United States of America.

CONTENTS

HOW TO BEAT BURNOUT

by

Frank Minirth, M.D.
Don Hawkins, Th.M.
Paul Meier, M.D.
and Richard Flournoy, Ph.D.

CONTENTS

CONTENTS

HOW TO BEAT BURNOUT

ACKNOWLEDGMENTS

The authors would like to gratefully acknowledge those whose contributions helped to make this book possible.

Special thanks goes to a number of people who risked burnout to type and compile the manuscript. Those include Carol Mandt, Teresa Pakiz, Debra Stack, Jim Schneider, and Kathy Short.

Further thanks goes to Marty Williams Anderson for extensive writing and editorial work, which included coordinating the efforts of four different authors.

INTRODUCTION

While in north Dallas recently I decided to take advantage of a couple of hours' free time to pay an old friend a visit. I hadn't seen him in several years, but a mutual friend had mentioned his name to me the previous week, and I decided to look him up.

An elevator gently whisked me into the heart of a glass-and-steel skyscraper, and I stepped off into the plush reception area of a major radio station. It was quite a contrast to the Spartan central Texas studios where Bob had first introduced me to radio broadcasting.

The receptionist smiled and asked, "May I help you?" When I explained that I had dropped by to visit Bob, I was shocked by her response. Her face reacted as if she had been hit. Her voice quivered, and tears came to her eyes. Choking, she whispered, "You haven't heard?"

"What happened?" was all I could reply.

It took her a minute to form the words. "Bob is dead! A little over a year ago. We just couldn't believe it."

Several memories flashed through my mind, like slides in rapid-fire sequence. Bob's pleasant laughter when I threw the wrong switch on my first encounter with a radio control board. Pleasant mornings spent drinking coffee and discussing the ins and outs of radio production. Bob's patience in handling equipment failures. Bob and I with our wives attending a Billy Graham Crusade at Texas Stadium. The smile on Bob's face when he told me he had been appointed operations manager of a major Dallas station.

My mind replayed tapes of numerous conversations, on subjects ranging from spiritual to political to nonsensical. Still, I couldn't quite grasp the full impact of what I had just been told. After all, Bob was only a few years older than I. The last time I saw him, he seemed in prime health. What happened?

Prodding back her tears, the receptionist continued. "We really miss Bob. We still can't believe it." She went on to explain that Bob had encountered two major job failures and the breakup of his marriage, all within a short span of time.

I waited for an opportunity to phrase my question. "Did he have an accident? A heart attack?"

I'll never forget her reply: "No," she said, "Bob died of natural causes. Even the doctor said Bob just burned out."

Burnout, a term heard with increasing frequency these days, is becoming a prominent fact of life in the fast-paced and stress-filled final decades of our twentieth century. In gathering material for this book, we discovered that people in all walks of life are experiencing burnout, perhaps as never before. We have found burnout within our own families, our counseling staff, our colleagues in ministry, and in the lives of a large proportion of those people to whom we minister. Most of us have experienced some degree of burnout, at least short term, or we have been close to someone who has. All of us writing this book know what burnout is firsthand.

Except for a few such as Bob, or those who use suicide as a way of escape, most of us eventually recover from burnout to some degree.

Yet many wait too long to counter its effects or try dead-end roads to ease the strain. They end up losing their jobs, their health, and sometimes their families. They may never recover from those effects.

That is the bad news.

The good news is that there is hope for recovery from burnout. And there are warning signs that can be used to prevent you or those close to you from ever experiencing burnout. That good news is our reason for writing this book.

DON HAWKINS

1

WHAT IS BURNOUT, AND WHO GETS IT?

No one expected Catherine to experience burnout; but that's exactly what happened. Raised in east Texas, the third of four daughters, Catherine grew up in a Christian home, trusted Christ as her Savior at an early age, committed and dedicated her life to Him in junior high, and served as the president of her church youth group in high school.

During her early years, however, another drive also began developing with her. As Catherine puts it, "My sisters did well, so I felt pressure to do well, to be smart like they were." Although personable and extremely attractive—enough so to later work as a model—Catherine had a poor self-concept. "I just didn't think very much of myself; I felt the need to prove myself all the time. Even though my parents were loving and accepting, I put a lot of pressure on myself to do well. For example, in school I expected to make A's even though I wasn't an A student."

Those internal pressures hit head on with external stress in college and nursing school, where Catherine began to experience the warning signs of burnout. "There wasn't a lot of time for rest. After classes all day there was work in the hospital, and I often skipped meals and sometimes slept four or five hours a night." During that time, Catherine also started modeling to help pay bills. That added more pressure to her time schedule. "There was no time for outside activities or hobbies, just for school and work."

Soon Catherine began having trouble sleeping. She says, "I just couldn't handle the pressure. I cried a lot; my grades began dropping; I just felt exhausted all the time. When I finally finished school, I didn't want to be a nurse, or even want to be around doctors, nurses, or medicine. In fact, I didn't care if I ever took my state board exams. I graduated from nursing school a semester late, decided to forget about nursing, and went to work as a secretary. I was really burned out."

Burnout is when one's attitude becomes "a job is a job is a job," according to Edelwich and Brodsky, authors of one of the first books on burnout. To them, job burnout is when people get to the point of just putting in their time, not making waves, and just barely getting by or going through the motions.

Psychologist Herbert Freudenberger, who claims credit for the term, says that burnout is a depletion of energy and a feeling of being overwhelmed by others' problems.

According to psychologist Christina Maslach, an early researcher of the problem, burnout is "a syndrome of emotional exhaustion, depersonalization, and reduced personal accomplishment that can occur among individuals who do 'people work' of some kind."[1]

In our own experience in counseling, burnout victims show those same three factors. Feeling physically and emotionally exhausted, victims frequently cannot face the future, and they detach themselves from interpersonal closeness. Sensing themselves to be drained emotionally, they also suffer spiritually.

1. Christina Maslach, *Burnout—The Cost of Caring* (Englewood Cliffs, N.J.: Prentice-Hall, 1982), p. 3.

The detachment leads to depersonalization—looking down on people, reacting negatively to them, and developing an attitude of "I wish people would go away and leave me alone."

That attitude toward others, coupled with a feeling of emotional exhaustion—especially when seen in compassionate Christians and workers in the caring professions—results in a reduction in personal accomplishment. A feeling of diminishing accomplishment leads to stronger feelings of personal inadequacy, which further reduces accomplishment. And thus the vicious cycle of burnout is established.

A well-known business consultant believes that burnout is a major reason American industry today has such a hard time achieving gains in productivity.

THE ROLE OF STRESS

One of the most common definitions of burnout describes it as a loss of enthusiasm, energy, idealism, perspective, and purpose. It can be viewed as a state of mental, physical, and spiritual exhaustion brought on by continued stress.

Although a certain amount of stress is common, perhaps inevitable, and some stress is positive, too much stress over too long a time can result in burnout. Too much burnout, without learning and applying certain coping techniques, can lead to clinical depression. We might view this on a continuum as follows:

Stress ⟶ Burnout ⟶ Depression

Dr. Hans Selye, probably the most widely recognized authority on stress, defines stress as our body's response to any demand made upon it. He divides stress into two types: (1) *distress*—excessive levels of continued, damaging stress, and (2) *eustress*—a good, positive kind of stress one feels at times of happiness, fulfillment, or satisfaction.

Although some stress is necessary for everyday living and, in lesser amounts, even for learning and growth, large, continued (chronic) amounts of stress, even eustress, can debilitate people mentally, physically, and spiritually. We do not, therefore, want to eliminate all stress from our lives, but we do need to learn how to better handle and manage the necessary stresses of life.

BURNOUT OF THE WHOLE MAN

Too much stress and burnout affect the whole person—physically, emotionally, and spiritually. Physical symptoms can include anything from ulcers and digestive upsets to coronary problems. Often a burnout victim experiences a constant sense of fatigue, coupled with an inability to sleep. Emotionally, a burnout victim often suffers from depression. That results from being angry with oneself because of an inability to function at one's previous high performance level. Spiritually, burnout victims often reflect what could be called a "Martha complex"—extreme anxiety over proving one's self-worth by serving God and others.

That syndrome is illustrated in the gospel of Luke, when Jesus visits the home of Mary and Martha. Martha became overly involved in housework and felt her sister Mary should help her instead of sitting and listening to Jesus teach. Not only did Jesus tell Martha that her priorities were wrong, but He gently and carefully explained to Martha that, because of her anxiety over work, she was "tied up in knots" (Luke 10:41). That is the literal meaning of Jesus' original words, which can be translated "cumbered about," "anxious and bustling," "worried and bothered," or "upset." Many people can relate to Martha's anxiety in trying to prove their self-worth through their work.

Each of us is a potential target for burnout. Increasingly we find symptoms showing up in ministers, lawyers, physicians, housewives, psychologists, social workers, police officers, parents, computer professionals, nurses, industrial workers, secretaries, counselors, corporate executives, managers, missionaries, teachers, and students. Half the parents in America—according to professor Joseph Procaccini, as well as one of five ministers today—according to an Alban Institute survey—suffer burnout.

One of the tragic paradoxes of burnout is that the people who tend to be the most dedicated, devoted, committed, responsible, highly motivated, better-educated, enthusiastic, promising, and energetic suffer from burnout. Why? Partially because those people are idealistic and perfectionistic. They expect too much of themselves as well as of others. Also, since they started out performing above average, others continue to expect from them those early, record-breaking results over the long haul, even though no one would expect a runner in the one-hundred-yard dash to keep up that same speed in a cross-country run.

Burnout is:

- a parent feeling overly responsible when a child does something seriously wrong
- a missionary who uses a relatively minor health problem as an excuse for escaping the burdens and frustrations of living in a foreign culture
- a pastor, who is idealistic and overcommitted, try-

ing to please everyone in his congregation and feeling guilty when he doesn't

- a nurse in a large hospital who takes her time or even ignores a patient's buzzer request for attention
- a mental health worker who just doesn't seem to care any more
- a factory worker who goes to lunch and doesn't return
- a doctor who finds himself avoiding certain patients
- an artist sensing that his creativity is expressionless
- an alcohol rehabilitation counselor drinking more and more, while complaining about his clients who drink
- a school principal griping about her teachers
- a teacher griping about her students
- a business executive who finds himself unable to function at his previous level
- a salesman who has become so depressed that he is considering suicide
- a homemaker who finds herself in total despair after taking on too many activities

These examples are taken from cases of burnout treated in our clinic. More about these individuals, their particular symptoms, and their recoveries will be given in later chapters.

BURNOUT IN HUMAN SERVICES

Burnout is the end result of prolonged job-related or personal stress. The helping professions—nurses, doctors, pastors, social workers, and therapists, for example—seem to be particularly prone to burnout.

Why? Human services workers, who deal with other people's personal problems, are employed in highly stressful occupations.

We've encountered a psychologist who left his profession to go to work in an oil field, a social worker who left her job to open up a ceramics shop, and a teacher who abandoned his field for a sales position. All of them had one thing in common: they were dedicated people in human service professions who left their careers, not just because of salary considerations, but because they were disillusioned and headed toward burnout if they did not change their outlook or their profession.

Many people change jobs because they are burned out. Although one person left his job as a psychologist to work in an oil field, another left a stable and secure administrative position in state government with a fixed salary to join a private psychiatric clinic. Even though his monthly salary would no longer be guaranteed, he preferred practicing individual and group therapy to doing reams of institutional bureaucratic paperwork, which was leaving him increasingly frustrated and burned out.

THE THREE BURNOUT AREAS

1. *Mental.* Burnout shows up mentally in the form of a feeling of disillusionment or failure as a person or worker. Signs of anger, cynicism, negativism, or increased irritability spring up. Burnout victims may feel frustrated by a sense of helplessness, hopelessness, or self-doubt, which then may lead to depression. Another common sign is guilt—false guilt over trying to be overly responsible or committed, a feeling of not doing something perfectly or well enough. Other symptoms of mental or emotional burn-

out include apathy, difficulty concentrating or pay ing attention, decreased self-esteem, feelings of disenchantment, disillusionment, disorientation, or confusion.

2. *Physical.* Throughout the years of our counseling, we have observed that continued stress and burnout may bring on backaches, neck aches, headaches, migraines, insomnia, loss of appetite (or a never-satisfied appetite), ulcers, high blood pressure, constant colds, digestive problems, allergies, or in the most severe forms of continuing stress and burnout, heart attacks and strokes.

In many people, unrelieved, unresolved tension and stress result in their turning to alcohol or drugs, either prescription or over-the-counter, for temporary relief. The decreased energy and fatigue symptomatic of drugs tend to worsen an already burned-out feeling.

3. *Spiritual.* Some people experience spiritual exhaustion with burnout. Such individuals seem to have lost perspective and have failed to recognize their own limits. They usually experience a gradually increasing feeling that God is powerless and that they themselves are the only ones with the power to help in their current situation. Without realizing what they are doing, they refuse—consciously or unconsciously—to rely on God's power and try to play God themselves. They may drop times of personal spiritual meditation and Bible reading, only to feel as if they are in a spiritual vacuum where nothing or no one appears to be able to help. Then as time passes, they realize that their own power, or energies, are not enough either. They become disillusioned or feel like giving up, believing that others, including God, have given up on them.

Like Solomon, they may describe the advanced effects of their burnout in terms similar to this:

> So I hated life, because the work that is done under the sun was grievous to me. All of it is meaningless, a chasing after the wind. I hated all the things I had toiled for . . . because I must leave them to the one who comes after me. And who knows whether he will be a wise man or a fool? Yet he will have control over all the work into which I have poured my effort and skill. . . . This too is meaningless. So my heart began to despair over all my toilsome labor under the sun. For a man may do his work with wisdom, knowledge and skill, and then he must leave all he owns to someone who has not worked for it. This too is meaningless and a great misfortune. What does a man get for all the toil and anxious striving with which he labors under the sun? All his days his work is pain and grief; even at night his mind does not rest. This too is meaningless. (Ecclesiastes 2:17-23)

At the beginning of this chapter we learned of Catherine's experience with burnout, which parallels that of many people today. Some never recover, but Catherine did. In fact, the secretarial job she took was at the Minirth-Meier Clinic. As she describes it, "It seems God put me in just the right place to be able to recover from burnout and to ultimately become involved again in my chosen field of nursing."

And how did Catherine recover from burnout? "I first recognized that I was burned out; then I began doing something about it. I learned to take care of myself physically. I cultivated my spiritual life. I developed outside interests. And perhaps most important of all, I learned not to be so hard on myself, to allow myself to fail occasionally, and to forgive myself when I did fail."

The rest of this book is dedicated to sharing the kind of insights Catherine discovered, insights that can help individuals beat burnout. We will explore the symptoms of burnout—the warning signs—to help those who may be approaching burnout recognize the dangers before they become devastating. We will examine significant causes of burnout, including early-life factors, personality factors, stress and environment factors, and a surprisingly significant element to which Christians can be particularly susceptible.

Finally, we will discuss positive steps for reversing burnout, steps that, if taken, can make it possible for former burnout victims such as Catherine to lead healthy, productive, balanced lives.

Burnout is serious, but for those who are feeling its effects, there is hope.

2

WARNING: DOWNWARD
SPIRAL AHEAD!

In the fall of 1900, a massive hurricane struck the Texas gulf coast. The city of Galveston, lying squarely in the path of the storm, bore the brunt of the hurricane winds and accompanying tidal wave. More than six thousand people lost their lives.

Today, more than eight decades later, when hurricanes roar across the Atlantic to hit the east or south coasts, only a few lives are lost. Why? Because advance warning techniques have improved vastly since the turn of the century. Now hurricane watches and warnings are widely broadcast. And people in threatened areas heed the storm warnings and evacuate to safety.

Just as meteorologists can now recognize certain signs as storm warnings of an approaching hurricane, so psychologists today can recognize storm warnings—symptoms of approaching burnout—that need to be heeded. Such warnings tend to build on top of one another. As Freudenberger notes, they involve:[1]

Exhaustion. Lack of energy associated with feelings of tiredness and trouble keeping up with one's usual round of activities are the first warning signs of burnout.

1. Herbert Freudenberger and Geraldine Richelson, *Burn-Out* (New York: Anchor, Doubleday, 1980), pp. 62-66.

Detachment. The next warning sign is putting distance between oneself and other people, particularly those people with whom one has had close relationships. People on the edge of burnout have less time and energy for relationships, since more and more of their time and efforts are concentrated on just "keeping up."

Boredom and cynicism. According to Freudenberger, boredom and cynicism are "natural companions. One begets the other; detachment begets them both." The burnout victim "begins to question the value of friendships and activities—even of life itself."

Increased impatience and irritability. Usually burnout victims are people who have been able to do things quickly. However, as burnout takes hold, their own ability to accomplish things diminishes, and their impatience grows and causes flare-ups with others. They blame family and coworkers for things that were their own fault more than the fault of others.

A sense of omnipotence. Some burnout victims may have thoughts such as "Nobody can do my job better than I," or "Only I can do it, nobody else." They may also think subconsciously—while denying it consciously—that "Not even God can do it, only me. I'm more powerful and see things more correctly than anyone, even God." Obviously, that form of exaggerated subconscious thinking, which is not unusual among burnout victims, borders on the delusional.

Feelings of being unappreciated. Burnout victims experience complex feelings of bitterness, anger, and resentment because they are not being appreciated more for their added efforts. Why not? Because those added efforts, instead of producing added results, are generating reduced results. Rather than acknowledging that, they blame others for their reduced results.

Change of work style. Reduced results and conflicts with colleagues and other work-related contacts will eventually cause one of two things to happen. Either the victim will withdraw from decisive leadership and work habits, or he or she will seek to compensate for the conflicts by becoming more and more tyrannical, demanding, or inflexible, which only causes the cycle of burnout to worsen.

Paranoia. Once burnout has taken long-term hold, it is a small step from feeling unappreciated to feeling mistreated or threatened. The advanced burnout victim may sense that someone is "out to get me."

Disorientation. As burnout continues long-term, the victim will have increasing difficulty with wandering thought processes. Speech patterns will falter, concentration spans will become increasingly limited, and the ability to remember names, dates, or even what he or she started to say will diminish. The victim may jokingly refer to having a problem of increasing old age or senility, but increasing agitation and inward stress are the problem.

Psychosomatic complaints. Physical ailments seem more conventional and therefore easier to accept than emotional ailments. The following physical complaints will flourish in the burnout victim: headaches, lingering colds, backaches, and similar complaints. These physical symptoms are frequently induced or at least prolonged by the burnout victim's emotional stress. The complaints may have real physical causes, but, more than likely, they are brought on by emotional stress, which the sufferer may not want to admit. Often, the victim focuses more on physical complaints than usual, as those become the "scapegoat," on one end of the spectrum, for the person's emotional condition and, on the other end, for the negative work results of his burnout.

Depression. There are differences between a generally depressed state and the form of depression that usually signifies burnout. In burnout, "the depression is usually temporary, specific, and localized, pertaining more or less to one area of life." The depression of most burnout victims is apt to be anger at other people for causing his or her problems.

Major depression. Some depressed burnout victims will experience major depression, a *generally* depressed state that is usually prolonged and pervades all areas of a person's life. Furthermore, the generally depressed person has turned blame for negative circumstances towards self. Instead of being angry with others, he or she tends to feel guilty for everything that is going wrong.

Suicidal thinking. As depression associated with burnout progresses, the result can be suicidal thinking. Suicide is the tenth leading cause of death in the U.S. Ten percent of individuals who make suicidal gestures eventually die of suicide. Certain personality types, such as the hysterical personality, may make suicide threats or gestures that are manipulative in nature only. However, obsessive-compulsive personalities are more likely to make actual suicide attempts.

CASE EXAMPLES

Some victims of burnout treated in our clinic were mentioned in chapter 1. Those include:

The parent who felt overly responsible when a child did something seriously wrong. A Christian mother, Mrs. A, did a reasonably good job in raising her children, as did her husband. Yet one child grew up and lived in total rebellion against God. When Mrs. A looked back on her life, she remembered circumstances in which she didn't act in the way she believed a perfect mother should have. As a result, she blamed herself totally for the child's failure. She suffered from false guilt and major depression.

The missionary who used a relatively minor health problem as an excuse for escaping the burdens and frustrations of living in a foreign culture. After several years of being a foreign missionary, Mr. B found he really did not enjoy missionary work as much as he thought he would and felt he had made a mistake. He thought he could serve God better in the U.S. in a different capacity. And yet he was embarrassed to come back and tell his supporters that he had decided not to be a missionary any more. He blamed a relatively minor health problem on his decision to return to the U.S. Then he felt guilty about using that as an excuse.

Mr. B's burnout symptoms included exhaustion from "culture shock" (which normally involves impatience and irritability when coming upon so many obstacles in a different or slower culture that make it impossible to accomplish as much as one can in one's own culture), withdrawal from decisive leadership, psychosomatic complaints (which had some basis, but relatively minor), and depression involving guilt—guilt from giving up and guilt from blaming his withdrawal on what was, at best, a half-truth.

The pastor who is idealistic and overcommitted, trying to please everyone in his congregation and feeling guilty when he doesn't. The Reverend C showed up for every meeting, for all the missionary society meetings and Sunday school meetings, and he felt guilty whenever he didn't. Whenever anyone asked him for counseling, he went ahead and saw them, even when his schedule was already full. As a result, he was ignoring his own personal needs, was not getting enough sleep, and was not spending enough time with his wife or children. He felt guilty about not spending enough time with his family, which was in danger of falling apart, and he also felt guilty whenever he said no to anyone in his congregation. Reverend C's symptoms included exhaustion, detachment (from family), and major depression (including guilt).

The nurse in a large hospital who was taking her time or even ignoring patients' buzzer requests for attention. A conscientious nurse, Miss D normally took good care of her patients. Because of her long working hours, however, and grudges she had toward her supervisor, she became clinically depressed. Her supervisor expected too much, including requiring her to work overtime too many weekends. Afraid of losing her job, Miss D said nothing about the long hours. Finally, she reached the point of losing her motivation, resulting in poor work. When she got to the point of ignoring patients' buzzers, she sought out our counseling help.

Miss D's symptoms included exhaustion, detachment (from patients), cynicism, feelings of being unappreciated, a change of work style, paranoia (fear of being fired if she requested fewer hours), depression (accompanied by anger toward her supervisor for her problems).

The mental health worker who just didn't seem to care any more. Mrs. E did a lot of counseling in a psychiatry unit. She helped many people who suffered from depression, and she loved her patients. Yet talking to people fifty to sixty hours a week about depression finally got to her. She started to get clinically depressed herself. Mrs. E's symptoms included exhaustion, boredom and cynicism, feelings of being unappreciated, and depression.

The factory worker who went to lunch and didn't return. An eighteen-year-old recent high school graduate, Mr. F had landed a factory job that paid well. At first he liked the job. It wasn't difficult, he had opportunity to meet people of all ages, and "it sure beat doing schoolwork." But spending all of his time on an assembly line, turning a screw on a part, repeating the process thousands of times a day, all day long, forty hours a week eventually began to get to him. Because of the monotony, the noise level, and the heat in the nonair-conditioned factory building, Mr. F became burned out. One day he went to lunch and didn't come back, planning to quit his job.

Mr. F's symptoms were exhaustion, boredom, feelings of being unappreciated, irritability, and depression (accompanied by anger toward those who were making him work in an undesirable work environment).

The alcohol-rehabilitation counselor who was drinking more and more, while complaining more and more about his clients who drank. For most of his life, Mr. G had not been a drinker. He enjoyed people and enjoyed working with them, but he was finding himself becoming more and more frustrated. A number of the alcoholics with whom he was working were poorly motivated and were not getting better. They would not do what they needed to do to get over their problems. That made Mr. G angry, because he wanted them to get better, both because he loved them and also because their refusal to get better made him feel powerless.

As a result, Mr G became increasingly angry and began drinking himself. The drinking brought on a greater depression, physically related, by lowering the serotonin level in his brain. He then began drinking to excess, which made him feel temporarily numb to his pain. However, the day after a drinking bout he would be even more depressed.

Mr. G's symptoms were detachment, impatience and irritability, feelings of being unappreciated, and major depression (from both physical and psychological causes).

The business executive who found himself unable to function at his previous level. A highly energetic and intelligent man, Mr. H had risen to the presidency of his company by the time he was forty. When he reached fifty, however, he was still trying to maintain the sixty-hour week that had helped carry him to the top of his company, and then maintain a multitude of outside activities as well. When he found he could no longer do all that, he began to get angry—angry at himself for getting older, angry at God for allowing him to get older, angry at the aging process itself, and angry because he was unable to concentrate quite as well. The anger brought on depression, which made his concentration level even worse.

Mr. H's symptoms included exhaustion, impatience and irritability, change of work style, disorientation (involving a lowered concentration level), and depression (related to his anger).

The salesman whose depression had led to suicidal thinking. A middle-aged man with some health problems, Mr. I, a Christian, occasionally had experienced bouts with depression over the years. After turning forty, he suffered two significant losses: his job and the impending breakup of his marriage. As a result, he had to work longer hours for less money at a job that gave him little satisfaction. His marital conflict aggravated his job-related burnout and left him with no emotional support. Mr. I's strong personal need to achieve, coupled with the hopelessness he felt concerning his circumstances, led to depression and suicidal thinking.

Mr. I's symptoms included exhaustion, detachment (from former colleagues, as well as from his wife), boredom (in a less than challenging job), feelings of being unappreciated, psychosomatic complaints, major depression (involving hopelessness and guilt for all his problems), and suicidal thinking.

The homemaker who found herself in total despair after taking on too many activities. A workaholic homemaker, Mrs. J had been the oldest daughter in her family. Her mother had been critical of her while she was growing up; no matter what she did it wasn't quite enough. Her school grades were usually A's with a few B's. Whenever she got a B, her mother criticized her. When Mrs. J married, she carried her workaholism and obsessive-compulsive desire to please into her marriage and motherhood experience. She did too much for her children, including home schooling. That allowed her to think for them, control them, and teach them herself, even though she lived in an area that had good public schools that were not offensive to Christians.

Mrs. J was active in a number of church organizations, taught Sunday school, was president of the women's missionary society, was the church organist, and sang special solos and duets. She was a workaholic career woman, even though it wasn't a paid career. As a result of her workaholism and striving to live up to her own mother's expectations of having a "perfect" daughter, Mrs. J suffered a major depression and burnout.

Mrs. J's symptoms included exhaustion, impatience and irritability, feelings of being unappreciated, change of work style, paranoia, disorientation, and major depression (accompanied by guilt from not doing everything perfectly).

All of these people, after a time spent under the care of our clinic, were able to reverse their burnout spiral and recover. Much of the information that helped them do that is shared in this book. Had this book been accessible to them, some of them would have had the information they needed to overcome their burnout without direct professional care. Others would have been helped by this information but would still have needed special care before their burnout spiral would have been reversed.

THE WORKAHOLIC—CANDIDATE MOST LIKELY

Although anyone can be subject to burnout, one personality type seems to be particularly prone to that condition. Most of the above case examples were "Type A" or obsessive-compulsive personalities. They are the ones who tend to be the most vulnerable for potential burnout. These individuals, often described as workaholics, are marked by four characteristics: (1) a hectic schedule, (2) a strong achievement orientation, (3) an inability to say no, and (4) a tendency toward frequent cardiac problems.

Such workaholic personalities often show the following symptoms of potential burnout.

The major source of self-esteem and pleasure is work and productive activity. Obviously, there is a valid amount of pleasure and self-esteem that should be received from work. However, since many people received only conditional love from their parents during childhood, when they were doing what pleased their parents, they condition themselves to feel significant only if they are being productive.

The major drive of obsessive-compulsive or workaholic individuals is a need for achieving control. That includes a need to control self, others, circumstances, and one's environment. (For a detailed list of characteristics of the obsessive-compulsive individual, as well as reasons behind these, see *The Workaholic and His Family* by Minirth, Meier, Wichern, Brewer, and Skipper [Grand Rapids: Baker, 1981].)

More than 90 percent of physicians and 75 percent of ministers who have been tested through the Minirth-Meier Clinic lean primarily toward these obsessive-compulsive personality traits. Many of these may tend to "play God" over their staff or congregations, refusing to delegate control over even the least significant responsibility or problem.

THE SPIRITUAL ELEMENT

A lack of spiritual "daily bread" often compounds the burnout victim's self-efforts. Often, when one feels the pressure of burnout, the first thing to be eliminated is the time for personal reflection, meditation, and spiritual devotion. The pressures of a busy schedule, coupled with an increasing inability to keep up, crowd out a time for meditating on the Word, which is essential in keeping a sharp edge spiritually, mentally, and physically. Rather than meditating on

Scripture, burnout victims often spend that amount of time worrying about the problems that are pressing in on them.

Perhaps, then, decreased times of spiritual devotion should be the first warning sign of a potential burnout victim. And since surveys show that only 5 to 10 percent of Christians practice daily times of Bible study and meditation, at least 90 percent of Christians should be considered more susceptible to burnout than they would be otherwise.

One successful businessman and Sunday school teacher, who was headed toward burnout, told us, "I realized that the shortened amount of time I was spending in the Word was being used only to find things to feed my class. All the while, I was starving spiritually and needed to feed myself. I decided that it was necessary, for a time, to give up my Sunday school class and spend time in the Word just feeding myself."

One sign of good mental, emotional, and spiritual well-being is a sense of day-to-day and moment-to-moment dependence upon God's enabling power for self and for others.

When individuals begin to experience burnout, one warning sign is an increasing sense of self-effort. Rather than trusting God or even others' God-given abilities in particular circumstances, burnout victims simply try harder, thinking they must depend more and more upon self. Interestingly, when committed Christians start depending more on themselves, they may start giving more lip service to their trust in God in order to cover up their decreased dependence on Him.

The classic example of that is seen in Moses' experience with the children of Israel during their years in the wilderness. There in the desert, God told

Moses to "speak to that rock" and water then would come out of it to refresh the Israelites. Weary and disgusted with the Israelites complaints about desert living, his leadership, and God's ability, Moses took credit for the rock's life-giving water, not by speaking to it but by striking it twice with his rod. Moses' statements to the congregation, "Listen, you rebels, must *we* bring you water out of this rock?" (Numbers 20:10, italics added), showed that he thought his efforts were needed on top of God's abilities to get the job done.

In verse 12, God reprimands Moses for that action. "Because you did not trust in me enough to honor me as holy in the sight of the Israelites," He denied Moses the right to lead the Israelites into the Promised Land, because He considered Moses' usurping of His own glory, in front of His people, reprehensible.

That example alone should be enough to cause a person in the burnout spiral to take heed when attempting to do God's work in personal strength alone. Trusting God for His inexhaustible provision of energy and enablement, either through self or through others, is not only the true practical way to handle a situation, but it is the way God wants it in order that His glory and power, instead of one's own, is demonstrated to others.

A TIME FOR ACTION

The time for taking action to break the downward spiral of burnout is at the first recognition of any storm warnings. Remember, burnout is a reversible spiral. The key is to begin action immediately to take care of oneself and to reverse the burnout.

God wants us to have peace. The Old Testament word *shalom* ("peace," a common Jewish greeting) is a term that indicates far more than simply the absence of hostility. It includes that (Joshua 9:15), but on a more positive note it suggests also a quality based on a strong relationship (Psalm 41:9; Jeremiah 20:10). That relationship leads to tranquility or contentment, which is one of three component parts of biblical peace (Psalm 4:8; Isaiah 32:17). It also includes the element of recompense, restoring, or making complete (1 Samuel 24:19; Joel 2:25). Finally, and most significantly, the biblical concept of peace includes completion. In fact, that is the basic concept of the Old Testament root word for peace. This is beautifully illustrated in the use of the word in 1 Kings 7:51 regarding Solomon's completion of the Temple.

How does that relate to us? God's will for the Christian is to experience the legacy of peace that Christ left for his followers. "But the Counselor, the Holy Spirit, whom the Father will send in my name, will teach you all things and will remind you of everything I have said to you. Peace I leave with you; my peace I give you. I do not give to you as the world gives. Do not let your hearts be troubled and do not be afraid" (John 14:26-27).

He wants us to experience tranquility, contentment, the absence of inner strife, and completeness. We must take steps to reverse burnout's downward spiral in order to fulfill that aspect of God's will. Inward peace of mind, plus fullness and abundance in life, is the will of God for Christians (Isaiah 26:3; Philippians 4:6-7).

Jesus said, "Come to me, all you who are weary and burdened, and I will give you rest" (Matthew 11:28). Those dedicated workers who consciously and without apology stop to take good care of themselves mentally, physically, and spiritually, will have, by far, the best chance of eventually fulfilling their life's purpose and calling. Theirs will be the experience of peace.

BURNOUT INVENTORY

If you believe you are headed for burnout, here is a way to test yourself for symptoms of a downward spiral ahead. Check those statements with which you agree.

1. More and more, I find that I can hardly wait for quitting time to come so that I can leave work.
2. I feel like I'm not doing any good at work these days.
3. I am more irritable than I used to be.
4. I'm thinking more about changing jobs.
5. Lately I've become more cynical and negative.
6. I have more headaches (or backaches, or other physical symptoms) than usual.
7. Often I feel hopeless, like "who cares?"
8. I drink more now or take tranquilizers just to cope with everyday stress.
9. My energy level is not what it used to be. I'm tired all the time.
10. I feel a lot of pressure and responsibility at work these days.
11. My memory is not as good as it used to be.
12. I don't seem to concentrate or pay attention like I did in the past.
13. I don't sleep as well.
14. My appetite is decreased these days (or, I can't seem to stop eating).
15. I feel unfulfilled and disillusioned.
16. I'm not as enthusiastic about work as I was a year or two ago.

17. I feel like a failure at work. All the work I've done hasn't been worth it.
18. I can't seem to make decisions as easily as I once did.
19. I find I'm doing fewer things at work that I like or that I do well.
20. I often tell myself, *Why bother? It doesn't really matter anyhow.*
21. I don't feel adequately rewarded or noticed for all the work I've done.
22. I feel helpless, as if I can't see any way out of my problems.
23. People have told me I'm too idealistic about my job.
24. I think my career has just about come to a dead end.

Count up your check marks. If you agree with a majority of those statements, then you may be feeling burnout and be in need of professional help or counseling or, at least, a change in life-style.

3

UNFULFILLED EXPECTATIONS: THE BURNOUT BURDEN

Burnout involves unfulfilled expectations, being worn down and tired out because what one thought would happen hasn't come about. Unfulfilled expectations relate basically to rewards that were expected but not received, rewards such as happiness, praise, attention, a sense of satisfaction, or a sense of well-being or security.

Often, unfulfilled expectations occur because those expectations have been too high. If you lower your expectations to more realistic ones, you are less likely to burn out. (Of course, if you lower them to the point that you want to "just forget the whole thing," you are already in burnout.)

But shouldn't Christians have high expectations? Oh, yes. We should expect God to work miraculously, but in His way, not ours. As Jeremiah learned: " 'For my thoughts are not your thoughts, neither are your ways my ways,' declares the Lord. 'As the heavens are higher than the earth, so are my ways higher than your ways and my thoughts than your thoughts' " (Isaiah 55:8-9).

Often a Christian's high expectations are not a reflection of God's thoughts so much as they are attempts to be involved in God's work in the world, in order to get praise from others (including the Lord) as a boost to one's own ego or shaky self-esteem. Sometimes the high expectations even started off from a right base, only to change their foundation later on.

In Romans 12:3, we are told: "Do not think of yourself more highly than you ought, but rather think of yourself with sober [sound] judgment, in accordance with the measure of faith God has given you." That doesn't mean you should not think of yourself highly, as someone God died for, but "not . . . more highly than you ought," not as if you are indispensable. Often, one approaches or experiences burnout because of the thought, "If I don't do it, no one else will," or "No one else will do it right." That is indeed thinking of self more highly than one ought to think. God has resources, as good as, if not better than, the ones He has given us, to complete a job (if He wants it done), resources that we know nothing about.

ELIJAH'S UNFULFILLED EXPECTATIONS

Certain events in the life of the prophet Elijah read like a modern-day case study in burnout, because of his unfulfilled expectations. In his interaction with Queen Jezebel, following his great victory over the prophets of Baal and his subsequent flight to the wilderness, Elijah exhibited many symptoms characteristic of what we today call burnout. A study of the events in 1 Kings that surrounded that interaction shows why he suffered that condition and what God did about it. Applying that divine "wellness program" to your life can start the reversal of your own burnout spiral.

In considering that and other passages of Scripture, it is important to distinguish between interpretation and application. Interpretation deals with what the specific passage means in its historical context to the individual or people to whom it was written. Application, on the other hand, has to do with the significant or relevant principles that can be drawn from the passages concerning life today.

Nearly a thousand years before Christ, Israel was ruled by the wicked king Ahab and his equally wicked queen, Jezebel, who had spread the worship of Baal throughout Israel. During these dark days, Elijah's character and ministry surfaced like a bolt of lightning, in startling contrast to the life-style of most Israelites. His words were characterized by boldness, his ministry by miraculous deeds. His commitment and willingness to stand for the true God of Israel, as well as his dependence upon Him, are illustrated in a challenge to the 450 prophets of Baal to a competition of miracles and in his prayers, for fire and, a short time later, for rain. One would think that an Elijah would never suffer burnout. However, Elijah was no super-human individual. As James 5:17 explains, Elijah was "a man just like us."

Elijah, in fact, is a vivid biblical example of Freudenberger's observation that burnout "is the letdown that comes in between crises or directly after 'mission accomplished.' "[1] Elijah was successful, a high achiever. He expended a great deal of physical, emotional, and spiritual energy in his conflict with the prophets of Baal in front of the Israelites gathered on Mount Carmel. His success caused the Israelites and their king to come back to the worship of the only true God. Shortly after that incident, he expended more energy by climbing to the top of Mount Carmel, spending an intense period of time in prayer for rain to end a three-year drought and, when that prayer was answered, running twenty miles from

1. Herbert Freudenberger and Geraldine Richelson, *Burn-Out* (New York: Anchor, Doubleday, 1980), p. 110.

Carmel to the city of Jezreel. In his excitement and in the power of the Lord, he even outran King Ahab's chariot.

Following all these strenuous but miraculously successful activities, Elijah received an unexpected jolt: Jezebel swore that she would have him killed. Expecting more success, he was instead rejected and threatened. His heady joy was replaced by fear. He turned and began running again, this time for his life, to Beersheba in Judah. And then, leaving his servant behind, he walked or ran for another day into the desert.

After courageously confronting 451 of his enemies—King Ahab and the prophets of Baal—why would he turn and run at a death threat? Instead of persisting in prayer, as he had done for rain (1 Kings 18:41-45), why did Elijah flee?

Existing on a physical and emotional high at that point, he had been caught off guard emotionally and spiritually. With the adrenaline still flowing, he depended upon the strength that had brought him to Jezreel, physical strength. So instead of praying, he ran.

ELIJAH BURNS OUT

As he ran from Jezreel to Beersheba for his life, he must have become more and more depressed, more and more burned out physically. That is easy to understand. Emotionally, his expectations of Jezebel had not been fulfilled. Spiritually, he had exchanged his dependence upon God for what little physical strength he had left. Compounding the problem, he abandoned his servant, withdrawing to the wilderness alone. With no close friend or associate, no one to help or encourage him, he was overcome by feelings of despair and self-pity. Note carefully in 1 Kings 19:3-4 the emotions experienced by Elijah as he came to a broom tree, sat down under it, and prayed that he might die. " 'I have had enough, Lord,' he said. 'Take my life; I am no better than my ancestors.' Then he lay down under the tree and fell asleep."

Elijah felt detached and isolated from everyone. The focus of his thinking was on himself. He was obsessed with a desire to be more successful than his ancestors. Setting and seeking to reach unrealistically high standards led to Elijah's burnout and frequently leads to burnout today.

Note how Elijah's self-centered thinking continued even forty days later, after God had given Elijah rest and food, and even insight, through the question recorded in 1 Kings 19:9-10: " 'What are you doing here, Elijah?' He replied, 'I have been very zealous for the Lord God Almighty. The Israelites have rejected your covenant, broken down your altars, and put your prophets to death with the sword. I am the only one left, and now they are trying to kill me too.' "

ELIJAH'S BURNOUT SYMPTOMS

A cluster of feelings associated with burnout find their expression in these verses. They include:

1. *Egotism.* Elijah's egotism was associated with feelings of being indispensable. Ultimately, God reminded the prophet that he was not the only one left, that there were still seven thousand who had not worshiped Baal. At that stage, however, Elijah felt that he was the only one. His sweeping generalization of Israel's apostasy was only partially accurate.

2. *Feelings of resentment and bitterness.* He resented the fact that others had abandoned God. And

his bitterness within drained away important emotional energy.

3. *Feelings of paranoia.* The prophet says, "And now they are trying to kill me too." It would seem that he had expanded one death threat into a national crusade to assassinate him.

4. *Feelings of self-pity.* Note the "I" emphasis in Elijah's words.

5. *Feelings of resentment and anger toward God.* Certainly, God did not need to be reminded of how zealous Elijah had been for His name. Asking God to take his life (v. 4), coupled with the complaint, "They are trying to kill me" (v. 10), demonstrated his dissatisfaction and lack of trust concerning God's supreme control over his life, as well as a desire to have personal control over when his life ended.

All these feelings are likely to be experienced by an obsessive-compulsive individual who feels burned out. Since "Elijah was a man just like us," it is easy to see how a study of his burnout case can give insight into coping with burnout today.

GOD'S REMEDY FOR BURNOUT

Observing God's compassionate dealings with Elijah can give us principles that we can apply in handling burnout today.

First, He met Elijah's physical needs—rest and then nourishment (vv. 5-6).

Second, God allowed Elijah to see that He still remained in control of circumstances and was still active in the prophet's life. The extended communication between the two of them (vv. 9-17) demonstrates God's continued concern for the prophet.

Third, during that communication, God prompted Elijah to ventilate his intense feelings. To get rid of negative feelings, it is important not to bury them but to express them (although not in a manner hurtful to others, which only compounds problems for both parties).

When we expose our feelings to others, only then can we begin to see them realistically—for what they are—and then to get rid of them. Often, however, an extended period of time is necessary for those feelings to come to the surface and dissipate. So it was with Elijah, as God patiently prompted him three times to open up and state how he felt (vv. 4, 10, 14).

Fourth, only after Elijah had exposed his feelings did God give him new but lighter tasks. God assigned Elijah a series of tasks that he was capable of handling—anointing two new kings and a new prophet (vv. 15-16). An individual who has experienced burnout should not be rushed back into situations involving major stress. However, taking on lighter tasks that can be handled more easily helps rebuild the self-esteem of the burnout victim.

And finally, God provided for Elijah something every burnout victim needs after his recovery: a genuine friend. From that point on, Elisha became Elijah's friend, fellow worker, and disciple (vv. 18, 21). Elijah had come to feel that he was alone. Those feelings, of course, did not reflect the true situation, since seven thousand other Israelites had also refused Baal worship. On the other hand, Elijah had been alone, but only because, like many burnout victims, he had brought about his own aloneness by abandoning other people (his former servant and others in his flight to the wilderness).

To summarize, God reversed Elijah's "burnout" by meeting his basic needs. Elijah needed rest and nourishment, which He provided. He needed fellowship with God, so God spoke to him through "a gentle whisper" (v. 12). Elijah needed a proper perspective of himself—a sense of self-worth—so God assigned him a task he could handle. Finally, the prophet needed close relationships with others, so God provided his friend and servant, Elisha.

Elijah, the successful high achiever, was almost at the peak of total success. He had been miraculously victorious in all his endeavors. All he needed was Jezebel's conversion to the true God, which he may have anticipated was at hand, to experience total success in his pursuits for God. When the major crisis was over, the main part of his mission accomplished, he dropped his spiritual guard, expecting smooth sailing. Instead, his expectation regarding Jezebel not only was unmet but was turned against him. When he saw that his expectations were to be unfulfilled, burnout came quickly, because he had exerted his physical and emotional resources to their limits, and he no longer trusted in his spiritual strength.

So it is with us when we expect success because of our own efforts and within our own time limits. When expectations are unfulfilled, whether those that were originally God-given or not, and we start depending less on God and more on ourselves, burnout is not far behind.

4
BITTERNESS: A HIDDEN ROOT

In our Christian psychiatric clinic, two women, Lucy and Linda,* were treated for suicidal depression. Both of them came from similar backgrounds. Although they grew up in different parts of the country, both were oldest daughters raised in Christian families active in the church. Both Lucy and Linda began participating in their church's music program at an early age and continued to do so after they were grown. Both were also involved in teaching.

Yet soon after becoming adults, both became severely depressed to the point of being unable to function. Lucy, in fact, had developed multiple personalities. Each came to our clinic as the result of strong suicidal thoughts.

After months and even years of treatment, both began making significant progress. Lucy ultimately became healthy and functional. Linda, however, continued to struggle.

In examining the similarities and differences between these two women, one key factor became evident. Both women had been sexually and emotionally abused by their fathers and by other male family members at an early age. For years, both had blocked out that repeated abuse from their conscious minds.

*Names have been changed.

When compassionate Christian counselors enabled them to remove the blocks that had led to their severe depression, consciousness of what had happened to them came to the surface.

When they became aware of what had happened, however, their responses were somewhat different. Over a period of time, Lucy chose to forgive her father and others for what had happened. Linda, on the other hand, retained a measure of bitterness and resentment. She continued to harbor feelings of anger and resentment and could think or talk of little else. As a result, her process of healing and restoration was severely hampered.

Both Lucy and Linda had experienced severe burnout as wives and mothers. However, one was able to recover and experienced restoration from burnout. The other did not experience the same measure of recovery. Why? Because of the relationship between bitterness and burnout.

In our counseling ministries, we have seen literally hundreds of examples that verify a close connection between bitterness and resentment and the experience of symptoms that we call burnout. The purpose of this chapter is to give a biblical perspective on bitterness, to show how bitterness leads to burnout, and to show how freedom from bitterness is necessary for effective recovery from burnout.

Sometime ago, one of our staff was speaking at a regional pastors' conference in the Midwest. A number of the pastors attending the conference expressed their enthusiasm when they discovered that the theme of the messages would be burnout. However, several pastors expressed surprise when the speaker drew attention to the connection between burnout and bitterness. As one pastor said, after the conference, "I've been feeling burned out for some time. I always thought of it in connection with serving the Lord and working hard in my ministry. I never thought part of my burnout resulted from being bitter or resentful toward the demands placed on me in ministry or towards several board members who had attempted to have me fired many years ago."

The word for *bitter* is used in both the Old and New Testaments for either a literal bitter taste or an attitude. For example, in Exodus 15:23 the Israelites attempt to drink "bitter" water. The same concept is used in illustrating a product of the heart in James 3:11: "Can both fresh water and salt (bitter) water flow from the same spring?" In a contrast between water that is bitter or brackish to the taste and that which is sweet, drinkable, and thirst-quenching, the term for bitter is used in a figurative sense of strong, negative emotions in both the Old and New Testaments. For example, Job asserts, "Even today my complaint is bitter" (Job 23:2). In Esther 4:1 the Israelites cry "loudly and bitterly." In a similar vein, Peter, after denying Christ three times, "went outside and wept bitterly" (Matthew 26:75; Luke 22:62).

One of the fundamental lessons learned in medical school is that fever indicates the presence of an infection. Therefore, simply to treat a fever without looking for its cause—the infection—is failing to practice good medicine. In reviewing the period of Israel's history between the Exodus from Egypt and the arrival of the new desert-raised generation in the Promised Land, Israel on several occasions demonstrated a characteristic that is related to bitterness in the same way that fever is related to infection. That characteristic, far from being outdated, is prevalent today even among many Christians. It is referred to in Scripture as "murmuring" or "grumbling" (in whispers).

Although each of us has had extensive Bible training, including seminary degrees, none of us, until recently, had ever heard or read a word study on "murmuring." As we began examining that term, we discovered that, with the exception of a reference in Joshua 9:18, all occurrences of the word *murmuring* were found in six chapters of Moses' two books: Exodus 15-17 and Numbers 14, 16, and 17.

We discovered also that the term is always followed by the preposition *against:* "murmured against." The subject of the verb, to murmur, was always the congregation Israel: "Israel murmured against." The object of the murmuring was usually an authority figure, either Moses or Aaron. At times, Moses alone was the object of murmuring (Exodus 15:24; 17:3). At other times, the Lord was the object of murmuring (Exodus 16:7-8; Numbers 14). As we examined that concept, we discovered that there was always some external reason for murmuring—bitter water, not enough food, or dissatisfaction with the decisions made by those in authority.

What is murmuring? Our definition for murmuring is to express resentment, dissatisfaction, anger, or complaint in low or half-muted tones. Murmuring is the opposite of unconditional obedience. It also stands in stark contrast to grateful trust. Our definition includes several component parts.

First, it involves opposition expressed in muted but audible tones. The Israelites' murmur against Moses and Aaron in Numbers 14:2: "If only we had died in Egypt! Or in this desert!" Although the passage infers that the Israelites communicated their murmuring to each other, it nonetheless was audible to and directed against Moses and Aaron and, ultimately, God.

In our teaching careers on the college and seminary level, we frequently witness murmuring because of an unexpected quiz or of an announcement of a difficult assignment. In fact, during our own student days, each of us engaged in murmuring. Another component of the biblical concept of murmuring is hostile opposition. In fact, in Numbers 14:9 Moses describes the nation's murmuring as an act of rebellion "against the Lord."

A third component of murmuring is that it constitutes unbelief. The Lord so labels the Israelites' murmuring in Number 14:11: "How long will these people treat me with contempt? How long will they refuse to believe me, in spite of all the miraculous signs I have performed among them?"

Sometime ago, the wife of a man engaged in full-time Christian ministry came for counseling about the pressures under which her husband labored. During the course of her initial conversation, she observed, "I really don't have any problems myself." However, she expressed complaints about several people in church, a couple of her office colleagues, and even about some incidents that had occurred in her family years before. During the counseling session, she asserted that both she and her husband were "burned out."

It took some time to demonstrate to her the connection between her feelings of burnout and her bitterness toward the people and incidents about which she had complained.

Murmuring is a common phenomenon today and is present in the lives of many of us who are Christians, including those who have experienced burnout.

Second, we are observing that, as fever indicates the presence of infection, murmuring can show the underlying presence of bitterness.

Few passages illustrate that relationship better than Exodus 15. The Israelites, under Moses' leadership, successfully crossed the Red Sea. They witnessed the miracle of deliverance from the Egyptian Army, then sang, under Moses' direction, a great hymn of praise to God for that deliverance.

Only three days after singing the words, "Who . . . is like you, O Lord?" (v. 11), they found themselves three days' journey into the wilderness without water (vv. 22-24). Coming to a place called Marah, they discover water. However, it was too bitter and distasteful to drink. Their response? "The people murmured against Moses, saying, What shall we drink?" (KJV).

That response to adversity—murmuring—was repeated numerous times during Israel's years in the wilderness. However, in that first incident, we discover a clue that demonstrates the connection between murmuring and bitterness. Exodus 15 does not say that the people were bitter, yet the name of the location in which Israel is first said to engage in murmuring is Marah, which means *bitter*. It seems unlikely that the Holy Spirit, in directing Moses to record these words, left us with the name of that obscure location by accident or without purpose. It seems that God went to great pains to point out the bitterness of the water. And we believe that was to highlight the underlying bitterness of the people.

Another factor present in Exodus 15, which is frequently connected with murmuring and, consequently, with bitterness, is a short memory. Just three days earlier, the Israelite nation had been electrified by the magnitude of God's deliverance. Now, it seems, they were complaining, "God, what have you done for us lately?"

In much the same way, a graduate student received a sizeable gift in the mail that enabled him to pay for almost an entire semester of studies. Less than two weeks later, he was bitterly complaining about his financial circumstances because he was not able to take his wife out to eat regularly.

In Psalm 103:2 the psalmist writes, "Praise the Lord, O my soul, and forget not all his benefits." Perhaps one of the most effective ways to reduce the possibility of burnout in our lives is to remind ourselves frequently of both the big and small ways that God "daily loads us with benefits" (Psalm 68:19, NKJV*).

THE CAUSES OF BITTERNESS

1. *Wrong motives or jealousy.* In counseling Christians, we frequently see bitterness associated with jealousy. The examples include successful attorneys who envy the abilities of their colleagues, Bible college and seminary students consumed with jealousy toward fellow students whom they perceive as having more insight into Scripture, and pastors or missionaries envious of others who have seen more outward evidences of success in their ministries.

2. *Wrong response to irritations; conditional love.* In Colossians 3:19 Paul instructs husbands to "love your wives, and be not bitter against them" (KJV†). The Greek word *pikroi* used here demonstrates "resentment or an incensed and angry attitude of mind." Frequently, we hear wives assert, "Nothing I do ever pleases him. I can't cook, can't keep house, can't take care of the children, or can't balance the checkbook to please him." Sometimes we

New King James Version.
†King James Version.

hear husbands in marital counseling making the same assertions. One husband even used such assertions to justify his having an affair with another woman. His rationale? "I'm not sure I love her any more."

We believe that kind of bitterness and petty criticism often results from an underlying lack of unconditional love. Unlike God, we often are guilty of having *conditional* love, based on the performance of the one we supposedly love. Conditional love produces harshness and bitterness both in husbands and wives. Frequently, that can lead to marital burnout. However, conditional love and marital burnout can be reversed.

3. *Wrong response to adversity.* In Hebrews 12:15, we discover a warning that "no bitter root grows up," instead of enduring "hardship as discipline" (v. 7). Although not all adverse circumstances are direct acts of divine discipline (e.g., Satan's attacks on Job to get him to disavow God, "When [God] has tested me, I will come forth as gold" [Job 23:10]) all adversities are designed to produce a proper response that leads to growth in grace and knowledge of God. As 2 Corinthians 4:17 tells us, "For our light and momentary troubles are achieving for us an eternal glory that far outweighs them all."

In calling for a proper response to circumstances of discipline, Hebrews 12:14 requires a response of peace with all men and *holiness* in our relationship with God. If we fail to diligently pursue these qualities, bitterness may take root. As that bitterness grows and develops, often beneath the surface of our conscious thoughts, it becomes more and more a part of our outlook on life. The results are devastating, both to us and to those around us.

4. *Misplaced strife.* James 3 provides a good illustration of the literal and figurative uses of the word *bitter* in the New Testament. In verse 11, bitter or salt water is used as an illustration of bitter conversation. In verse 14, the underlying attitude in the heart is demonstrated. In that section, James is calling for a demonstration of wisdom through meekness. However, when jealousy and selfish ambition are present in the heart, it often leads to strife, which in turn presents "disorder and every evil practice" (v. 16).

We have seen churches that for years have been crippled in their effectiveness for Christ because of "bitter envying and strife" on the part of church leaders. Even missionary and other organizations composed of Christian leaders are frequently rendered less than effective because of petty jealousies. In one local church, one of the elders, motivated by jealousy, refused to recognize the good job other leaders were doing and sought to disqualify every candidate but himself from the upcoming church election. He was unable to see his own bitterness until his pastor lovingly showed him how he, too, could be disqualified.

5. *An unforgiving spirit.* Often in counseling we hear about insults or offenses that have occurred years before. Sometimes we hear the words, "I just can't forgive." Invariably, when we hear those words, our response is to encourage our counselee to insert the more accurate word, "I *won't* forgive." Forgiveness is always a choice. Like love, it involves an act of the will.

Ephesians 4:31-32 draws a clear connection between bitterness and what is perhaps its most basic underlying cause, a refusal to forgive. "Get rid of all bitterness, rage and anger, brawling and slander, along with every form of malice. Be kind and compassionate to one another, forgiving each other, just as in Christ God forgave you."

That passage connects bitterness with underlying anger, outbursts of temper, ill will, and evil speaking. The contrast in verse 32 shows how conflict, anger, and unkindness are so frequently related to a refusal to forgive.

It is in that passage, and specifically in verse 31, that we see the ultimate solution to bitterness. The choice to which Paul calls believers who have been wronged is clear. First, we must choose to *put aside* or *get rid of* all bitterness and associated anger, outbursts of temper, ill will, and unkind words. Frequently, bitterness will grow and develop for years simply because we nourish it by talking about those offenses that have occurred. We voice our hurts to anyone who will listen and often to those who would rather not. In quiet moments, rather than meditating on Scripture, we spend our time meditating on those hurtful moments and how we felt.

EXPRESS ANGER APPROPRIATELY

Bitterness and its underlying emotion, anger, is unhealthy. Repressed anger needs to be appropriately and properly expressed. That's why earlier in Ephesians 4 Paul says, "In your anger do not sin: do not let the sun go down while you are still angry" (v. 26). If we are angry with our mate, with other Christians, with a family member, with our neighbor, or with a colleague at work, we should confront those persons, if at all possible, and carefully and lovingly express our feelings before the sun goes down (or before the day is over). To do otherwise is unhealthy spiritually, mentally, or physically.

CHOOSE TO FORGIVE

The second choice we must make is the choice to forgive. That choice first involves an approach of kindness and tenderheartedness. Frequently, we have seen individuals who, having been injured in the past, develop what might be called "a hard edge." They become calloused and insensitive to the feelings of others, or even to their own need for relationships with God and with other people. That hardened emotional state is often difficult to reverse.

Our pattern for forgiving is none other than Christ Himself. "Be kind and compassionate to one another, *forgiving each other*, just as in Christ God forgave you" (v. 32, italics added). The words of His prayer from the cross come vividly to mind: "Father, forgive them, they do not know what they are doing" (Luke 23:34). Peter, who experienced Christ's forgiveness firsthand, reminds us of how Christ, "when they hurled their insults at him, he did not retaliate; when he suffered, he made no threats. Instead, he entrusted himself to him who judges justly" (1 Peter 2:23). Surely, none of us have suffered wrongdoing to the extent of that suffered by our perfect and holy Savior.

What then is forgiveness? The word itself means to send or put away. It does not necessarily mean that we will forget. Frequently, forgetting is impossible, because the hurt has become burned into our long-term memory. However, we can choose to maintain consciousness of harmful events, or we can choose to do as Christ did and act as if they had not occurred. Forgiveness is a matter of the will; it is a choice. Furthermore, when we choose to forgive, we relieve a great deal of the ongoing mental and emotional stress that is required for nursing grudges. As a result, we are far less susceptible to burnout.

Elizabeth was a pastor's wife. For years she gave herself to her husband, her children, and the various churches and individuals to whom they ministered. Over a period of years, the ministry began to take its toll. There were times when her husband was less than sensitive about her physical and emotional needs. Church members were frequently harsh and critical, especially toward her husband and children. Yet, many of those same people often demanded hours and hours of her time. Elizabeth soon became burned out.

A change in her husband's schedule, followed by a move to another ministry, helped some. However, it was not until Elizabeth consciously *chose* to forgive a number of people—including her husband and children—and expressed a willingness to give up the bitterness that she admitted she felt that she began to actually recover from burnout.

We are far more likely to overcome burnout if we *choose to forgive* rather than choose to hold on to bitterness.

5

THE WORKAHOLIC AND HIS WORKPLACE

When most people hear the word *burnout*, they think of the hard-driving business person who never stops for coffee breaks or relaxing lunches, and who insists on taking work home at night, or even on vacations. There are, of course, occasional situations where such a workstyle is necessary. If that workstyle has been practiced long term, however, its necessity is as much in the mind of the workaholic as in the reality of the situation.

Seemingly logical explanations of, "That's the only way to get the job done," "That's the only way to get ahead in my profession (or company)," or "We need the extra money," are all too often cover-ups for the feeling, "That's the only way to prove to them what I'm worth," which ties in with the feeling, "That's the only way to prove to *myself* and others what I'm worth."

Many times a workaholic will try to make a virtue out of his overdependence on work (for a feeling of self-worth) by exalting work, the "Protestant work ethic," and even capitalism, to a far higher plane than in the mind of God. We are in favor of all three but not in order to excuse someone's destructive workaholic habits.

Work itself certainly is not to be shunned or downgraded. The apostle Paul knew that when he said:

We were not idle when we were with you, nor did we eat anyone's food without paying for it. On the contrary, we worked night and day, laboring and toiling so that we would not be a burden to any of you. We did this, not because we do not have the right to such help, but in order to make ourselves a model for you to follow. For even when we were with you, we gave you this rule: "If a man will not work, he shall not eat." (2 Thessalonians 3:7-12)

However, workaholism for the purpose of glorifying or exalting self is unnecessary and wrong, just as it was wrong for the Tower of Babel to be built "to the heavens," in order to "make a name for ourselves" (Genesis 11:4).

WORKAHOLISM AND GUILT

To verify the rightness of their workaholic tendencies, strong obsessive-compulsive individuals point out that whenever they slow down, they feel guilty for not accomplishing all that they *should* be doing, or even all that they believe God gave them the ability to accomplish. Yet, nowhere does God say that it is His will to carry out work that causes us to neglect Him, our families, and our health.

That unnecessary guilt or false guilt, felt whenever workaholics slow down, may be related to an anxiety regarding their fear of facing what had *not* been accomplished during their times of frenetic workaholic activity, things such as spending time with God, with family, and improving one's own mental and physical health. Also, many of the accomplishments of workaholics later on are found to be all for nothing, because not enough time was spent in planning and prioritizing for long-term accomplishment. To the workaholic, everything seems extremely important and urgent at the time.

One burnout victim, president of a fairly large company, told us the harsh realization that all his work was not what the Lord had in mind for his life had come slowly. God instead wanted him to work at being successfully balanced in work and family life. Allowing himself to become one-dimensional and obsessed with work, even to the detriment of everything else in his life, had seemed like a good quality to have previously. Now, however, he saw it for the selfish sin it was.

OBSESSIVE-COMPULSIVE PERSONALITY TRAITS

That executive's personality, such as that of all workaholics, is heavy with obsessive-compulsive personality traits, some good and some bad.

To discover whether or not your personality is primarily obsessive-compulsive, which may make you susceptible to workaholism and eventual burnout, see if a majority of the following traits apply to you.

1. is perfectionistic, neat, clean, orderly, dutiful, conscientious, meticulous, and moral.
2. does a good job but works too hard and is unable to relax.
3. is choleric, overly conscientious, overly concerned, inflexible, has an overly strict conscience and rigid thinking.
4. rationalizes to deceive and defend self and intellectualizes in order to avoid emotions.
5. is a good student, well organized, and interested in facts and not feelings; seems cold and stable and tends to split hairs.
6. is anti-authority at times and is pulled between actions of obedience and defiance. Obedience

usually wins, but occasionally defiance wins. The obedience leads to rage and the defiance leads to fear. The fears lead to perfectionistic traits and the rage leads to non-perfectionistic traits. A basic problem is defiant anger.

7. displays many opposite traits: conscientiousness and negligence, orderliness and untidiness.

8. has three central concerns: dirt (he or she is very clean), time (he or she is punctual), and money (he or she wants a feeling of security).

9. has feelings of helplessness, needs to be in control of self and others who are close to him or her, needs power, and is intensely competitive.

10. keeps emotions a secret from others, feels with the mind (is too logical), and, as a defense, isolates feelings from whatever he or she is experiencing.

11. has other defenses including: magical thinking—thinking he or she has more power than reality dictates; reaction formation—adopting attitudes and behavior that are opposite to the impulses the individual consciously or unconsciously harbors; and undoing—unconsciously acting out in reverse some unacceptable action that occurred in the past.

12. struggles to bring conversations around to the level of theories.

13. is afraid of feelings of warmth (which occurred in dependent relationships in early life), expresses anger more easily (because it encourages distance), postpones pleasure (out of unconscious guilt), lives in the future, lacks spontaneity, and is insecure.

14. may have unspontaneous and routine sex with little variety. Female perfectionists have difficulty with orgasm and male perfectionists some-

times have difficulty with premature ejaculation. That is a result of anxiety, which is related to their fear of loss of control.

15. usually had a parent or parents who were obsessive and demanded total devotion but gave minimal love, and who made the person feel accepted on a conditional basis (only when doing what the parent wanted him or her to do).

16. often leans, theologically, toward an extreme Calvinistic position, in which God chooses who will be saved and the individual's own actions, even the action of freely choosing to be saved, means little or nothing. (That is because he or she has a longing for some control in his or her uncertain world, as well as a desire to avoid personal responsibility.) Emotionally, however, he or she feels like an Arminian, not good enough to warrant God's continuing salvation.

17. needs respect and security.

18. craves dependent relationships but fears them at the same time.

19. needs to feel omnipotent and substitutes feelings of omnipotence for true coping.

20. has trouble with commitment, fears loss of control, and frequently focuses on irrelevant details.

21. often uses techniques to conceal anger, such as shaking hands frequently with a handshake that is rigid.

22. has feelings of powerlessness and avoids recognition of personal fallibility. He or she fears the possibility of being proved wrong, so lives in much doubt about personal words and actions. Even door latches are checked and rechecked to achieve certainty and security.

23. is extraordinarily self-willed, uses his or her defense mechanisms to control aggressive impulses,

and avoids real conflicts by dwelling on substitute obsessive thoughts. If these defense mechanisms do not work, the result is depression.

24. is stubborn, stingy (with love and time), frugal, persistent, dependable in many ways, and reliable.

25. has an overdeveloped superego, feels comfortable only when knowing everything, and tends to insist on ultimate truth in all matters.

26. has exaggerated expectations of self and others.

Our alcohol-rehabilitation counselor, Mr. G, was just such a person. He expected to cure his alcoholic patients and he expected them to do what was necessary to be cured. When that didn't happen, he had to admit that he wasn't perfect, which to him was to be contemptible (see number 29). He received some psychiatric help, quit drinking himself (following his own advice), and resolved his anger and frustrations. He came to realize that when dealing with alcoholics, some of them will respond and want to get over their problem and will do very well, and some of them will not. He came to accept his limitations and realized that the responsibility for his patients' recovery was really on their shoulders, not on his. His responsibility was to point out to them what they needed to do and then to leave it up to them whether or not to obey God and to work out their problems. As a result, Mr. G returned to his work and was able to function well without feeling burned out.

27. appears strong, decisive, and affirmative, but is not; rather, he or she is uncertain, uneasy, and wavering. Rigid rules are followed to control uncertainty. He or she needs to appear perfect.

28. exaggerates the power of personal thoughts.

Words (spoken or unspoken) become a substitute for responsible action.

29. has a grandiose self-view and strives to accomplish superhuman achievements to overcome insecurities. To that person, accepting one's limitations amounts to being average—and contemptible.

Our case example, Mrs. A, the mother who felt overly responsible when a child rebelled against God, had just such a grandiose self-view. She thought the success of her children depended upon her alone. When one child rebelled, she not only blamed herself but saw herself as less than a perfect mother, one with limitations and therefore contemptible. That self-view brought on depression and burnout. She didn't realize that every child is born depraved and that all parents make mistakes in parenting. Mrs. A was encouraged by our staff to quit carrying all the guilt and blame for her child's wrong choices.

That is not to say that parents should overlook their parenting mistakes. They should ask God for forgiveness for their mistakes, pray for their grown children, encourage them to commit their lives to Christ, and love them unconditionally, whether or not they accept Christ. Then they need to turn the burden for their grown child's future success over to their child.

30. is cautious in love relationships, because love results in concern about another's feelings that are not under one's own control.

31. has a single-minded style of thinking, is good at tasks that require intense concentration, and believes that everything is either black or white, completely right or completely wrong.

32. has a tendency to respond to extremes.

33. is critical but cannot stand criticism.
34. has strong rituals in his or her personal religious system. Rituals are considered important in many other areas of life.
35. considers commitment tantamount to dependency and being out of control. Marriage commitment is difficult; coexistence is preferred.
36. lives in the future, saves for a tomorrow that never arrives, discounts limitations of time, and denies death.
37. insists on honesty in marriage, which results in telling all, at times.
38. has trouble admitting mistakes.
39. uses excessive cautions or restraints in courtship.
40. gives minimal commitment in relationships but demands maximal commitment. As a result, each marriage partner pursues his own interests, and intimacy is limited. He or she is careful to *do* only a minimal share in marriage but wants to *think* for both self *and* spouse.
41. is legalistic in dealing with himself and others.
42. is (a) pecuniary—obsessed with money matters, (b) parsimonious—frugal or stingy, and (c) pedantic—overly concerned with book knowledge and formal rules.

THE WORKAHOLIC'S INNER VOICES

Inner "voices" or convictions are what keep workaholics going. They tell workaholics, who are usually the oldest children of their sex in the family, that they need to do something to be worthwhile. These voices or convictions do not let him or her rest in just *being* someone. *Doing* is the key to being worthwhile.

The cause usually lies in unrealistic expectations for a first child by parents who try to get the child to *do* or accomplish new activities before a child could normally accomplish them. That is partly out of anxiety—to be sure the child is normal—and partly out of parental pride—to improve their own self-esteem through raising an above-normal child. By the time a second child comes along, these desires and anxieties have been somewhat satisfied and the parents are more realistic about what to expect from a child at different stages. Meanwhile, that first child grows up with the following inner voices that drive him on.

1. *Voice from childhood.* That unhealthy voice or driving message says, "You're a nobody. What can you do to prove you're a somebody?" When the workaholic then starts to do something to prove self-worth, the voice says, "Keep doing more, more." When the workaholic reaches a goal, the voice says, "That's good, but it's not enough." Workaholics never reach the point of doing enough to prove that self is a "somebody" and relax in that knowledge.

The only way workaholics (or anyone else, for that matter) can truly prove they are somebodies is to accept the fact that *God sees them as somebodies*—so much so that He gave His only Son to die so that He could fellowship with them eternally. True self-worth can be experienced only as we understand and acknowledge our position as *accepted* or *acceptable* to Jesus Christ, because we claim, for ourselves, the payment that He made for our sins by dying on the cross.

2. *Voice of the depraved self.* That voice says, "I'll do what I want to do. I'll have fun or do my own thing." That conviction, reinforced by Satan, comes

into dominance when the workaholic out of exhaustion gives up on the first voice—in other words—when he is approaching burnout. The burned-out workaholic may still be going to work in order to receive a paycheck, but he or she is no longer exerting as much effort.

3. *Voice of colleagues.* That inner voice, also unhealthy, says, "Don't take time off; you can't afford it. People won't understand." Actually, that voice may or may not be the actual thoughts of the workaholic's colleagues, but only what he or she assumes colleagues would say. To overcome that voice, the workaholic must consider what are his or her actual priorities in life and in the particular task at hand.

When new therapists are hired at the Minirth-Meier Clinic, we caution them (1) that the number of cases they have affects the profit the clinic makes as well as their own salary, but (2) if their case load becomes so heavy that it is affecting their home life, they are to call a halt to accepting new cases. Those priorities must be recognized and followed daily.

4. *Voice of reality.* Another voice that workaholics and all of us hear, at times, will be the voice of reality, a healthy voice that we all need. That voice tells us to "face the music" and realize that mounting debt or some other problem means that we will need to work harder or longer for a particular period of time. When that period of time is up, however, we will again need to slow down to a normal pace. The problem with workaholics, however, is that when a crisis is over they keep finding more reasons to continue the extra exertion and long hours.

5. *Voice of the Holy Spirit.* That voice, which all Christians have, says, "What does God want you to

do?" In order to hear that "still, small voice," however, the workaholic must recognize its authority over all the other voices inside and separate what it is saying from the urging of the other voices. To do that, the Christian workaholic must continually stay familiar with the basic guidelines God sets down for all Christians in His written Word.

Our case example, Mrs. J, the workaholic housewife, illustrates how a workaholic can change from listening to the voice from childhood to the voice of the Holy Spirit.

After a month of hospitalization, Mrs. J was cured of her workaholism and depression by becoming aware of her anger toward herself and forgiving herself for not being perfect, and by becoming aware of her anger toward her mother for expecting her to be perfect and forgiving her mother for not being a perfect mother. After that, she and her mother actually became better friends. She learned to see her mother as a human being, one with good traits and bad traits. She learned to be just herself with her mother, even when her mother was demanding or was giving her occasional "guilt trips" or rejection. She learned not to accept those and to choose not to feel guilty when her mother displayed such actions. She let her mother's guilt trips go in one ear and out the other and learned to enjoy her mother instead.

Mrs. J also asked God to show her her own "light and easy yoke." She decided to put her children in the local public school, which was a good one, and continue teaching Sunday school, a ministry that she enjoyed. She gave up her job as church organist, sang only occasionally, and spent more time with her husband and children sharing their basic feelings with one another. Mrs. J became a better wife, mother, person, and witness for Christ, as a result of reorganizing her priorities and reprogramming her mind to listen to God's Holy Spirit rather than to her mother's parental injunctions.

CHECKLIST FOR WORKAHOLIC BURNOUT

If you have been wondering about your own tendencies toward workaholic burnout, see how many of these four statements you agree with. True or false:

1. I feel that the people I know who are in authority are no better than I am.
2. Once I start a job, I have no peace until I finish it.
3. I like to tell people exactly what I think.
4. Although many people are overly conscious of feelings, I like to deal only with the facts.

It is interesting that several of these statements would be considered good qualities to have in an employee. However, they are actually tendencies of a person susceptible to early burnout. Following are the reasons a person is likely to agree with these statements.

I feel that the people I know who are in authority are no better than I am. Burnout includes an underlying cynical attitude and a rebellion against authority figures. That attitude revolves around one's expectations not having been met.

Once I start a job, I have no peace until I finish it. If you will work day and night until you finish a job, it not only shows that work comes before everything else, but it may be related to authority rebellion as well. It could be tied in with an *"I'll* show him!" attitude or with a boss giving unrealistic time limits and demands. It may also be tied in with an idea that "if I can just get that project put into a nice, neat little package, it will show *him* (and *me*) that I'm a worthwhile person."

I like to tell people exactly what I think. As workaholics become more burned out, they become more irritable and more likely to say anything without holding back, because so much is pent up inside that there is no room to store more. Also, the more burned out, the more omnipotent and right they feel about personal viewpoints. As growing insecurity about decreasing abilities mounts, the victim becomes more arrogant. "I am right and everyone else is wrong!" Just as Jeremiah 17:9 said, "The heart is deceitful above all things."

Although many people are overly conscious of feelings, I like to deal only with the facts. If you take the emotional part of a workaholic's personality away, you would notice no difference. A workaholic represses feelings (except for irritability, and he or she doesn't recognize the basis for the irritability).

These four questions are the first in an inventory we give to suspected workaholic patients.[1] Complete the rest of this inventory as quickly as possible. Your first response is often your most honest answer. True or false:

5. I worry about business and financial matters.
6. I often have anxiety about something or someone.
7. I sometimes become so preoccupied by a thought that I cannot get it out of my mind.
8. I find it difficult to go to bed or sleep because of thoughts bothering me.

1. Presented first in *The Workaholic and His Family,* by Frank Minirth et al. (Grand Rapids: Baker, 1981), pp. 23-26.

9. I have periods in which I cannot sit or lie down—I need to be doing something.
10. My mind is often occupied by thoughts about what I have done wrong or not completed.
11. My concentration is not what it used to be.
12. My personal appearance is always neat and clean.
13. I feel irritated when I see another person's messy desk or cluttered room.
14. I am more comfortable in a neat, clean, and orderly room than in a messy one.
15. I cannot get through a day or a week without a schedule or a list of jobs to do.
16. I believe that the man who works the hardest and longest deserves to get ahead.
17. If my job/housework demands more time, I will cut out pleasurable activities to see that it gets done.
18. My conscience often bothers me about things I have done in the past.
19. There are things that I have done that would embarrass me greatly if they become public knowledge.
20. When I was a student I felt uncomfortable unless I got the highest grade.
21. It is my view that many people become confused because they don't bother to find out all the facts.
22. I frequently feel angry without knowing what or who is bothering me.
23. I can't stand to have my checkbook or financial matters out of balance.
24. I think talking about feelings to others is a waste of time.
25. There have been times when I became preoccupied with washing my hands or keeping things clean.

26. I like always to be in control of myself and to know as much as possible about things happening around me.
27. I have few or no close friends with whom I share warm feelings openly.
28. I feel that the more one can know about future events, the better off he will be.
29. There are sins I have committed that I will never live down.
30. I always avoid being late to a meeting or an appointment.
31. I rarely give up until the job has been completely finished.
32. I often expect things of myself that no one else would ask.
33. I sometimes worry about whether I was wrong or made a mistake.
34. I would like others to see me as not having any faults.
35. The groups and organizations I join have strict rules and regulations.
36. I believe God has given us commandments and rules to live by, and we fail if we don't follow all of them.

Now go back and count the number of statements you answered "true," including the ones you agreed with of the first four statements. A score of 10 or less reflects a fairly relaxed person. A score of 11 to 20 is average. A score of 21 or more reflects a definite tendency toward workaholism. If you scored in the twenties or beyond, you are also likely to become a victim of burnout.

"FACTS ONLY" THINKING ENCOURAGES BURNOUT

Unfortunately, the business world today makes a virtue out of "facts only" type of thinking. Most graduate business programs teach the student to use the "scientific method" alone in solving business problems, using only facts and logic. That means the emotional side of the employee, as well as of the supervisor, is totally ignored. We agree with a well-known executive management consultant's assessment that if business would deal with the emotional side of an employee, the whole person, the business would have a much more productive worker.

In his consulting business, this man deals with how clients and their employees are feeling. He says that too often business and industry take great employees and continually push them to make increased productivity levels until they burn out and start producing less and less. When that happens, industry usually thinks that they'll simply fire them and hire replacements. However, statistics show that it takes about two years to get a new employee to the point of productivity of an established worker. He recommends that, instead of firing employees who are not producing well, it is more productive to find a niche for them that is better suited for their personality strengths. That means paying attention to the way employees feel about and relate to the world around them. That policy is one followed by Japanese businesses, which today are experiencing a far higher productivity average than are American businesses.

CARING FOR THE WHOLE WORKER

Another policy followed in Japan is that no one works after hours and employee exercise periods and other breaks are adhered to strictly. Psychiatric studies have proved such workstyles are superior to those generally followed in American business, where employees are much more susceptible to burnout.

An example from this consultant's own experience, one with an ironic twist, validates that thinking. He was working for a Fortune 500 company, where all the other junior executives came early, stayed late, and always carried home briefcases filled with papers to work on at night. He, however, worked only regular hours and, although he took home a briefcase every night just to let everyone know he wasn't shirking, there was never anything in it!

He had already realized that competing with many others to become an officer of the company wasn't a worthy goal. Spending a half-hour in the Word every morning, he was seeing what priorities were all about, that life on earth is like the snap of a finger compared with life eternal. As he is fond of saying, "The only things you're going to be able to take into eternity with you are your spouse and children."

As a result, he concentrated on the Lord, his family, and his health outside of regular office hours. He then showed up every morning at work feeling rested and ready to put his all into his job during the regular work day. He laughs when he goes on to say that he was then given one of the first promotions among the junior executives, with a bonus of an extra week's vacation. Why? Because his superiors were sure he must be spending too much overtime on his work in order to accomplish as much as he did!

There are numerous examples of biblical characters—Joseph, Daniel, Nehemiah—who spent time with God every day and who, as a result, were among the top in the business worlds of their day. God wants people with a balanced life-style to be able to show the world that He is in control. For some, that will mean that He will see to it that they will reach the top and be able to do a good job from that position. For others, of course, He will have a simpler position in life from which they can glorify Him best.

When workers are young, it is easy for them to work hard, fast, and long and not spend time to pause and reflect on what they are doing. They hope that work pace will get them the prestige and prosperity they want in their career within a certain number of years, at which time they hope to be able to sit back, relax, and enjoy life and their families. Meanwhile, their health deteriorates and their families desert them, either physically or emotionally, for families can't wait all those years for satisfactory relationships. In his later years, the president of a large, successful, construction company in the Midwest, often said, "Slow down and take time to think. I wish I had done that when I was young, instead of working fifteen to twenty hours a day."

Another company president, Mr. H, our case example, also learned the value of slowing down and accomplishing more. When he received our psychiatric help, he came to realize that, at age fifty, there were certain things he should not be able to do as well and as rapidly as he could at thirty, but there were other things that he should be able to do better. He accepted his physical limitations but was made aware that he was now a lot wiser than he was at thirty. At fifty he should be using his wisdom and experience to bring success to his company rather than his "elbow grease."

So Mr. H cut down to a thirty-five-hour work week and began accomplishing a significant amount of good through decision-making and learning to delegate more to people under him. In fact, his company did better, and so did his family, after he slowed down to thirty-five hours a week than it had done when he was working sixty hours a week.

That proves another point that is counter to the thinking of most workaholics and burnout victims. No one is indispensable. There are other people who can do their jobs, or at least part of their jobs, as well if not better than they can. That doesn't mean the burnout victim isn't needed. It means only that he or she can be more successful in a more concentrated area while using much less energy.

As Howard Hendricks, professor at Dallas Theological Seminary, says "When you play the game of climbing the ladder to success, you may reach the top and find that, all the time, the ladder was resting against the wrong wall." Almost always, family members who take the time to enjoy one another and the simpler things in life, even if they have to sacrifice materialistic niceties to do so, are happier than those who are bringing in more money but have to sacrifice time with one another.

Of course, there are times when career transitions may make it necessary to work harder or longer for several months or so, but even then, a time limit should be set on how long one will continue to keep up such a pace and ignore or give lesser attention to other important areas of life.

One area of burnout experienced by too many today is that involving the start of a new business venture. Often, a new entrepreneur will work day and night to make a new venture profitable in a shorter amount of time than is needed. The time constraint usually has to do with financial considerations. Not enough money was available at the beginning of the venture to keep it afloat for the reasonable amount of time needed to start turning a profit. A word of warning might be to make sure enough money has been saved or raised before entering a new venture, rather than burning yourself out trying to make the new venture profitable in too short a time.

LOOKING FOR EMPLOYEE BURNOUT

An employer or supervisor may suspect burnout when an employee exhibits frequent absenteeism, more indecision, and less attention to personal grooming and health. The Monday "blahs" or blues may be an indication of approaching burnout. Of course, by the time the Monday "blahs" last all week long, the employee is in the midst of burnout. If the burnout victim is a supervisor, he or she should realize that burnout symptoms probably exist in those that report to him or her, as well. The supervisor should consider what can be done to encourage employees to want to come to work. It may include changes in reporting relationships, in office environment, and in allowing employees to have a say in the best way to accomplish projects.

Often, the relationship between employee and supervisor is to blame for burnout. The employee, if unable to change the relationship with the supervisor, should still ask, "What purpose for the Lord do I have in this job?" Often, the strains of the situation may be endured more easily when we know that God has a purpose for our being in that particular place at that particular time.

As for our nurse case example, Miss D (who was working overtime too much and was ignoring patients' buzzers), therapy helped get in touch with the anger she had toward her supervisor. After that she was able to be more helpfully assertive and not fear her supervisor's wrath or power. She let her supervisor know that she could not function working that many hours. Miss D told her that she either had to work a forty-hour week or find another job, and her supervisor agreed to allow her to work a reduced schedule. Through therapy, learning to forgive her supervisor, and cutting down her work schedule, Miss D was able to overcome her burnout and, again, become an important part in the healing of her patients.

GOD'S WILL FOR THE WORKAHOLIC

The crux of the consideration for Christians who don't want to burn out may be to consider if they are in the job God has for them. If you think you'll be fired if you spend sufficient time with family and on rest and relaxation, then it is unlikely that it is the job God has for you. Before quitting the company, however, it may be fruitful to consider if there is another type of position in the same company that would suit you better. One young Christian accountant in a large company realized that his chosen career was giving him little opportunity to deal with people on a personal level. Because he needed such contact, he asked to be switched to the human relations or personnel department of the company as a trainer. Today, he has won many awards for his innovative work efficiency programs and methods of motivating factory workers.

When we put God, family, and work in any other order, we have diminished our faithfulness to God and are saying, "I don't trust God to meet my needs." God would much rather we have less income and a more enjoyable life-style. If you quit the road to burnout, you may indeed face the possibility of being fired. However, you may be surprised to find that your rating in the company will go up instead of down, as you enter each day fresher and more ready to give your best to producing during the part of the day that should be allotted to work.

One former burnout victim and workaholic, a company chief executive officer, uses the following checklist to get his life in balance.

1. Realize that you don't have to be perfect to be "somebody." You are already "somebody" in Christ because He says you are.
2. Realize that you don't have to be completely neat in order to have other people and yourself approve of you.
3. Look at life from the eternity perspective. What will you take with you?
4. Learn to relax with activities that are relaxing to you.
5. Get in touch with your hidden anger, then forgive others for their part in it, and forgive yourself for having it.

Learning a new way of life comes hard for a workaholic, but it is necessary. A workaholic has to practice being relaxed, practice saying no to others' expectations of him, schedule time with God, schedule eight hours of sleep, and schedule time with family. The alternative is to become progressively less productive and of less benefit to loved ones and to himself as a result of burnout.

6

BURNING OUT FOR GOD

Some of the prime candidates for burnout are those people who want to serve the Lord "full-time" with all their heart, soul, and mind. Christians in vocational ministry often find themselves on the edge or in the depths of burnout. Among young, zealous Christian workers, the desire to "burn out for God" is often considered even an admirable trait and goal. The realities of carrying that goal long term, however, can be disastrous personally and to a ministry.

Several years ago, at a pastors' conference, one minister bragged to his colleagues, "I haven't taken a vacation in ten years. The only time I take off is a day once or twice a year." He then laughed at the warnings of his colleagues about keeping such a schedule. The next year at the pastors' conference, the news was passed around that that pastor was no longer in the ministry. He had suffered a physical and emotional collapse.

Another Christian worker, Jan Markell, wrote a book about her experience. She explains that she became so ministry-oriented she "was determined to serve God full-time, at least eighty hours a week."[1] As a result, she came close to suffering permanent physical damage.

1. Jan Markell and Jane Winn, *Overcoming Stress* (Wheaton, Ill.: Victor, 1982), p. 24.

The desire to burn out for God can be a costly one, for that is not what He calls us to do. Too many Christian workers burn out long before their time, spending only half a career or less in Christian service. If they continue in vocational ministry, often a long recovery period is needed before they begin to feel effective again. As one ministry-burnout victim explained it, "The usual problem with burning out for God is that you don't burn *out*, you just burn *down* to a flicker. Then you spend frustrating months and even years doing nothing but sputtering or flickering for God."

BURNOUT HABITS START EARLY

The seeds for that kind of problem, according to Dr. Archibald Hart, are usually planted during the first few years of one's career, when ministry habits and work styles are formed.[2] With a lot of textbook knowledge, hope, and untried faith, new pastors straight out of seminary or Bible college tend to look upon their calling idealistically. They believe they can solve immediately—with the flipping of Scripture pages—any and all problems they confront.

When reality proves them wrong, they continue striving to solve all problems, even though the amount of effort needed is much greater than what they had anticipated. Too late they realize that instead of doubling up their work efforts in order to keep their idealistic goals, it would have been better to have tempered their goals and recognized that *solving* other people's problems is not their calling. Being a *part* of the solution is all they are called to do. God will also use other people plus the Holy Spirit's

2. Archibald Hart, *Coping with Depression in the Ministry and Other Helping Professions* (Waco, Tex.: Word, 1984), p. 14.

leading in the life of the hurting persons to solve the problem.

Dr. David G. Congo surveyed ministers in thirty-two denominations in thirty-eight states to discover the significant factors involved in ministry burnout. His study isolated a number of significant factors involved in burnout.[3] Of the pastors surveyed:

- 70 percent worked more than sixty hours per week.
- 85 percent spent two or less evenings per week at home.
- 75 percent spent less than one evening a month purely for social time with their wives and other couples.

With such schedules, it's no wonder that many pastors experience burnout because they "grow weary in well-doing."

Of course, two other factors in ministry burnout include (1) working with a lean staff because of tight financial restrictions, and (2) everyone expecting Christian workers to put their all—heart, mind, body, and soul—into their work, since it is "for" God. Christian workers have to evaluate the work and opportunities that come to them with the question, "Is that what the Lord wants me to do at this time, or am I doing it just because it *seems* like such a great opportunity and need?" What the Lord leads you to do is not always the same as what you want to do *for* Him, especially if you are doing it in order that He or others might be more pleased with you, or that He or others might remain pleased with you.

3. David G. Congo, "What Causes Burnout?" *Theology News and Notes,* March 1984, p. 7.

Many people end up on the mission field because they see "the great need," and assume "the need is the call." That point of view is even stressed in some mission societies, often ones that have a high drop-out and burnout rate. That may well have been the problem with Mr. B, our missionary case example, who had been overwhelmed by the responsibilities and cultural differences on the mission field. Instead of using his minor health problem as an excuse for leaving the field, we encouraged him to prayerfully consider where he personally could serve God most effectively and then make arrangements to do that. Mr. B decided that he could serve God better in the U.S. as an associate pastor of a church, concentrating on counseling, at which, we assured him, he was gifted.

To relieve the guilt caused by exaggerating his health condition, he was encouraged to tell his financial and prayer supporters the truth of his mission field problems and that his physical health was not the decisive factor in his leaving the field. We told him that he might experience some hostility from a few supporters, but that most of them would welcome his honest openness with appreciation and would encourage him in his future ministry even more. And that is just what happened.

ON CALL FOR BURNOUT

The sense of being constantly "on call" is another major factor in ministry burnout. Ministry workers are almost constantly in contact with the sick, the hurting, the poor, the distressed, and the dying. Frequently, one crisis call is interrupted by another, with little time in between for recuperation. Many have described to us that sick or anxious feeling that occurs whenever the telephone rings, that sense of, "Well, who or what is it this time?" which may indicate approaching burnout.

Frequently, a feeling of indispensability accompanies these constant demands. People assume that they cannot face or overcome their problems unless they have personal help from their pastor. Sometimes, those to whom Christian workers minister initiate that thinking. Most commonly, however, it is the Christian workers themselves who generate that thinking in others. One pastor, feeling that he was becoming burned out, asserted, "I can't trust any of my staff members to take care of our people's problems." Since that pastor also communicated those feelings to his people, it's no wonder that they all tended to come to him directly.

As we mentioned earlier, more than three-fourths of the ministers tested through our clinic lean primarily toward workaholic, obsessive-compulsive tendencies. Work and productive activity are their major source of feelings of satisfaction and significance. Since they formed that attitude in early childhood communications with their parents, they assume their heavenly Father, too, is satisfied and pleased with them only when they are busy *doing* something *for* Him. They have inherited the "mantle of Martha," who was tied up in knots over much serving, rather than assuming the easy yoke of Christ that was meant for them.

THE DRIVE FOR CONTROL

The workaholic's main drive is a need for *achieving control*. Thus, workaholic ministers, as much as they would deny it, tend to "play God" over their congregations, often refusing to delegate control over even the least significant responsibility or problem. When instructed to delegate, they may *assign* control to others, but they then will insist on keeping on top of every detailed effort of the assignee.

Or, if one small assigned project is done to less than their own standards, they will usurp the authority they have given, take over the project themselves, and bemoan, "It seems I'm the only one who can get the job done." They refuse to see that God may be working in the other person's life, allowing him to learn from his mistakes in order to do better the next time, or if someone else needs to take over, it shouldn't be themselves.

BALANCING THE BURDEN BEARING

David Congo's pastoral burnout survey also showed that 61 percent of pastors spend less than one hour a week talking with other pastors.[4] A second key factor, then, can be observed from Congo's survey. Besides becoming burned out because they "grow weary in well-doing," many pastors receive little support from their peers in similar occupations.

The demands on a pastor often makes it difficult to carve out time to spend with fellow pastors, yet time so invested can be invaluable in keeping them from burning out. That situation is often even more acute in the case of foreign missionaries, who may find geographical, cultural, and financial barriers to peer fellowship and support. The difficulty comes when they allow the ever-increasing pressures of more to do and less time in which to do it to crowd out time when they and other fellow servants of

4. Ibid.

Christ could be "bearing one another's burdens." Such loners often reap the harvest of their failure to sow seeds of mutual support. Frequently, that harvest will involve burnout.

John D. Carter and Janelle Warner studied a selected group of Presbyterian pastors, their wives, and church members, to assess the differences in loneliness, marital adjustment, and vocational burnout. Their conclusion was that both pastors and pastors' wives experienced significantly more *loneliness* than those in non-pastoral roles, and that pastors' wives experienced higher levels of *emotional exhaustion* than non-pastoral males and females. Thus their statistical survey substantiated the premise that burnout is related to a lack of support.

According to the Carter/Warner study, "The pastor and his wife . . . spent less time together because of the demands of their efforts in Christian service. Subsequently, they may begin psychologically to withdraw from each other and from friendships due to burnout; he being overly involved and she being emotionally exhausted. As a result, they experience loneliness and less marital satisfaction."[5]

Christian workers know that the Creator has established certain fundamental laws upon which things operate. They don't try to defy the law of gravity or assume that, if they refuse to recognize it, it won't operate. However, they often try personally to defy or to refuse to recognize God's principle of sowing and reaping. They may teach it to others, putting great emphasis on Galatians 6:7, "Do not be deceived: God cannot be mocked. A man reaps what he

5. John D. Carter and Janelle Warner, "Loneliness, Marital Adjustment and Burnout in Pastoral and Lay Persons," *Journal of Psychology and Theology,* Summer 1984.

sows." They fail to recognize, however, that in Galatians 6 the apostle Paul is relating the principle of sowing and reaping to the *imbalance in carrying each other's burdens*.

Paul explains how Christians should function in relationship rather than in isolation.

> Brothers, if someone is caught in a sin, you who are spiritual should restore him gently. But watch yourself, or you also may be tempted. Carry *each other's* burdens, and in this way you will fulfill the law of Christ. If anyone thinks he is something when he is nothing, he deceives himself. Each one should test his own actions. Then he can take pride in himself, *without comparing himself* to somebody else, for each one should carry *his own load*. (Galatians 6:1-5, italics added)

In the process of explaining the overall implications of spiritual sowing and reaping in connection with other people, Paul shows a knowledge of what today we call burnout. He exhorts us to "carry [bear] each other's [heavy] burdens," in order to help Christians who have fallen into sin regain spiritual health without being tempted to sin again (because of having to carry too heavy a load).

To *disperse* and *balance* the carrying of one another's loads within the Christian community, Paul also urges us *not* to carry *too much* of others' burdens. "Watch yourself, or you also may be tempted" (v. 1). Then he warns against the opposite extreme— allowing others to take on too much of *our own* responsibilities. "Each one should carry his own [light or manageable] load" (v. 5).

Then, in verse 9, Paul brings the sharing of burdens exhortation and its accompanying principle of spiritual sowing and reaping to bear on symptoms that we know to be involved in burnout. He states,

"Let us not become weary in doing good, for at the proper time ["in due season," KJV] we will reap a harvest if we *do not give up*" (italics added).

The implications of that verse for burnout sufferers is obvious. First, they become "weary" in doing good. Pouring themselves into the quest for accomplishing more and more, they are overcome by exhaustion. They take increasingly less and less time for having personal, physical, and spiritual needs met.

LOSING ONE'S PERSPECTIVE

That leads to the second factor, they lose their long-term perspective, unable to see that "in due season, we shall reap." They sacrifice the future on the altar of the present.

An example of that second factor is Ed, a dynamic young Bible college graduate, who had overcome a speech impediment, and who was called to serve as pastor of one of only two Bible-teaching churches in a medium-sized city. At first, things went well. However, after several months, Ed discovered the existence of deep divisions in the church body. The harder he tried to heal those divisions, the more he discovered that the people on both sides turned against him. He and his wife became the targets of frequent criticism, which led to further discouragement. Hours and hours of meetings with the various factions failed to do anything but deepen the divisions.

After less than two years in the pastorate, Ed gave up, even though two fellow pastors had encouraged him to "hang in there." As one of the church leaders put it shortly after Ed's resignation, "He had already been through the worst of it; in fact, things were about to turn around. We probably would have lost one more family and, I think, after that, there would have been harmony." Unable to see that his persistence was about to pay off, today Ed is out of the ministry, divorced from his wife, and selling insurance.

GIVING UP

Ed's case also illustrates the third factor isolated for us by the apostle Paul in Galatians 6:9. He simply gave up. Paul says, "We will reap . . . *if we do not give up*" (italics added). Giving up is the culmination of the burnout process Paul described for us in Galatians 6:9. The process begins with *doing well*, but as well-doing escalates, we *become weary;* we then *lose the perspective* of "reaping in due season" and, ultimately, we "faint" or give up.

REVERSING MINISTRY BURNOUT

Please note that the answer is not to cease doing well. It is the contrary. Paul explains in verse 10, "As we have opportunity, let us do good to all people, especially to those who belong to the family of believers."

WORK FOR NEED, NOT APPROVAL

Often, the problem arises when we go beyond opportunity, endeavoring to gain the approval of self, God, or others on a performance basis. In his survey, Congo observes that some pastors have personality tendencies that make them more vulnerable to burnout. These are pastors who "have a high need for approval, pastors who derive their self-esteem from their work, pastors who are unassertive and feel controlled by others, and pastors who believe that the only way a job will be done right is if they do it themselves.[6] That, he says, answers the question why in a given church one pastor burns out and another thrives.

According to Congo, one way to avoid burnout is, "Turn the rat race into a relay."[7] His suggestions mirror the principles articulated by the apostle Paul in Galatians 6:9. One involves not trying to do it all yourself. Certainly, in that context, Paul's emphasis on bearing one another's burdens is one often overlooked by pastors who consider themselves the bearer of burdens for all those to whom they minister and who consider it inappropriate to share their own burdens with others. Those patterns, obviously, are prime candidates for burnout.

One of us found that true in his own ministry. His workaholism was all right while he was in college, graduate school, medical school, and during a hospital residency in psychiatry. But then he began experiencing burnout. His main symptoms were exhaustion and anger. His worst experience was when he was teaching pastoral counseling in a seminary, carrying on a part-time private practice, counseling students at home at no charge, taking theology courses, and speaking at seminars nearly every weekend. He said yes to every chance to minister.[8]

He then would read in Matthew 11:28 that God's "yoke is easy and his burden is light." That verse, he said, made him angry because he thought God's burden was overwhelming. Then he began to see that not all his burdens were from God. Many burdens he had taken on were a result of his own insecurities

6. Congo, p. 7.
7. Ibid., p. 8.
8. For further information see the introduction from *The Workaholic and His Family,* by Frank Minirth et al. (Grand Rapids: Baker, 1981), p. 13.

and subsequent desire to please everybody.

At that point, he learned to prioritize things better, to put his own relationship with God first, his family next, and his work or ministry third. That took several years to bring to complete reality. Now, instead of saying yes to everybody, he says no most of the time. When his schedule gets to the point of being a full "light" burden, then he says no to everything else, in order to keep time for his family.

A sidelight to his decision was that, at first, he had the following negative results:

1. He felt false guilt over not doing as many things as he had previously, when he thought that God wanted him personally to "rescue the world for Christ." He realized that if he personally were to try to meet every need he saw, he would soon be only one more needy person. Occasionally, he still feels a twinge of false guilt, however, when he can't meet others' demands or expectations.
2. He received hostility from other Christians, who were not used to his saying no (or who didn't think he should) to requests to minister to specific needs, to serve on boards, or to attend Christian meetings.
3. As he cut his work load from seventy-five to forty hours a week, he started having more time for contemplation. As a result, he began getting painful insights into himself, as he got in touch with his feelings. He saw selfishness there. He often had done good deeds not out of a genuine expression of compassion for people's needs but as an attempt to gain the approval and praise of others, in order to compensate for feelings of inferiority. It took him three years to work through those reactions.

Was his decision worth it? Yes. He now experiences great peace and joy in his life. He enjoys intimate fellowship with his wife. He experiences mutual love with his children. He has learned to trust God—not himself—to rescue the world, while he still desires to play the part that God has for him. And he now accomplishes, through half the effort, many times more than he was accomplishing then, a feat he would have previously considered impossible.

His experience has been used in his own counseling ministry since that time, including with Reverend C, our case example. When Reverend C came for counseling, he was encouraged first to become informed about his obsessive-compulsive, perfectionist personality by reading the book, *The Workaholic and His Family.* Then he was helped to work through some of the conflicts his personality created.

Through counseling, he too came to realize that he needed to make priorities in his life and really find God's "light and easy yoke" for him. We encouraged him to work a forty- to fifty-hour work week and then spend the rest of his time with his family, in personal devotions, and seeing to other personal needs. He was encouraged to go ahead and say no to parishioners when he didn't have time to do certain things. When he did that, he felt guilt at first, and he had a few church members who became angry with him for not meeting all their needs or demands immediately. Having made the choice to put up with any such hostility, however, he was able to work through his own false guilt.

Reverend C discovered that, with more time to think and to feel, he also became more aware of his own depravity and selfish motives. He had to work through those and begin growing more toward Christlike maturity. He has done fine in his ministry since that time, has recovered from burnout, and now has the insights to prevent burnout from happening again.

Another suggestion by Dr. Congo is to "gain a clear sense of your purpose and priorities."[9] That is the apostle Paul's perspective on "reaping in due season." When a pastor drags in the front door at 11:00 P.M. following an unpleasant board meeting, only to discover urgent messages to return calls to three church members—two of whom are having major life crises and the third who is a major critic—it is difficult to maintain perspective. However, that is precisely the point at which he must focus on "due season."

Second, Paul maintained his perspective. Instead of focusing on the present, "what is seen" (2 Corinthians 4:18), his perspective was eternal; he focused on "what is unseen." Frequently, whether in vocational ministry or not, our focus is on the pressures, problems, conflicts, and frustrations that invariably will lead to burnout. Why didn't Paul burn out with all the adversities he experienced? His perspective enabled him to catalog his sufferings as "our light and momentary troubles are achieving for us an eternal glory that far outweighs them all" (v. 17). Such a perspective answers Dr. Congo's question, "Why, in a given church, does one pastor burn out and another thrive?" In summary, we can avoid burning out if we maintain perspective beyond present adversities.

Another important point to remember is that perspective is easier to maintain in relationship than in isolation. Dr. Herbert Freudenberger explains that when we experience burnout, we often seek detachment from support. He explains, "When you separate

9. Congo, p. 8.

yourself from people and events, you strip them of the power to hurt you. Unfortunately, you also diminish their power to affect you in positive ways."[10]

Based on what he wrote to the Galatians, if Paul were conducting a seminar or workshop on burnout today, he would not only underscore the importance of maintaining a perspective, he would urge those experiencing burnout, especially those in vocational ministry, to "carry one another's burdens." He might even point to his own example of keeping such men as Luke, Timothy, and Titus with him, or quote his call to Timothy to "get here before winter" (2 Timothy 4:21). To underscore the urgency of allowing time for peer support in ministry, Paul might add that the alternative is burnout.

In most churches, 80 percent of the work is done by 20 percent of the people. And, if the pastor feels that he himself is doing that 80 percent, then he needs to spread out the work, not just to one or two church members, who may then reach burnout themselves, but to many people. If the work doesn't get done, he should let the people see that. God will not have one hand tied behind His back and the world will not crash and disintegrate if we roll it and its burdens off our shoulders.

Finally, the temptation to quit always lurks just behind the next problem. The apostle Paul himself certainly experienced a multitude of pressures and faced the temptation to give up. However, in discussing the ministry he had received from God, he shared with his Corinthian readers the dynamic that enabled him to continue serving Christ despite adversity. As he explains in 2 Corinthians 4:16, "Therefore

10. Herbert Freudenberger and Geraldine Richelson, *Burn-Out* (New York: Anchor, Doubleday, 1980), p. 62.

we do not lose heart. Though outwardly we are wasting away, yet inwardly we are being renewed day by day." Despite being "hard pressed on every side, but not crushed; perplexed, but not in despair; persecuted, but not abandoned; struck down, but not destroyed," Paul did not give up. His outward man was "wasting away," but he was experiencing the inward renewal of the power of God's indwelling spirit. Paul had tapped into the source of inexhaustible spiritual power available to the inner man.

A minister's role is "to serve God," not to "burn out for God." Continued stress and burnout diminish a Christian worker's capacity to render effective service to others. Furthermore, for those in vocational ministry always to give out and not allow others to minister or give to them ignores the fundamental biblical truth that the body of Christ is to have different parts that minister to one another.

7
JESUS TREATS TWELVE
TIRED MEN

During college days, one of our therapists suffered an arm injury during a basketball game. The arm was X-rayed by an orthopedic surgeon, who said no bones had been broken. After a few days' rest, the student resumed his basketball activities, as well as a job that involved lifting heavy boxes.

When, over a period of weeks, pain in the arm persisted and then worsened, the student returned to the orthopedist. A new set of X-rays showed the wrist now had a complete break. The arm had to be immobilized, and the stress of lifting boxes and playing basketball had to stop.

So it is with burnout. As seen in previous chapters, the stresses of life can lead to physical, emotional, and spiritual symptoms of burnout. Then, when these symptoms persist, it is imperative that stress levels be lightened so that recovery can begin.

Jesus recognized that when He saw His disciples return from a missionary trip on which He had sent them. In Mark 6:7, Jesus' great Galilean ministry is drawing to a close. Multitudes had thronged to hear His words and witness His miracles. The stress of those busy days for Jesus and His followers was compounded by a rising opposition on the part of the Pharisees, the official religious leaders of Israel. During that time, our Savior was particularly gripped with feelings of compassion toward the multitudes, whom He characterized as "harassed and helpless, like sheep without a shepherd" (Matthew 9:36).

At that point, Christ implemented a new phase of His ministry. It is described in Mark 6: "Calling the Twelve to him, he sent them out two by two. . . . They went out and preached that people should repent. They drove out many demons and anointed many sick people with oil and healed them. . . . The apostles gathered around Jesus and reported to him all they had done and taught" (vv. 7, 12-13, 30).

Mark interrupted the telling of the disciples' mission to explain to his readers of the death of John the Baptist (vv. 14-29), which evidently came about the time the twelve had set out on their mission. It's not difficult to sense just how stressful that time must have been for the twelve.

Several factors indicate how their stress may have risen to burnout levels. First, Mark's use of the word *apostles* in verse 30, coupled with the description of Christ's giving them authority (v. 7), indicates that that was their first official mission on their own. They were like novice salesmen who had completed their training and just set out with their materials into their assigned territory, or like a college quarterback who suddenly finds himself, after many practices, at the helm of the offensive team during the first regular-season game.

Coupled with the pressure to do well was the reality of spiritual opposition—"and gave them authority over evil spirits" (v. 7); the necessity of trusting God for providing their day-to-day needs—"Take nothing for the journey except a staff—no bread, no bag, no money in your belts. Wear sandals but not an extra tunic" (vv. 8-9); the constant drain of living out of a suitcase—"Whenever you enter a house, stay there until you leave that town" (v. 10); and the ever-present threat of personal rejection—"And if any place will not welcome you or listen to you, shake the dust off your feet when you leave, as a testimony against them" (v. 11). Then, after busy months of ministry and travel, they returned to Jesus and were informed of the tragic death of John the Baptist. By that time, they were prime candidates for burnout.

Although Mark's account of their debriefing (v. 30) indicates that Christ wanted to hear their report, it also indicates that He was more concerned about the effects their mission had on them than He was about hearing what they had done. None of the gospels record that any of Christ's comments were critical of their ministry. However, Mark indicated that Christ's immediate concern was to relieve their pressure.

That incident highlights an important principle for employers, supervisors, and Christian leaders. It is often easy to become so concerned with "getting the job done" or "doing it right" that we lose sight of the needs of the people who are actually carrying on the work. That is especially true if the employer or supervisor is an obsessive-compulsive workaholic too. Our Savior displayed a type of personal concern and compassion needed today when He said to His disciples, "Come with me by yourselves to a quiet place and get some rest [or 'rest a while,' KJV]" (Mark 6:31). He sensed that the burnout factor was present in them, so, although there was a vast number of people still unreached, He instructed them to take a break.

A close examination of Christ's brief statement shows there are three key elements that, when combined, can relieve the stresses that lead to burnout. These are (1) a change in location, (2) a change in activity or responsibility, and (3) a certain amount of time.

A CHANGE IN LOCATION

It is significant that Christ did not simply say, "Take a break." He specifically told His disciples to come aside, or change location, to a quiet place. In fact, the term Christ uses for the location to which the disciples were directed suggests that it was a remote or solitary place. Christ knew His disciples would be unable to experience relief from stress as long as they were in contact with "so many people . . . coming and going that they did not even have a chance to eat" (v. 31).

Regular vacations with a change of locale and even occasional "getaways" or "mini-vacations" are an important part of preventing burnout or of relieving burnout once it has occurred.

How does a psychiatrist escape burnout? One has developed a mountain retreat in a neighboring state to which he makes regular visits. For him, that change in location from a busy urban ministry to the quiet solitude of mountain greenery is an important key to preventing burnout.

Whether your getaway place is a nearby campground, the mountains, the beach, or just a weekend "escape package" at a nearby hotel, it is important to carve out time for a change of scenery.

A CHANGE IN ACTIVITY

The second factor seen in Christ's instructions is a change in activity or responsibility. It is significant that the same person who sent them on their ministry mission now tells them to rest up. The particular word used by Christ, which can be accurately trans-

lated "rest up," indicates that the disciples themselves needed to take the initiative to do that. So it is
with an individual experiencing stress today. Often, a
person may know he or she should rest, but there is a
temptation not to take time to do so. Eventually, the
discovery is made that failure to get proper rest is a
shortcut to burnout.

For years, a minister in a busy pastorate also
carried an early morning radio ministry. Late night
board and committee meetings, as well as ministry
phone calls, were followed by the sound of a 4:00 A.M.
alarm clock to prepare for radio ministry that began
at six. When years of that frantic schedule began to
take its toll, the concerned advice of friends was
heeded. The radio ministry and schedule were modi-
fied and burnout was averted.

A CHANGE FOR A TIME

The third element in Christ's instructions to his
disciples is an amount of time. The tense of the verb
"to rest" indicates a relatively short period of time.
The point is that a planned amount of time should be
taken for a change in location and activity. That was
particularly needed in light of the description of their
surroundings during the debriefing—crowds of people meeting each other coming and going, leaving the
disciples with no spare moment to call their own,
even in order to eat.

That description of the disciples' circumstances
may strike a responsive chord with you. If so, perhaps Jesus is also telling you, "Come with me by
yourselves to a quiet place and get some rest."

A final glance at the disciples in this chapter
surfaces two important facts. First, they did take action to alleviate the stresses that lead to burnout. "So

they went away by themselves in a boat to a solitary place" (v. 32). However, when they reached that solitary place, there were already crowds there waiting for them, so their getaway didn't last long. Nevertheless, the boat journey itself was at least a short time of change of location and activity away from the crowds.

The continued demands of people for ministry, however, ultimately contributed to the dulling of their spiritual perception. When they saw Jesus feed the five thousand in that solitary place, with only five loaves of bread and two fish, they were still too numb to take it all in. As a result, when they saw Jesus walking on the water later that night, "they were completely amazed, for they had not understood about the loaves; their hearts were hardened" (vv. 51-52). Burnout can leave one so hardened or disillusioned with the world that one has little emotional or spiritual energy left to comprehend the supernatural or the meaning behind it.

The lesson to be learned from these twelve tired men is evident. When the stresses of life are building to the burnout level, it is time to consider a change of location, a change in activity or responsibility, and an amount of time in which to take a break. The alternative may be burnout.

8

STARTING THE UPWARD SPIRAL PHYSICALLY

Escaping or reversing burnout primarily involves taking care of yourself physically, mentally, and spiritually, allowing God and others to help you in that task. But, first of all, you have to decide to take the initiative yourself, realizing that taking care of self is a responsibility given us by God. Without meeting that responsibility, we will never be able to succeed in the life-long purposes He has for us.

TAKING CARE OF YOURSELF

At our clinic, we have patients complete a "Taking Care of Yourself" test, which gives them and us some idea of how well they are accomplishing that God-given task. We have divided these test questions into three categories: the physical, emotional, and spiritual, even though some of the questions include elements of more than one category.

The following are the questions to the physical parts of this questionnaire and the advice we give our patients, including those suffering from burnout. Except in cases of suicidal thinking (discussed in the next chapter), we advocate making changes in the physical areas of a burnout victim's life first. Just feeling better physically often begins to change a person's burned out emotions and gives them the strength to begin other changes—physical, emotional, and spiritual.

PHYSICAL CARE

1. Did you exercise three times this past week?
The medical profession has maintained for years that being in good physical condition makes a noticeable difference in longevity, and good health. Exercise can help keep off weight, keep blood pressure under control, keep the heart healthy, and even ward off other diseases.

We have known that individuals become addicted to negative things, such as drugs and alcohol. However, we now know that they can become addicted to positive things also. William Glasser showed that people can become addicted to jogging. Such an addiction has a physical reason. Certain chemicals are released from the body during jogging and other healthful exercise that cause a sense of well being.

Scripture also indicates that physical training is of some value (1 Timothy 4:8). Being in good physical shape will aid your effectiveness for Christ.

2. Did you eat a balanced diet this week?
Diet is a major factor in the realm of physical health. Most nutritionists agree that the best diet is a balanced one that includes a little of all the food groups—meat and other proteins, vegetables, fruit, dairy products, and bread, cereals, and other grain products.

If you need to be on a weight-reducing diet, make sure it includes all the food groups, but less of each. The only way to lose weight and keep it off, healthily, is to reduce your calories and to exercise more. An important tip to remember is to ask yourself as you start to eat something, "Am I eating this to please God or to please myself?" Another important factor is not to base your self-worth on your physical appearance but on your position—who you are in Christ.

3. Did you get eight hours of sleep per night most nights this week?

Many people boast that they can get by on little sleep, but studies show that most adults need about eight hours of sleep per night to function at their best and to stay healthy. Children need even more. For example, an elementary school child may need ten or eleven hours, a junior high school student nine or ten, and a high school student eight to nine. Some elderly people, however, can get by on less than eight hours.

When we don't have enough sleep, we tend to be irritable, more critical, more depressed, have a harder time concentrating, work less efficiently, and enjoy life less. Actually, we can't serve God well if we aren't getting proper rest. Sleep is essential to sound mental, emotional, and spiritual health.

God Himself set a good example for us when He rested after creating the world over a six-day period. "On the seventh day he rested from all his work" (Genesis 2:2).

4. How much of a "Type A" personality are you?

The medical profession defines a "Type A" personality as one who is time oriented and never seems to have enough time. He tends to be competitive and success-oriented, a workaholic, often doing two or more things at once. That type of personality may experience a great deal of underlying anger behind the success orientation and have a stronger need to produce in order to feel succesful. Such persons are prone to heart disease and, statistically, are more likely to die young.

It is important for the Type A personality to slow down, relax, and put priorities in proper order. Type A personalities tend to move, walk, and eat rapidly. They also tend to hurry those with whom they are talking. Type A's get upset when waiting (in traffic or when placed on hold in a telephone conversation) and when they must perform repetitive tasks. They try to schedule things tighter and tighter in order to get more things done. Even taking a short break from work or taking time to relax and do nothing produces guilt.

Since Type A persons usually live life on a schedule—a tight schedule—they must rearrange that schedule to include time to relax, time with the Lord, time with children and mate, time just to goof off, and after all that, then their scheduled time for work. For most people, of course, that will involve the normal forty-hour work week, and when absolutely necessary, up to fifty hours—but no more. Then, after rearranging their schedule according to priorities, they must determine to follow it.

If you are a Type A, you need to develop an ability to slow down. To do that, become aware of your need to take life slower. Take deep, slow breaths to aid in the slowing down process. Review your former priorities and be determined to be content with completing or accomplishing perhaps half as many tasks a day as you would normally try to do, remembering that taking care of yourself and the emotional and spiritual needs of your loved ones is your first priority. For some, that means getting away for a while, for others, it means saying no to heading up that committee yet another year. Each of us is responsible for finding ways to be responsible toward himself.

LEARN TIME MANAGEMENT SKILLS

To spend less pressured time with work, time management skills may need to be sharpened. Will Rogers once said, "It's not so much what you do each day, it's what gets done that counts." Although this is not a book on time management, some practical suggestions are in order.

1. *Take inventory of your usage of time.* Invest time in scheduling, making lists of things to be accomplished, and prioritizing that list. Plan ahead, allowing sufficient time for interruptions. Beware of "time bandits," those things that intrude into your schedule and rob you of precious minutes and hours that could be used to accomplish the task at hand.

2. *Learn to concentrate on the task at hand.* Work at screening out distractions. Learn to distinguish between essential details and nonessentials.

3. *Be able to grasp the big picture.* Work at "majoring on the majors." Be sure to relate your daily tasks to overall life goals and even to "five-year goals."

4. *Work at being decisive.* Get all the information available and then make a decision. Don't put it off. Avoid procrastination.

5. *Learn to delegate, particularly those things that can be done effectively by other people.* Don't spread yourself too thin. Concentrate your time and energies on doing those few things you are best at doing.

Making changes in all these physical areas of your life will take time. However, as you start them, you will begin to find the physical strength to start making changes emotionally and spiritually as well.

9

STARTING THE UPWARD SPIRAL EMOTIONALLY

Before addressing those things that you can do to take care of yourself emotionally, we must address an emotional problem of the most severe burnout victim, that of suicidal thinking.

REVERSING SUICIDAL THINKING

A woman phoned in to our radio talk show recently to tell about her daughter who had been burned out and depressed. The depression had become a major one. She had voiced suicidal thoughts to her family on several occasions, but, partly because she was a Christian, they had not taken her seriously. Eventually, the daughter killed herself. The woman who phoned in did so to warn listeners to take seriously the suicidal thoughts of loved ones.

Anyone who is talking about suicide or who admits to having suicidal thoughts should be under professional care, preferably by a Christian psychiatrist or psychologist. Anyone who has a "suicide plan" should be hospitalized immediately.

To the severely depressed who have lost hope, suicide may seem the only way out of their situation. A severely burned out and depressed Christian may even become convinced that it is God's will, that God no longer wants him or her in this world. The Bible, however, shows that suicide is a sin equivalent to murder. The Scriptures record seven suicides: Abimelech (Judges 9:54), Samson (Judges 16:30), Saul (1 Samuel 31:43), Saul's armor bearer (1 Samuel 31:5), Ahithophel (2 Samuel 17:23), Zimri (1 Kings 16:18), and Judas Iscariot (Matthew 27:3-5). It is clear that none of those were in the will of God.

A common misconception involves the fear that to mention suicide to a depressed person will bring about thoughts that have not occurred previously or will increase the likelihood of a suicide attempt. Actually, to lovingly confront a person with a question about suicidal thoughts can be the first step toward reversing suicidal thinking, as it was with the depressed salesman, Mr. I, our case example whose pastor questioned him. Mr. I then spent four weeks in the hospital under our care. He was able to reverse his burnout and depression and to put his marriage and life back together.

In our ministry, we have developed ten warning signs of individuals who are most likely to attempt suicide. Several of these, as you will notice, have a close relationship with burnout.

WARNING SIGNS OF SUICIDE

1. Intense emotional pain, as seen in severe depression
2. Intense feelings of hopelessness
3. A prior history of a suicide attempt, or voiced warnings of suicidal intentions
4. Severe health problems
5. A significant loss—death of a spouse, loss of a job, and so on
6. Forming of a suicide plan
7. Chronic self-destructive behavior—alcoholism, an eating disorder, and so on
8. An intense need to achieve

9. An excess of disturbing life events within the past six months
10. Someone who is single, male, white, and more than forty-five years of age, who has experienced some of the above signs

TAKING CARE OF SELF—EMOTIONALLY

If your burnout has not reached the severe stage of suicidal thinking, our "Taking Care of Yourself" test includes a number of steps you can take personally to help reverse the emotional part of your burnout.

1. Have you laughed several times today?

A wise man once compared a cheerful or merry heart to good medicine (Proverbs 17:22). Laughter is a sign of good mental health. Medical studies indicate that laughter releases chemicals called endorphins in the brain, promoting feelings of well being. Author Norman Cousins helped himself recover from a debilitating disease by watching old film comedies and cartoons, allowing himself to laugh every day as part of his healing process. The absence of frequent laughter may be an external symptom indicating the presence of deeper emotional conflicts.

2. What percentage of your self-talk was positive today?

Each of us talks to ourselves. The way in which we talk to ourselves has a great deal to do with how we feel. Self-talk that is negative, derogatory, or critical fosters depression. Make an effort to be more positive, kind, and forgiving in the things you say to yourself. Why not set aside a time to consider how you talk to yourself? Look for specific changes. Forgive yourself when necessary and move on from personal failures.

3. What amount of time this past week did you spend living in the present?

Many people focus on past failures or past accomplishments. Either focus can be damaging to good mental health. Often when we are depressed, we focus on the past. It is important that we live in the here and now.

Another misplaced focus is dwelling only on what may happen in the future. Jesus says in Matthew 6:34, "Therefore do not worry about tomorrow, for tomorrow will worry about itself. Each day has enough trouble of its own." Anxiety causes that misplaced focus on the possible problems of tomorrow. Because of God's sovereign control, however, tomorrow will take care of itself.

Learn to deal with your past, look forward to your future, and live properly one day at a time in the here and now.

4. Did you do something three times this week for relaxation and recreation?

Maintaining good mental health often involves learning to relax. It is worthwhile to plan, at least three times a week, activities specifically dedicated to enjoyable recreation, something not connected with your usual line of work. If you are experiencing burnout or near burnout, try some recreational and relaxing activities other than your usual, since they obviously are not helping your situation.

That is particularly true of the one who views a lot of television, trying to forget the worries of the day through watching the traumas of make-believe characters. Watching make-believe, or even someone else's real life, is never a substitute for experiencing life yourself. Instead, shoot some baskets with your kids or play some table games with the whole family. Do those activities for fun, without a highly competitive attitude. Occasionally, you might even play less than your best in order to let the other person win. It will be good for his or her self-esteem and sense of pleasure, and for your sense of values.

If a job or vocation is exceedingly stressful, tiring, frustrating, or boring over a long period of time, perhaps a change in responsibilities, activities, job, or career needs to be considered. If possible, a sabbatical may be in order. But make sure the change is to positive types of activities, although less demanding ones. Don't act on a burnout impulse to become a full-time hermit, beach bum, or occasional tinkerer.

For two of our case examples, consideration of changing jobs brought different decisions.

The eighteen-year-old factory worker, Mr. F, did go back to his job temporarily. Meanwhile, he received vocational testing at our clinic and found that he had gifts in some other areas. Also, he discovered that his type of personality would not tolerate a monotonous job. (Some people can do monotonous work and even seem to thrive on it. They block out the monotony and just seem to enjoy themselves. Other people need new and different challenges.)

Eventually, Mr. F quit his job and began work as a carpenter, where he could do different things each day and see the work of his hands begin to make a house take shape. Only when he changed jobs to one more compatible with his personality did he recover completely from his burnout.

Mrs. E, the mental health worker who counseled depressed people, was encouraged to take a different tack. To continue working in such a specific and difficult area, she found that thirty hours of counseling a week, instead of her former fifty to sixty hours, was all that she could handle effectively. She was then able to spend more time relaxing and working in her church. A change of pace and rearrangement of her schedule, rather than a change of job, was the key to reversing her burnout.

LEARN STRESS MANAGEMENT

Although a certain amount of stress is necessary and even good, our response to stress can make us capable of meeting more of the necessary stresses of life successfully. And although a lifting of as much stress as possible may be necessary to recover from current burnout, stress management needs to be learned to avoid future burnout. That involves:

- learning when it is appropriate to say no, both to yourself and to others who may place demands on you
- learning when it is appropriate to settle for limited objectives
- being able to distinguish between situations in which you should respond with your "flight or fight" defense mechanism in gear and those in which you should take a less concerned approach

We must learn to recognize our limitations as human and, when we sense that we are close to our limit, take a deep breath, relax, and seek—at least temporarily—a change of pace, a change of place, and a change of perspective. If you think you can't afford a vacation, then make it a financial priority and plan and budget for it.

5. How often were you stuck on "Plan A" this month?
"Plan A" is your routine schedule. It includes all

the things you normally do each day from the time you get up to the time you go to bed. Plan A includes the events of your day, your activities, your habits, and your appearance. People often become depressed because they are following Plan A.

If your Plan A is leading to frequent bouts with burnout and depression, it may be time to form a Plan B. That may involve coming up with five to ten specific things you can do in a given period of time, say a week, to change how you feel. Recreational activities mentioned above would be a part of that. Other changes to your plan may include just rearranging your before-work activities. If you feel sluggish until you eat breakfast, eat breakfast when you first get up. If you have trouble keeping your eyes open when reading your Bible first thing in the morning, take a shower first. If finding something to wear each morning is a great frustration, start laying out clothes the night before.

When developing Plan B, set aside specific time to invest in time with the Lord. Include one meaningful social contact each day, by phone if necessary. Develop a daily routine that includes some variety and is more personally satisfying, if only in the little things. People who are more emotionally oriented tend to become bored more quickly. Variety in daily life helps that.

Plan B should also include refreshing Sundays or whatever day you have off. Scripture says the "Sabbath" should include refreshment, no work, celebration of our relationship with God, assembling together with Christian friends and with relatives, and enjoying life.*

---

*Note: although the New Testament doesn't mention the Mosaic command to observe the Sabbath, the Sabbath-rest principle existed in the Mosaic law.

6. How much change have you experienced during the past year?

Because of the mobile society in which we live, change is a major factor in life. Changes in residence, employment, or schools all produce stress points. Medical studies show that if too many stress points accumulate during any one year, there is a great likelihood of developing significant physical or emotional problems. The Holmes-Rahe Stress Test was designed to identify the number and severity of stress factors experienced by an individual during the preceding year. A total of two hundred or more stress points can indicate the presence of or likelihood of burnout.

THE STRESS OF ADJUSTING TO CHANGES[1]

Events	Scale of Impact
Death of a spouse	100
Divorce	73
Marital separation	65
Jail term	63
Death of close family member	63
Personal injury or illness	53
Marriage	50
Fired at work	47
Marital reconciliation	45
Retirement	45
Change in health of family member	44
Pregnancy	40
Sex difficulties	39
Gain of new family member	39

1. Reprinted with permission of T. H. Holmes and R. H. Rahe, "The Social Adjustment Rating Scale," *Journal of Psychosomatic Research*, II:213. Copyright 1967, Pergamon Press.

Business readjustment	39
Change in financial state	38
Death of close friend	37
Change to different line of work	36
Change in number of arguments with spouse	35
Mortgage over $10,000	31
Foreclosure of mortgage or loan	30
Change in responsibilities at work	29
Son or daughter leaving home	29
Trouble with in-laws	29
Outstanding personal achievement	28
Wife begins or stops work	26
Begin or end school	26
Change in living conditions	25
Revision of personal habits	24
Trouble with boss	23
Change in work hours or conditions	20
Change in residence	20
Change in schools	19
Change in recreation	19
Change in church activities	19
Change in social activities	18
Mortgage or loan less than $10,000	17
Change in sleeping habits	16
Change in number of family get-togethers	15
Change in eating habits	15
Vacation	13
Christmas	12
Minor violations of the law	11

7. Is the sexual part of your life healthy?

Proper sexual function plays a role in preventing burnout. For married people, that involves application of the principle explained by Solomon in Proverbs 5:15-21. In that section, Solomon established two important principles regulating our sexual nature.

Principle 1: Since God created us male and female, it is both normal and desirable for husbands and wives to enjoy the romance and excitement of marital love.

That principle is consistent with what Paul explains in 1 Corinthians 7:1-5. It is also talked about by Solomon in the following verses. Note the vivid word pictures used by Solomon to capture the essence of marital romance:

> Drink water from your own cistern,
>   running water from your own well.
> Should your spring overflow in the streets,
>   your streams of water in the public squares?
> Let them be yours alone,
>   never to be shared with strangers.
> May your fountain be blessed,
>   and may you rejoice in the wife of your youth.
> A loving doe, a graceful deer—
>   may her breasts satisfy you always,
>   may you ever be captivated by her love.
>   (Proverbs 5:15-19)

Principle 2: Sexual misconduct displeases God and will produce serious consequences.

For the married person that means remaining true to one's mate not only physically but in thought, word, and deed.

For the single person, that involves a discipline and commitment to purity consistent with 1 Corinthians 6:19-20. Public opinion seems to indicate that a majority of adults—61 percent, including 78 percent of young adults, according to a recent Roper Organization survey—now believe that premarital sex is not morally wrong. That, however, does not change the negative feelings premarital sex produces. These include feelings of unease, frustration, and guilt—real guilt—which involves holding back, a less than complete and unending commitment to the present and future well-being of the other person. As Dick Purnell says in his book *Becoming a Friend and Lover,* in the marriage relationship,

> there is safety and security . . . without fear of abandonment. There is also total freedom from guilt in sex. You can know that God smiles on and is pleased with your sexual relationship. . . . Outside of marriage, guilt eats away at the individuals until the relationship is either destroyed or crippled. . . . Stimulated by lifetime commitment and the absence of guilt . . we are able to be ourselves totally and to be emotionally "naked" without fear. . . . When we have sex outside the boundaries that God has set up for our protection and provision, we end up cheating ourselves.[2]

Such feelings of unease, frustration, and guilt produce added stress in a single person's life instead of relieving it. The added stress of a sexual relationship lacking lifetime commitment adds to those factors that can create burnout and make it harder to recover from burnout. God's laws regarding sex are meant as a protection (physically, emotionally, and spiritually), not as a limitation to our pleasure and fulfillment.

In Proverbs 5, observe the graphic way in which Solomon describes the consequences of sexual misconduct.

Why be captivated, my son, by an adulteress?
    Why embrace the bosom of another man's wife?
For a man's ways are in full view of the Lord,
    and he examines all his paths.

2. Dick Purnell, *Becoming a Friend and Lover* (San Bernardino, Calif.: Here's Life, 1986), pp. 58-59.

The evil deeds of a wicked man ensnare him;
  the cords of his sin hold him fast.
He will die for lack of discipline,
  led astray by his own great folly.

> (Proverbs 5:20-23)

For singles, maintaining sexual purity and learning how to relate to others in close friendships before marriage alleviates stress and burnout, as Purnell's *Becoming a Friend and Lover* so aptly shows. For married couples, maintaining marital romance, and cultivating the sparkle of an intimate relationship can add zest to life and help prevent burnout. For help in that regard, see the book, *Sex in the Christian Marriage*.[3]

8. Have you done something good—physically, psychologically, or spiritually—for one person this week?

The age in which we are living is a self-involved, "me" generation. The selfish spirit of this age can be mentally unhealthy. The apostle Paul expresses his concern for an "others orientation" in Philippians 2:4: "Each of you should look not only to your own interests, but also to the interests of others." Physically, you might help someone with chores or errands. Psychologically, you might provide someone with counsel or just a listening ear. Spiritually, you might share what the Lord has been teaching you. We are emotionally enriched when we invest ourselves in others. Christ reminds us in Luke 6:38 that giving comes back to us in like measure and more.

---

3. Richard Meier et al., *Sex in the Christian Marriage* (Richardson, Tex.: Today Publishers, 1985). Distributed by Baker Book House, Grand Rapids.

9. Have you forgiven the last three people who offended you?

Forgiveness is important because, if we don't forgive others, we tend to turn our anger inward, which results in bitterness and then in depression. Forgiveness involves, by an act of the will, choosing to no longer hold a grudge against an offending party. It is inaccurate to say, "I cannot forgive," since forgiveness is a matter of the will. We can say, "I will forgive with God's help." The measure of forgiving each other is "just as in Christ God forgave you" (Ephesians 4:32). It is important when we were offended to quickly choose to forgive rather than to harbor grudges.

10. How many times has envy affected you this year?

Allowing envy towards others to continue leads to depression. Solomon said, "A heart at peace gives life to the body, but envy rots the bones" (Proverbs 14:30). Solomon recognized the effect of positive or negative emotions on our physical being. A proper response to the success of others is to be happy for them. Solomon says in Ecclesiastes that when we desire to prove that we are more important than others, which is the basis for envy, we are like a person chasing the wind, which is futile. It is important to be grateful for what we have received from the Lord. When envy surfaces, remember that none of us deserves anything. Whatever we get from life is a gift from the Lord.

11. Did you talk with your spouse (or, if single, a close friend or relative) three times this week about your feelings?

Emotional problems often come when we have

repressed our feelings instead of dealing with them. It is important to sit down with our spouse (or roommate or close friend) and share both the good and bad events of the day. Sharing feelings also is important when resolving areas of marital conflict. Men generally tend to hide their feelings more than women and may need to work specifically at that.

Tips for conflict resolution include:

- Use "I" messages—"I feel," "I need," "I want"—instead of "you" statements—"you should," "you shouldn't."
- Avoid attacking each other's character; explain only the specific behavior that offends.
- Ask for some kind of specific change, keep the issues to the present, and avoid bringing up the past.
- Listen to your spouse.
- Don't let your emotions get out of hand.
- Resist the temptation to keep track of who won past conflicts. Recognize that when someone wins a marital conflict, everyone loses.
- Ask for and give feedback to each other.
- Schedule time to discuss feelings with your mate.

12. Did you share your burdens with a friend this week?

A successful, intelligent, hard-working businessman suffered a major heart attack. During his recovery he become close friends with one of us. During a telephone conversation, he remarked, "You are about the only person I feel I can really call a close friend." What is remarkable about his statement is that his experience typifies that of many candidates for burnout.

Most people who experience depression or burnout do not have even one friend to whom they are close enough to share their personal feelings and still feel loved and accepted. An important step in maintaining an emotional balance is to develop close friendships. Each of us needs about six people with whom we can share our true feelings and still feel loved. It is hard for any person, even a mate, to have the full burden of all our feelings, particularly if he or she is going through an emotionally heavy period, too.

Of course, if you are already in burnout, building a friendship may be hard to do, although if someone offers friendship and unconditional understanding at this time, don't rebuff it. It's what you need, even if you have little emotional energy to offer them anything in return. Allow others to give friendship to you. After you recover from burnout, the give and take of friendships will be important to keeping your life balanced.

If you still have the emotional energy, start looking for friends, ones who will be good listeners, who will be loyal, and who will care, but also who will be willing to give a viewpoint different from yours if they feel it is needed. The book of Proverbs has a great deal to say about friendship, including the reminder that "a friend loves at all times" (Proverbs 17:17), and "wounds from a friend can be trusted, but an enemy multiplies kisses" (Proverbs 27:6). Find someone with whom you can relate, then spend time with that person developing a growing friendship and building mutual trust.

Beginning a relationship may involve challenging another person to become involved in helping balance each other's lives. If you both need to reduce your weight, you might agree to call each other every evening to list what you have eaten that day. If you need to spend more time in the Word or in quality time with family members, work out a similar reporting arrangement with someone from your workplace, church, or neighborhood. Such a reporting system may get you active in making personal changes, be a helping hand to someone else, and help build a casual relationship toward becoming a closer friendship, all at the same time.

13. Did you do at least one specific thing this week to become closer to a relative—a parent, brother, sister, or other close relative?

Each of us has a family heritage, one that has tremendous bearing on our mental health. Often a need exists to go back and mend or repair relationships, building a new way of relating that can lead to good mental and emotional stability. It is important to take the initiative to build a closer relationship with your family, rather than waiting on others in the family to take the lead. Doing at least one thing per week—perhaps a phone call, a letter, a visit, or an outing—with extended family members can build closer relationships and foster emotional health.

ACTIONS LEAD TO EMOTIONS

If you see a lot of areas above that need changing in your life, you may think, "But I just don't feel like doing all that!" particularly if you are already feeling the effects of burnout. However, an important principle to improving one's life is that proper actions lead to proper emotions. We frequently find that true in our counseling. The most dramatic illustration of that, perhaps, is in marital counseling. Often, a husband or wife will say, "I just don't feel like trying any more. I've lost that feeling of love for my mate." In such cases, our counsel is to act like you love your spouse and, pretty soon, you will begin to feel like you love your mate as well. Many initially respond with unbelief to that statement but come back later saying in joyous astonishment that it works.

The same approach can work in your own relationship with God, with others, and with yourself. Begin taking some of those needed steps to revitalize your life, to begin to reverse that burnout spiral, whether you feel like doing them or not. The actions of doing the right thing will soon be followed by the desire to do them, and you'll be on the upward spiral, moving away from the depths of burnout.

10
STARTING THE UPWARD SPIRAL SPIRITUALLY

The spiritual part of burnout victims' lives has been neglected, although sometimes they don't realize it. Some burnout victims do realize it but believe that their special situation made it completely impossible to keep up an adequate spiritual life. Usually, changing one's priorities and even canceling out activities that were previously thought to be important priorities, as mentioned in the previous chapter, are necessary to finding the time to recuperate from burnout spiritually.

If you doubt that the quality of your spiritual life has had any effect on your burnout, see how many of the following questions from our "Taking Care of Yourself" test you can answer positively.

1. Does the Word of God still give you a thrill?
Although emotions are not always an accurate guide for gauging response to the Scriptures, the nature of the Word of God indicates that it should give us an emotional lift. Meditating on the Word of God allows God to speak to us personally through the words that apply, in one way or another, to all of us. Do you look at God's Word as His love letter to you?

One danger faced by many Christians, especially those in vocational ministries, may be over-familiarity with and a loss of wonder at God's Word, produced by the constant handling of Scriptures. We should work at developing an attitude of awe toward the Scriptures. The book of Psalms begins, "Blessed is the man . . . [whose] delight is in the law of the Lord; and on his law he meditates day and night. He is like a tree planted by streams of water, which yields its fruit in season and whose leaf does not wither."

A number of factors may be involved in causing us to lose that thrill over the Scriptures: depression, sin in our lives, a habit of neglecting to spend time with God in the Word, approaching the Scriptures only from an academic or teacher's viewpoint, or never having been genuinely saved.

If you have not trusted Jesus Christ as your personal Savior and Lord, acknowledge that to do so is not only the key to overcoming burnout but also the ultimate answer to meaning and purpose in life.

Acknowledge to God that you are a sinner (that you have not and cannot, on your own, live up to His desires for your life), and that you yourself cannot bridge the gap that your sins have caused between you and God. Realize that Christ's death was the punishment you deserve for your sins. Having taken your punishment upon Himself, His death and resurrection became the basis for the forgiveness of your sins and for your coming into a close and completed relationship with God. Depend on His death and resurrection to cancel your debt to God.

Then trust Him as your personal Savior from a life, here and eternally, without God. Realize that His Holy Spirit then resides in your life to lead you, comfort you, empower you, and to allow you to feel God's love for you.

It is worth the effort to work to recapture joy in personally communicating with God through Bible reading and study.

2. Do you enjoy the old hymns of the faith?

In addition to reflecting on our relationship with God through the Bible, the old hymns of our faith can produce good psychological and mental health. The composers of those hymns wrote them, not because they had a job to do, but because the thoughts and concepts about God they express thrilled them so much that they were compelled to share their spiritual joy with others in that manner. The next time you sing a hymn or just read the words of one, think of the joy and devotion to God that those words produced in the composer.

The older hymns, generally, are characterized by simple but profound messages; by easy memorization, because they contain a great deal of repetition; and by drawing biblical truth together with human experience, which can produce a satisfying spiritual and emotional response. Try singing a hymn to God as you begin and as you finish your daily devotions. You might even keep a hymnbook with your Bible for such a purpose.

3. Did you apply the Word of God to your life daily this past week?

Contrary to the opinion of some specialists in both fields, the Bible and psychiatry are not incompatible, as long as the Bible is the final authority. Scripture memorization can be a useful tool for maintaining good mental health. As Solomon exhorted, regarding God-given instructions: "My son, pay attention to what I say; listen closely to my words. Do not let them out of your sight, keep them within your heart; for they are life to those who find them and health to a man's whole body" (Proverbs 4:20-22).

God promised Joshua prosperity and success through meditating on and applying God's Word.

Be careful to obey all the law. . .do not turn from it to the right or to the left, that you may be succesful wherever you go. Do not let this Book of the Law depart from your mouth; meditate on it day and night, so that you may be careful to do everything written in it. Then you will be prosperous and successful. . . . Do not be discouraged, for the Lord your God will be with you wherever you go." (Joshua 1:7-9)

Set a goal of memorizing three verses a week to bring your perspective back into focus, and then consciously apply those verses to your life over several days' time. Don't start out, however, as many Type A's might, trying to memorize too many verses a week, giving little time to really meditate and apply each verse memorized. Also, setting too high a goal, if not met, can cause false or unnecessary guilt and even cause you to give up on the whole process.

Memorized verses can help keep you from sin, especially when, because of tiredness, you are more prone to temptation. Memorized words popping back into your mind become a special hedge against temptation.

Also, as you study the Bible each morning, over and beyond the verses you memorize, look for one or two special concepts and commands that you can apply to your life that day.

4. How often this past month has Proverbs 8:36, "He who sins against me injures himself" (NASB*) applied to you?

Many individuals, including Christians, fail to understand the reasons for God's laws. They think they were set up only to test our blind and unquestioning obedience to God—that His primary desire is

**New American Standard Bible.*

for complete dictatorship, and so He sits in heaven with a big stick, just waiting for us to get out of line. That there are loving, caring, and reasonable bases behind His laws and that they were set up for our best interests does not occur to them. God knows that if we live in light of His principles, life will be more enjoyable and meaningful. When we sin against God, we are indeed hurting ourselves. When we disobey God, our self-concept is lowered and we experience a lower sense of self-worth. By claiming God's power through His Holy Spirit, we can resist temptation and yield to God.

5. *When needed, how quickly do you apply 1 John 1:9 to your life?*

"If we confess our sins, he is faithful and just and will forgive us our sins and purify us from all unrighteousness."

When we do sin, God's forgiveness is always sufficient and immediately available. Although some Christians tend to ignore sin in their lives, others have a hard time applying the principle of 1 John 1:9 because of a desire to punish themselves. "Confess" doesn't mean saying, "I'm sorry." It means "to agree with God" that what we have done is wrong. It also requires a desire to change that behavior. We need to determine that by His grace we will confess—agree with His assessment of what we've done—and then accept His forgiveness, forgive ourselves, seek to make needed changes, and, finally, forget the situation and move on.

God is a just God, but He also is a loving Father. He waits with outstretched arms for us to come back to Him and agree with Him that our sin, which severed our fellowship or companionship with Him, was wrong. It is important to remember that Christ has paid for our sins already, in full. Consequently, it is not our place to try to punish ourselves or pay for our own sins. Also, because Christ has already paid for our sins, we never lose our salvation, no matter how much we sin. We accepted salvation as a free gift, neither earned or deserved. Although fellowship or companionship with God can be broken, confession of sin restores that fellowship with God, and that leads to good mental health.

6. How often this past year have you felt that God was with you?

When individuals first come to trust Christ as Savior, they sense that God is with them, that He is watching over them, and that He is going to take care of them. As time passes, sometimes that feeling fades and they forget that God is personally involved with them every day in every activity.

It is good for your mental health to realize and feel that God is present with you right now. If you've lost that feeling, make sure you talk with Him every day, through prayer, and that you allow Him to talk with you each day—through the Word, the prompting of His Holy Spirit, and the circumstances that He brings into your life. However, make sure that the latter two ways in which He speaks to you, which easily can be interpreted subjectively, according to our own desires, always agree with what He tells us through His written Word.

7. Can you pinpoint several instances this week in which you accomplished something "through Christ," as Paul proclaimed he did in Philippians 4:13?

"I can do all things through Christ which strengtheneth me" (KJV).

Amid the stresses of life, we must realize that our ability to do anything comes only "through Christ." In discussing the ups and downs of his experiences, Paul related all ability and achievement to the enabling of Christ. To live the Christian life apart from Christ's power is impossible. But to give over the responsibility of living the Christian life to divine power alone, apart from human responsibility, was never intended, either. That verse shows that divine enablement and human responsibility work hand in hand.

THE BURNOUT ESCAPE METHOD

Until you can put all the principles of chapters 8, 9, and 10 at work in your life (which will take time), you might memorize or carry with you this outline, to check how you are doing in escaping from burnout.

1. Use time wisely.
2. Keep priorities straight.
3. Relax more.
4. Realize I am someone in Christ.
5. Watch perfectionistic tendencies.
6. Look at the true meaning of life.
7. If truly suicidal, make immediate arrangements for hospitalization (through your doctor, pastor, or a nationally-recognized Christian therapy clinic).

Remember that your priorities start with those things that are eternal and, besides God Himself, only two things will last with you forever: the Word of God and your relationships with other Christians, including your family.

11

THE REKINDLING OF HOPE

When an individual experiences burnout, he or she invariably becomes "I" centered. In fact, many burnout victims sound like the prophet Jeremiah in Lamentations 3:16: "He has broken my teeth with gravel; he has trampled me in the dust." They may not always think that of God, but they will think it of some person in authority over them or of someone who is more powerful than they. We have been encouraged to see, however, that in our personal experience and in our ministry to others, redirecting our attention toward what God has for us, as manifested in His Word, can rekindle hope and help alleviate the symptoms of burnout.

One of the most common characteristics of advanced burnout is the loss of hope. Over recent years we have heard of hundreds of individuals, housewives, students, pastors, missionaries, lawyers, businessmen, accountants, executives, and others express the same thing: "I just don't feel that there's any hope of changing the situation."

Hope is an essential ingredient, we've observed, to withstanding the difficulties and pressures of life. The author of Hebrews refers to hope as "an anchor for the soul" (6:19). We see severe emotional traumas and disorders overcome, seemingly irreparable marital conflicts healed and homes restored, and one tragedy after another endured—but only when there is hope.

A Midwestern businessman recently told us of the tragedies that had marked him and his wife. First, his son was killed in a traffic accident. Soon thereafter a daughter took her life on Christmas Day. Within a matter of months, another son took his life. How could he and his wife survive? Certainly, they had grieved over their losses, but as this man expressed it, "We didn't lose hope. We believe our children have trusted Christ as their Savior. Even though tragedy took them from us, we will see them again." Can such hope really exist and not falter, even after such tragedy?

A SETTLED HOPE

The word for "hope" commonly used in Scripture does not mean a sense of wishing something were so. The biblical concept of hope is more of a settled anticipation, a "favorable and constant expectation."[1] The Greek verb form for "hope" used in the New Testament frequently is closely related to the concept of *trust* (John 5:45; 2 Corinthians 1:10). The noun form in the New Testament is frequently associated with the specific prospect of Christ's return to earth, as in Titus 2:13, "The blessed hope—the glorious appearing of our great God and Savior, Jesus Christ."

JEREMIAH: OUR MODEL FOR HOPE

One of the most extensive developments of the subject of hope occurs in the Old Testament, in Jeremiah's book of Lamentations. Here, set against the

1. W. E. Vine, *Expository Dictionary of New Testament Words* (Old Tappan, N.J.: Revell, 1966), p. 232.

backdrop of a nation facing disaster and ruin, a prophet whose eyes are saturated with tears discovers that his hope, which has been depleted and even obliterated by the tragic end of the nation, is rekindled and refocused in his God. The prophet Jeremiah's experiences, recorded in Lamentations 3, give practical suggestions for people today who have experienced burnout.

Most burnout victims can identify with the words of Jeremiah in Lamentations 3:1: "I am the man who has seen affliction by the rod of his wrath." Although Jeremiah is designated in that passage as a representative of the nation, he is nonetheless describing the personal sorrows he experienced under the hand of God. Verses 1-24 contain almost forty references to *I, me* or *my.* Notice the graphic terms, in verses 2-16, with which Jeremiah decribes his perception of the circumstances in which he finds himself.

> He has driven *me* away and made *me* walk
> in darkness rather than light;
> indeed, he has turned his hand against *me*
> again and again, all day long.
> He has made *my* skin and *my* flesh grow old
> and has broken *my* bones.
> He has besieged *me* and surrounded *me*
> with bitterness and hardship
> He has made *me* dwell in darkness
> like those long dead.
> He has walled *me* in so *I* cannot escape;
> he has weighed *me* down with chains.
> Even when *I* call out or cry for help,
> he shuts out *my* prayer.
> He has barred *my* way with blocks of stone;
> he has made *my* paths crooked.
> Like a bear lying in wait,
> like a lion in hiding,
> he dragged *me* from the path and mangled *me*

and left *me* without help.
He drew his bow
    and made *me* the target for his arrows.
He pierced *my* heart
    with arrows from his quiver.
I became the laughing stock of all *my* people;
    they mock *me* in song all day long.
He has filled *me* with bitter herbs
    and sated *me* with gall.
He has broken *my* teeth with gravel;
    he has trampled *me* in the dust.

(Italics added)

HOPE EXHAUSTED

Certainly Jeremiah's language vividly describes what victims of burnout frequently feel, even in the way in which adversity is attributed to God or someone else more powerful than they.

Lamentations 3:17-19 summarizes what many victims of burnout feel.

I have been deprived of peace;
    I have forgotten what prosperity is.
So *I* say, "*My* splendor [strength] is gone
    and all that *I* had hoped from the Lord."
I remember *my* affliction and *my* wandering,
    the bitterness and the gall.

(Italics added)

The victim loses peace, prosperity, and strength. He gains misery, bitterness, and pain. That is a situation where hope has been exhausted.

HOPE REKINDLED

Against this "death of hope" backdrop, Jeremiah suddenly says, "Yet this I call to mind and therefore I have hope" (v. 21). It is as if Jeremiah spots a light in the distance, toward which he now focuses attention.

The word used here for "hope" is one most closely associated with the concept of waiting and carries the idea of an expectation, thus leading from faith, to trust, to patient waiting. The meaning of that kind of hope is not a pacifying wish of the imagination to drown out troubles, nor is it uncertain, wishful thinking. That kind of hope, instead, refers to a solid ground for expectation directed towards God.[2] The significance of that inward shift is obvious. Although the agony of his experiences brought hope to an end, it was rekindled when the prophet's mind was directed toward certain truths about God rather than toward his present circumstances.

HOPE REFOCUSED

Jeremiah then goes on to examine four significant truths in Lamentations 3:22-23. Notice that, by that time, his "I" outlook had changed considerably.

> Because of the Lord's great love *we* are not consumed.
>   for *his* [God's] compassions never fail.
> They are new every morning;
>   great is *your* faithfulness.

>   (Italics added)

With hope rekindled and refocused:

1. *He examines God's great, loyal love.* The term *loyal love* is one of the most significant concepts in the Old Testament. It is a term used frequently of God's covenant relationship with his followers. Its parts include loyalty, love, and mercy (kindness or compassion). It is seen in God's relationship with Israel and with us (Psalm 85:7; 98:3).

2. R. Laird Harris, ed., *Theological Wordbook of the Old Testament*, vol. 1 (Chicago: Moody, 1980), p. 373.

The point Jeremiah is making is that those to whom he was writing (and by application, those of us who belong to God today), can count on God's loyalty, love, and mercy toward us, no matter how desperate our circumstances. Even in the midst of burnout, we can still look to God who is never unloving or disloyal to us. He will never stop loving us unconditionally.

2. *He observes God's compassion.* God not only is loyal and trustworthy, but He feels our emotions. He will never fail to be moved with kindness and compassion in His actions toward us.

3. *He realized God's compassionate concern is unending.* No matter how dark the day, they are "new every morning." They never grow old, wear out, or become obsolete. God is always loyal, loving, and compassionate.

4. *He knows, consequently, that God is greatly to be trusted.* As the apostle Paul also came to realize, God is sovereign and, because of that, all things can be counted on to "work together for good to them who love God, to them who are the called according to his purpose" (Romans 8:28, KJV).

During times of stress and burnout, we have found these truths to be fundamental in rekindling hope and alleviating the spiritual and emotional stresses of burnout. We personally have applied them, as did Jeremiah. "The Lord is my portion; therefore I will wait for him" (v. 24).

BURNOUT REVERSED

We have shared these words with countless individuals with positive results. Certainly, physical and

emotional needs must be met, too, as in the case of
Elijah, when God provided food and rest, encouragement, and comfort of a friend (such as Elisha). However, the essence of reversing burnout is expressed in
Lamentations 3:24-26:

> I say to myself, "The Lord is my portion;
>   therefore I will wait for him."
> The Lord is good to those whose hope is in him,
>   to the one who seeks him;
> it is good to wait quietly
>   for the salvation of the Lord.

Even though circumstances may have our "face
in the dust" (v. 29), when we focus beyond our circumstances we will be able to say "I have hope." Although the characteristics of burnout may vary in
intensity and combination, although they may be cyclical or progressive, although they may come over
weeks, months, or even years—whatever the case—
through focusing on God and hoping in Him, burnout
can be reversed.

When the principles we have shared in this book
are applied, particularly those in the spiritual realm,
we have seen hundreds of people *regain* hope, *refo-
cus* their perspective, *center* their attention on the
Lord and on waiting for Him, and *renew* their
strength.

It has been like music to our ears to hear men
and women echo the words of David, "He restores my
soul" (Psalm 23:3). We are convinced that by taking
the initiative while depending on the Lord, you *can*
beat burnout.

12

RECOVERY FROM BURNOUT

The term *burnout* is never found in Scripture. However, there are many biblical examples of people whose symptoms parallel those of today's burnout victims. When someone undergoes burnout, it involves the loss of two important elements from that person's life: strength and hope. The Bible gives many examples of individuals who lost those two important elements and who lost, as a result, much of their effectiveness in serving God. One of the most vivid of those, along with one of the most practical biblical prescriptions for overcoming the loss of strength and hope, is not given in an account of an individual, however, but of a nation—Israel. That account is found in Isaiah 40.

A major thrust of the Old Testament is the fact that God called Israel as a nation to be His representative in the world. During the glory days of the nation's deliverance from Egypt under Moses, the conquest of the Promised Land under Joshua, and the establishing of the kingdom of David and of his son, Solomon, the nation functioned as God's servant with a relatively strong degree of effectiveness.

However, by the time Isaiah appeared on the scene, the nation had experienced hundreds of years of spiritual indifference, misplaced priorities, compromise, and a lack of personal commitment to God.

Consequently, the law of sowing and reaping was in full operation. The ten northern tribes had been scattered by the Assyrians when the prophet Isaiah wrote the comforting words of Isaiah 40. He was seeking to prepare what was left of the nation for the impending disaster of captivity by the Babylonians.

We are not suggesting that the nation of Israel was a victim of burnout, but we do see a strong parallel between what occurred to Israel and their circumstances, to which Isaiah spoke, and the spiritual factors that frequently contribute to burnout today. When Christians neglect appropriate spiritual priorities, compromise biblical convictions, and allow their personal commitment to Jesus Christ to be weakened by such factors as personal pleasures, desire for material possessions, and efforts to achieve power and influence (1 John 2:15), the results will be a loss of spiritual strength, which ultimately can lead to a loss of hope.

That does not mean a Christian will ever find his salvation in jeopardy; it is secured by Christ's death on the cross, by the full payment for all our sins, including those we will commit as Christians. Israel was still God's chosen people, even though as a nation she was powerless to be an effective witness for God and even though her inhabitants felt hopeless in their circumstances.

Isaiah's message to Israel was designed to call the nation's attention to God, who alone can provide the physical, emotional, and spiritual healing necessary for those without hope or strength. It is significant that in Isaiah 40 the prophet spends the bulk of the chapter—through verse 26—pointing a spotlight toward Israel's God, showing Him to be both powerful (the Creator) and caring (The Shepherd).

Then, in verse 27, Isaiah lovingly confronts his people with their problem. He personifies Israel the nation as an individual suffering from attitudes generally present in what we now call burnout. They are feelings of isolation and of injustice.

The feeling of isolation is expressed by Isaiah's question to Israel, "Why do you say, O Jacob, and complain, O Israel, 'My way is hidden from the Lord' " (v. 27). In much the same way, today's burnout victim also feels isolated and unappreciated. He or she says, "Nobody appreciates me. No one understands me." Those thoughts relate to family, employer, fellow employees, teachers, friends, and others. The feeling of isolation often is most intense when the people closest to the burnout victim are involved.

Closely paralleling the feeling of isolation is the feeling of injustice. That is also reflected in Isaiah 40:27: "Why do you say, O Jacob, and complain, O Israel . . . my cause [rights] is disregarded by my God'?" All too often, today's exhausted burnout victim says, "It's just not fair!" That feeling can be related to family matters, studies, work, and even to successes enjoyed by friends.

After sharing those statements symptomatic of Israel's condition, Isaiah shifts the focus from what the nation says to what Israel actually has in the Lord. Again, a parallel can be made in the symptoms experienced by the nation and those experienced by the individual whose spiritual condition has brought on burnout today.

> He gives strength to the weary ["faint," KJV]
>   and increases the power of the weak.
> Even youths grow tired and weary,
>   and young men stumble and fall.
>   (vv. 29-30)

Four significant characteristics, "faint," "weary," "weak," and "stumble and fall," are given in those words from Isaiah. Each of them can apply to those suffering from burnout today.

Faint. This term, used again at the end of the chapter, "and not be faint," describes one who is about to pass out from a lack of nourishment. Most of us have experienced times when we went many hours without proper nourishment and perhaps without rest. Today's burnout victim, because of long hours, inability to sleep, and perhaps poor eating habits tends perpetually to feel at the point of fainting.

Weary. An individual suffering from burnout is characterized by perpetual exhaustion. Like a rubber band stretched beyond its capacity, he or she has lost elasticity. A college student drove himself during two rigorous semesters of work, study, and ministry, climaxed by several all-night stints of study in preparation for exams. After staying up all night cramming the night before his most crucial exam, he fell asleep a half-hour before the exam was scheduled to begin. He slept through the exam, failed the course, and eventually dropped out of school. He suffered the consequences of his burnout.

Weak. The burnout victim suffers a drop in his concentration level and in his ability to produce. Since we often tend to judge people on their ability to produce, there is often a parallel drop in feelings of self-worth. The decline in the ability to concentrate often results from, and enhances, anxiety. In Matthew 6, our Savior three times commands. "Do not be anxious" (NASB). The term He uses in those three commands is a Greek word signifying division. The anxious individual has become distracted, divided in his attention. As a result he or she is unable to function at previous levels of efficiency.

Stumble and fall. The student who slept through his exam also illustrates a fourth significant characteristic that parallels those of today's burnout victims. The individual suffering from burnout is like an accident looking for a place to happen, to "stumble and fall." He is headed for a disaster—a blowup in a personal relationship, a physical collapse, or even a spiritual or moral failure. That individual is likely to crash unless his burnout is dealt with properly. Isaiah adds that even the youth of his day faced the possibility of major disaster without feeling how close they were to the brink. So it is with potential burnout victims today. Indeed, college age and other young, dedicated Christians are among the most likely to suffer from burnout and its devastating characteristics as they start out life on their own with all their might, not knowing their own limitations.

As Christina Maslach so aptly put it,

> Burnout—the word evokes images of a final, flickering flame; of a charred and empty shell; of dying embers and cold, gray ashes. . . . Once fired up about their involvement with other people—excited, full of energy, dedicated, willing to give tremendously of themselves for others . . . [burnout victims] did give . . . and give and give, until finally there was nothing left to give any more. The teapot was empty, the battery was drained, the circuit was overloaded—they had burned out.[1]

Despite the bleak picture painted in Isaiah 40, the prophet does hold out hope for those who were experiencing the symptoms brought on by the years of spiritual decline and failure in Israel. In verses 28-31, Isaiah presents the solution, which starts with this basic reminder:

1. Christina Maslach, *Burnout—The Cost of Caring* (Englewood Cliffs, N.J.: Prentice-Hall, 1982), p. 3.

Do you not know?
  Have you not heard?
The Lord is the everlasting God,
  the Creator of the ends of the earth.
He will not grow tired or weary,
  and his understanding no one can fathom.

It is marked by the character of a gift:

He gives strength to the weary
  and increases the power of the weak.

It is experienced by those who wait on the Lord.

But those who hope in [wait upon] the Lord
  will renew their strength.
They will soar on wings like eagles;
  they will run and not grow weary,
  they will walk and not be faint.

RECOVERY STARTS WITH A REMINDER

As in the case of many physical, emotional, and spiritual problems, the prophet Isaiah points out to Israel ("Do you not know? Have you not heard?") that the information necessary for solving their burnout problem is already at hand.

The prophet is doing what was needed for Israel then, which is the solution to the spiritual aspect of burnout today. He is refocusing attention from the nation to God, from the nation's inability to God's infinite ability. If a burnout victim is experiencing the following symptoms, he or she can profit greatly from applying the principles that Isaiah shared with God's weak and hopeless people of his day.

| The burnout victim is about to give up and feels the end has come. | The prophet presents God as everlasting. |

The burnout victim perceives self as forsaken by God and man.	The prophet presents God as "Yahweh," the covenant-keeping God.
The burnout victim perceives self as helpless.	The prophet presents God as Creator of the ends of the earth.
The burnout victim perceives self as at the point of fainting—utterly weary.	The prophet presents God as neither fainting from overexertion nor growing weary from overwork.
The burnout victim perceives self as confused, unable to figure out a solution to the dilemma.	The prophet presents God as possessing infinite understanding.

In many pastoral and clinical counseling situations, individuals experiencing burnout have come to feel and experience hope when their attention has been focused beyond their circumstances to the characteristics of the God they serve. Indeed, for the person who has placed personal trust in Jesus Christ, burnout is a problem that can be solved.

RECOVERY IS MARKED BY A GIFT

The second facet of Isaiah's solution, as it applies to modern burnout, is that by nature it is a gift. "He gives strength to the weary and increases the power of the weak." Just as salvation is a gift from God, received by His grace through faith, and it is in no way of ourselves (Ephesians 2:8-9), so the power and energy necessary to overcome burnout must be received as a gift from God.

RECOVERY IS EXPERIENCED BY WAITING

Finally, the prophet reaches the heart of his solution for Israel. He explains that renewal of strength and hope is experienced by those who "hope in [wait upon] the Lord" (v. 31). One of the primary irritations confronting us in our fast-paced society is waiting. We wait for elevators and traffic lights, find ourselves placed on hold and waiting when using the telephone, stand in line and wait at the checkout counter of grocery stores, sit and wait in reception rooms of doctors' and dentists' offices, and otherwise occupy a great deal of time just waiting. Few of us enjoy it. Many of us become extremely impatient and irritated when forced to wait.

Yet one of the most important biblical principles found throughout the Bible involves waiting. A profitable study involves considering the Old and New Testament words for "wait" and the contexts in which they are used. Waiting is an important ingredient in our personal spiritual growth and development. It is designed by God to build into our lives a number of important traits. He uses waiting to produce such important fruits of the Spirit as longsuffering, meekness, and self-control. Throughout the Psalms, David makes frequent reference to the blessings that will befall those who wait on the Lord. In Lamentations 3, Jeremiah explains that "it is good to wait quietly for . . . the Lord."

The word used by Isaiah for "wait" is an illustrative Hebrew term describing a rope stretched taut. It is closely related to the term used for the scarlet thread, the cord hung from Rahab's home in Jericho in Joshua 2. The significance of that is that the waiting process is a stretching one, one that is often extremely difficult but one that ultimately has a good end.

Isaiah promises renewal of strength to those who

wait upon and hope in the Lord. Here he utilizes another vivid Old Testament term that is related, in its root meaning, to the concept of "passing through." It was used of a change of clothes and of a knife cutting or passing through meat or other material. A related term in Job 14:7 refers to the second growth of a tree that has been cut down.

The significance of that term to today's burnout victim is important. Like an old and battered car, the burnout victim's strength is depleted. He has been many miles and feels he cannot long continue on. The Lord's promise is that waiting on Him will bring renewal of strength. His old, faltering strength will be traded in for God's limitless energy. Physically, emotionally, and spiritually, he will become like new by waiting upon the Lord.

Waiting thus becomes an expression of trust in the God who is described by Jeremiah as being "good to those whose hope is in [who wait on] him" (Lamentations 3:25) and who, according to David, strengthens the heart of those who wait on Him (Psalm 27:14).

The picture of these Israelite individuals who were faint, powerless, weary, and experiencing complete disaster, now soaring as eagles, running long distances without growing weary, and walking without fainting, completes the description of a spiritual principle that, when applied today, provides a workable cure for the spiritual dimension of burnout.

Don't despair. There is hope! There is a solution available to the child of God. By turning attention away from self and one's seemingly hopeless, helpless condition and onto the everlasting God, the burnout victim can find strength renewed. By waiting on the Lord, he or she can find a constant supply of wisdom and strength from the God who faints not, who is never weary, and who Himself will never experience burnout!

BEFORE BURNOUT

by

Frank Minirth, M.D.
Don Hawkins, Th.M.
Paul Meier, M.D.
Chris Thurman, Ph.D.

To our many good friends
from among the obsessive-compulsives
whose lives have impacted and
shaped us to balance our obsessions
by living life one day at a time
with an eye on eternity

CONTENTS

BEFORE BURNOUT

FOREWORD

When most of us take the time to read a book on burnout, we look for it to do at least two things: present concepts clearly enough so anyone can understand them and compel us to change and/or renewal.

I found that both these elements abound in *Before Burnout*. This is the second in a great series by these authors, and each book has helped me rediscover two life-changing truths that are essential to beating burnout.

I speak from the heart here. I never realized how easy it is to slip into burnout, but I've also suffered from what the authors say is its number one cause: unfulfilled expectations. That *fact* wasn't new to me, but the *skills* needed to detect the subtle ways it can creep into your life were; and that's what makes both these books so valuable.

In *How to Beat Burnout*, I was taken on a journey that helped me rediscover the thousands of expectations I had. It offered valuable insights on how to cope with the tremendous emotional burden unfulfilled expectations can create in life. Those were sobering lessons for me, especially because I travel the country teaching people the damage unfulfilled expectations can bring to their lives and relationships. Somehow, I

failed to see the overwhelming number of expectations
I had allowed to be a part of my life.

To my amazement, I realized I had expectations
about everything: traffic flow, store clerks, machines,
government employees, my family, my staff, how many
people should attend our seminars, read our books,
rent our film series—the list could go on. No wonder I
was burned out!

But the good doctors didn't just leave me hanging
by a thread. After insightfully helping me realize where
I was, they skillfully guided me back to where I needed
to be—firmly resting on the marvelous truth of Isaiah
40:31. "Yet those who wait for the Lord will gain new
strength; they will mount up with wings like eagles,
they will run and not get tired, they will walk and not
become weary."

Before Burnout nobly takes the torch from its pre-
decessor and offers gems that can help you beat burnout *before* it happens. Each intriguing chapter will
take you through the pages of Scripture and shine a
clear, transparent light on the secrets to heading burnout off at the pass.

In reading this book I was reminded of two of my
favorite truths about contentment. The first is, *if we're
not satisfied with what we have today, we'll never be
satisfied with what we want tomorrow.* The second is
equally powerful, *contentment is knowing I already
have everything I need in Christ.*

In this worthy sequel, Drs. Meier, Minirth, and
Thurman, along with their good friend and long-time
colleague Don Hawkins, give us the knowledge we need
to believe these truths and the skills necessary to apply
them.

There are more books out there on burnout than
any of us have time to read; but this one is worth your

time. Learning how to beat burnout before it beats us is something we all need help with; you're holding a tool right now that can help you do that. If you're grappling with the same issues of peace, contentment, and fulfillment I have, this book is for you.

GARY SMALLEY

PREFACE

The purpose of our previous book, *How to Beat Burnout*, was to address a problem that has reached epidemic proportions in today's society: burnout. In that book we showed burnout victims how to overcome their burned-out condition and return to successful Christian living.

In this book we zero in on one of the three major causes of burnout—an obsessive-compulsive personality, along with related Type A characteristics—to show individuals with those traits how they can prevent their tendencies from resulting in an initial or cyclical burnout.

We know a group of obsessive-compulsive individuals who regularly check themselves by asking, "Why be 'O-C' about this situation?" In other words, they ask, "Is it really necessary for me to practice extreme obsessive-compulsive—hard-driving and perfectionistic—behavior in this situation?"

The answer clearly is no. It isn't necessary to be O-C in our work, thought, and actions to prove to God or to other people the worth of our work or ourselves, which is the general motivation for O-C behavior. The alternative is to be the person God wants us to be today.

To do that, we will take a close look at how the obsessive-compulsive and Type A personalities think,
feel, and act, and how their tendencies toward extremes in certain areas can become more balanced. In
today's society we see more and more individuals with
obsessive-compulsive personality traits, so it's likely
that you are among them or interact closely with someone who is. We cannot give individuals with these personality traits entirely new personalities, nor would we
want to. But we do hope to show how they can adjust
their more extreme and potentially harmful traits so
that they can experience more balanced and fulfilling
lives.

Part of this book was written during a hurried
plane trip. The last part was written sometime later
during a restful Saturday afternoon at a Bible conference. In between were a number of personal struggles
with obsessive-compulsive behavior, of which we all
will undoubtedly experience more. But the process of
writing this book has helped enlighten us and give us
direction in overcoming our own obsessive behavior.
We trust that this beginning in our own lives will extend to those who read this book.

After all, why be so O-C when it is healthier and
biblical to be more balanced in our behavior? May we
all gain the insight and motivation to make balanced
living a daily reality.

1
THE BURNOUT-PRONE PERSONALITY

Several staff members of a Christian radio station had been working almost nonstop for weeks to develop a multi-media presentation for a Christian college. Hundreds of slides had been taken, processed, selected, and carefully sorted. They had recorded interviews with numerous individuals. Thousands of feet of audio tape had been auditioned and edited. The staff had worked hard to select carefully a wide variety of background music. Finally, all the ingredients were coming together.

As they neared the end of the project, the exhausted crew stopped about three o'clock one afternoon for a quick bite of lunch. Turning to his secretary, the project manager said, "Debi, why don't you ask God's blessing on this food."

"Sure" she replied, then quickly prayed, "God, help us to get everything done, now please, and in order. Amen." Immediately the crew broke into laughter.

"What's so funny?" asked the manager.

His administrative assistant replied, "Why, that was the perfect workaholic's prayer. That is *exactly* what you would expect from a group of obsessive-compulsives* like us."

Sometimes being obsessive-compulsive is stimulating, interesting, and a lot of fun. Many times it can be highly productive. Our research at the Minirth-Meier Clinic has shown us that obsessive-compulsive individuals tend to be the most productive, conscientious workers.

But obsessive-compulsive (perfectionistic) behavior can be destructive, both to obsessive-compulsives and to those around them. Though obsessive-compulsives are unlikely to fail at a job through irresponsibility, carelessness, or neglect, they are likely to bring about a catastrophe by working themselves to the point of burnout. In fact, this book came into existence partially as a result of the harried experience of those radio-station workaholics putting together that multimedia presentation.

THE CHRISTIAN TENDENCY TOWARD BURNOUT

Although obsessive-compulsive personality traits can be seen in men and women, college students and farmers, hard driving executives and overstressed housewives, a large percentage of evangelical Christians have an overabundance of obsessive-compulsive personality traits.

One such workaholic was Paul Meier. We'll let him tell his own story.

> When I first started my residency in psychiatry at Duke University, I still had a lot of extreme obsessive-compulsive traits, but I had no idea that I was obsessive-compulsive. When I began reading the standard psychiatry textbook on the obsessive-com-

---

* Please see the glossary at the back of this book for definitions of this and other special or technical terms used in the text.

pulsive personality, I carefully studied each page for at least twenty minutes, trying to memorize everything on it.

Two weeks later, I had covered only about forty pages when I read that obsessive-compulsives seldom finish a book. They accumulate a lot of books, but they seldom finish reading one, because they spend so much time poring over each page, trying to memorize everything. Suddenly that information hit me between the eyes. I had to admit that I had all the traits I had been reading about for the past two weeks. That made me so angry that I slammed the book shut. And to this day I haven't finished reading it.

Even though most obsessive-compulsives stress the importance of objective thinking, they often find it hard to take an objective look at themselves. Paul Meier is not the only O-C ever to have difficulty identifying the strengths and weaknesses in his own personality.

WHO IS THE OBSESSIVE-COMPULSIVE?

What is the origin of the term *obsessive-compulsive?* Clinically speaking, an obsession is a particular thought repeated over and over to the point that it is difficult to dislodge from the mind. Such *obsessions* usually result in frequently repeated behavior patterns. Those are known as *compulsions.*

Obsessive-compulsives come in all shapes and sizes and manifest all degrees of obsessive-compulsive behavior. In its extreme, obsessive-compulsive behavior takes the form of agoraphobia (a fear of open places), panic attacks, anxiety attacks, an inability to sleep, and sometimes even difficulty in functioning at all. If the latter occurs, the obsessive-compulsive individual may need to be hospitalized or to receive intensive insight-oriented counseling to discover the root cause of the obsession and the resulting compulsions.

Needless to say, most obsessive-compulsives don't go nearly that far. Examples of relatively normal obsessive-compulsive behavior include the man who frequently pats his hip pocket to see if his wallet is still there, the housewife who calls her husband's office three times to remind him to be sure to get home early to visit with his in-laws, the Sunday school teacher who checks and cross-checks every Scripture reference that will be used in the upcoming lesson, and the football coach who watches the preceding week's game film twenty times, trying to pick up clues to reverse his team's three-game losing streak. And as you can see, obsessive-compulsive behavior isn't necessarily negative.

Dr. Frank Minirth, who admits to being "O-C," has developed a 129-point list describing the major characteristics of the obsessive-compulsive personality trait. Particularly significant is item number 128. It reads, "The obsessive-compulsive likes lists."

The following test of obsessive-compulsive behavior helps us to get to know the O-C a little better.

1. An O-C will figure out a numbering system for almost anything, from wardrobe planning to reading all the research papers in his chosen field. He is especially O-C if he writes research papers.

2. He takes intensive notes in his devotional time. He is especially O-C if he periodically rereads those notes.

3. He takes psychological testing each year just to see if he has grown more obsessive-compulsive.

4. He averaged more than forty pages of class notes for each high school, college, or graduate class. He is especially O-C if he typed up those notes.

5. He always makes it a point to arrive within sixty seconds of the exact time of an appointment. He

is especially O-C if he becomes almost clinically depressed when he is unable to fulfill this commitment.

6. He makes intensive lists of things to do. He is especially O-C if he categorizes his lists on carefully filed 3 x 5 index cards.

7. He feels a desperate need to reorganize his filing system several times a year.

8. He keeps his checkbook balanced—to the penny. If he finds that impossible, he may postpone examining his checkbook figures at all.

9. If he takes a psychological stress test, he will regularly score in the top 5 percentile.

10. He constantly finds himself trying to do two things at once. He dictates letters into a cassette recorder as he drives through rush-hour traffic on a suburban expressway, or writes a research paper on a flight from Tampa to Dallas—at the same time he eats a snack.

11. He finds himself saying, "I'll do it myself, and I'll do it right." If he is blessed with a "Type A personality" as well—with its chronic competitiveness, high achievement orientation, and impatience—he will add, "Right now!"

12. He checks the time more than twice an hour. He is especially O-C if he does this on his day off.

13. He eats while he works. He is especially O-C if he sneaks a granola bar in the elevator, or a Big Mac in rush-hour traffic.

14. He wants to name his children alphabetically from oldest to youngest. He is especially O-C if he wants to alliterate all their names.

If you can identify with a majority of those traits, then the person gazing back at you from the mirror is probably a certified obsessive-compulsive. Now that we have introduced ourselves, let's learn more.

2
TWO KINDS OF PERFECTIONISTS

In college Harry wanted to participate in almost every campus activity. He played on the basketball and the baseball teams, was active in the campus church, was a member of the college debate team, sang in a choir, took every possible elective course, dated every weekend, and even managed a small business on the side. When Harry finished college, his grade point average hardly reflected his intelligence level. In high school he had been able to keep up his grade level while carrying on numerous outside activities. Too late he discovered that high intelligence alone wasn't enough to ensure his success in college. That would have required that he spend a good deal of time on one goal—his studies.

Julie was in college with Harry. Her grades were good. Whenever Julie worked on an assignment, she'd spend hours on background research. She was never satisfied that she'd done enough. When she typed a paper, it had to be letter perfect. Indeed, typing caused her great anxiety and distraction, for each page had to be error-free. If it wasn't, she'd retype the whole page. She was proud of the fact that she didn't use correction fluid or make erasures on her papers.

But Julie found that her O-C behavior limited her overall college experience. She spent a great deal of her time tidying up her dormitory room and doing her laundry. She shied away from most of the extracurricular campus activities, and as a result met few people except at church on Sundays. Even then she barely became acquainted, for she didn't have much experience in developing close friendships. Julie didn't see the big picture of how other college activities could develop the interpersonal skills she would need throughout her life.

Believe it or not, Julie and Harry were not personality opposites. Instead, both of them had obsessive-compulsive personality traits, the main one being a desire to exhibit "perfect" behavior to prove one's personal worth. They both experienced anxiety about not being accepted, about not being good enough.

Their personalities looked different because they defined "being good enough" from opposite points of the spectrum. Harry defined "being good enough" quantitatively. His biggest worry was that he might not be participating in enough activities in college. Julie defined "being good enough" qualitatively. Her biggest concern was that she might not be doing any one thing well enough. Not surprisingly, though they came from opposite extremes, they shared a difficulty in dealing with time. Neither one had achieved balance in the way they regarded and used time.

Put another way, Julie was a *quality* perfectionist and Harry a *quantity* perfectionist. Julie's obsessive-compulsive extremes were mixed with some passive-aggressive behavior. She felt aggression toward doing what she felt she "ought" to do, so she showed that aggression passively by dragging her feet when she worked on a project she thought she should complete. Because she was also obsessive-compulsive and thought that everything should be done perfectly, the two personality traits fed on one another.

Julie took a long time to complete her projects because she could not easily accept her work as good enough to consider any one job completed. In addition, drawing out a project allowed her to act out her negative feelings toward "oughtness" or authority through passivity, that is, by taking longer than necessary to complete what she thought she *should* do.

Harry's Type A behavior consisted of O-C tendencies combined with hysteric or histrionic behavior. He was excessively competitive and highly achievement oriented as long as others could see and appreciate those achievements. He suffered from a chronic sense of time pressure and often was impatient with the pace of life. He wanted to prove to the whole world how good he was at what he did—and how quickly he could do it.

The quantity perfectionist is the one who gives himself twenty things to do in a day, completes nineteen, and then wants to kick himself that night for not getting the twentieth task done. He is usually a firstborn child.

And he does not simply want to do many things. He wants to do many things at once—without concentrating on doing as thorough a job as he might. He wants to please or to win approval from everybody—to have everyone's attention and applause. That can best be done, he thinks, by a flurry of activity, not by doing one thing well. To the Type A obsessive-compulsive, more is better and most is best.

Traditional obsessive-compulsives like Julie usually zero in on accomplishing one thing absolutely perfectly. But they cannot decide what is absolute perfection, so they never consider a project completed, for there might still be some way it could be further perfected. An only child, or the only boy or the only girl in a family, tends to have the combination of O-C and passive-aggressive traits that lean toward this type of quality perfectionism. Such a child is likely to have had perfectionistic parents who did his thinking for him—and who made most of his decisions.

As a consequence, the child has strong obedience-defiance conflicts. Part of him really does want to please the authority figures in his life. So he strives to do what he thinks will please God and his parents and at the same time bring himself personal satisfaction. Yet all the while, he resents the perceived demands of authority figures. So in an unconscious resort to rebellion and vengeance, he acts passively by never actually finishing those tasks he thinks would be pleasing to authority figures.

In Romans 7 the apostle Paul describes such behavior when he says, "I do not understand what I do. For what I want to do I do not do, but what I hate I do. . . . For I have the desire to do what is good, but I cannot carry it out. For what I do is not the good I want to do; no, the evil I do not want to do—this I keep on doing. . . . Who will rescue me from this body of death?" (Romans 7:15; 18b-19; 24b).

THE PROBLEM OF TIME

Obsessive-compulsives tend to take an extreme approach to time. Type A people easily become slaves to the clock. They are constantly looking at their watches, checking calendars, reviewing their daily diaries and lists of things to do, crossing off this and adding that, and endeavoring in every way to cram more and more into less and less time. Evidence that a Type A mentality is flourishing in today's society can be seen in the success of such books as *The One-Minute Manager,* *The One-Minute Mother,* and *The One-Minute Father.* Each of those books contains simple, easy-to-use principles for dealing with relationships in the workplace or the home. Our purpose is not to criticize such books. They contain much that is useful. But built into the concept of the one-minute person is the principle that it is possible to do more in less time, a major preoccupation of the Type A obsessive-compulsive. Yet even *The One-Minute Father* recognizes that "these . . . methods of personal communication with your children are just a slice of the parenting pie. Being a good parent takes a good deal more than spending a minute now and then with your children."[1]

Can you imagine what it would be like to have a book called *The One-Minute Christian?* Perhaps we should consider such a project. Chapter titles might include "Instant Spirituality," "Fifteen-Second Devotions," "How to Share Your Faith in Half a Minute," "The Forty-Five-Second Prayer Life," "Instant Maturity," "How to See Positive Growth, Grace, and Knowledge in Less Than a Minute." Sounds absurd, doesn't it? But it is not far off the mark as a description of life from the point of view of the Type A obsessive-compulsive struggling to cope in a fast-track society.

Contrast the one-minute mentality with the mindset of the founder of the Procrastinator's Club of America, Les Waas. He believes that the people who fail to relax are the people who die early. So he doesn't mind if you refer to him as the "late" Mr. Waas. In fact, the slogan for his organization is "Procrastinate Now." Procrastinators like Mr. Waas tend to be basically passive-aggressive, and their approach to any deadline is "There's always tomorrow."

Now the basic obsessive-compulsive usually has some passive-aggressive traits. Though he may be

1. Spencer Johnson, *The One-Minute Father* (New York: Morrow, 1983), p. 99.

more conscientious than the basic passive-aggressive person, his personality still leans toward the Procrastinator's Club thinking—that of wanting to rebel against time and deadlines, even reasonable ones.

At the heart of both Harry's and Julie's problems was an inability to focus on what was truly important. Both filled up their days with activity, but neither one used time strategically. Harry ran from activity to activity, and Julie methodically perfected each detail of the tasks she attempted, but neither one achieved a balance of emphasis (focusing one's time strategically) and breadth (participating in a variety of activities) in his total college experience. To do that they would have had to balance the extremes of quality and quantity, something neither one could do.

Jesus and many other biblical figures were able to balance those extremes, however. Jesus demonstrated a significant consciousness of time and of the seasons of the year. He arrived at each destination at just the right time, but He was never rushed, never dilatory. The principles that guided Him can help us achieve a similar balance in our lives.

But before we look at those biblical principles, it will be helpful to deal with certain "road hazards" inherent in the obsessive-compulsive personality. That will be the topic of the next chapter.

3

ROAD HAZARDS OF THE OBSESSIVE-COMPULSIVE

After sitting in on a radio program in which a panel of Christian counselors discussed the obsessive-compulsive personality, a Christian college administrator turned to a friend on the panel and said, "I don't like being an obsessive-compulsive, or whatever it is." Replied his friend, "I'm probably obsessive-obnoxious, and I'm not sure I like it either." During that call-in program, several people had phoned in to voice their dissatisfaction with the obsessive-compulsive personality traits in their lives.

All of those people missed an important point. Though we may not like certain aspects of our personalities, it is important that we accept ourselves. After all, God allowed us to grow up in families where we developed the particular collection of personality strengths and weaknesses we have.

We gain most of our personality traits between the ages of three and six as we learn to relate to our parents and siblings. The obsessive-compulsive personality is usually formed in an oldest child or in the oldest boy or girl. New parents, who often expect more of a small child than he or she can give, drive their first-born to excel early. The child sees that he is more likely to be praised and attended to when he strives for "perfection" than when he simply does what he can with no particular emphasis on perfection. Reaching for perfection to please others becomes a habit early in life.

It is important to remember two overriding principles. First, we need to think of ourselves not with selfish pride or false humility but with sober judgment. God made each of us for a purpose, one that is neither more nor less important than the purpose He has for other individuals. God made us for His glory, and He knew the type of personality each of us would develop. With that in mind, we need to remember the exhortation of the apostle Paul: "Do not think of yourself more highly than you ought, but rather think of yourself with sober judgment [realistically], in accordance with the measure of faith God has given you" (Romans 12:3).

Second, we need to continue in a process of development. As 2 Peter 3:18 puts it, "Grow in the grace and knowledge of our Lord and Savior Jesus Christ." We need to strengthen the strengths we have and work to overcome our weaknesses.

O-C PERSONALITY TRAITS

On first impression, the obsessive-compulsive seems to be a conscientious and dutiful individual, highly motivated toward obedience. He is likely to be a hard worker (usually working too hard), to have a strict conscience, and to be highly motivated. As one hard-working O-C frequently told his children, "Work makes life sweet." The O-C tends to be self-sacrificing and more willing to give up personal gain or desires than some other personality types, which lean toward more selfish behavior.

One of the results of such self-sacrificing behavior is that obsessive-compulsives tend to be extremely successful. Statistically, obsessive-compulsive personalities in mid- to upper-level management positions in American business and industry are outnumbered only by paranoid personality types. Paranoid personalities are afraid of other people's controlling them, so they strive to take control themselves.

The Scottish missionary Eric Liddell, who won a Gold Medal for Britain in the 1924 Olympics for his running, was a classic, dedicated, Christian O-C. He once told an audience, "I believe God made me for a purpose, but He also made me fast. And when I run, I feel His pleasure." He proved that he didn't run to be glorified by others when he sacrificed an opportunity to win an Olympic medal by refusing to run the race on Sunday. His conviction was that Sunday was the Lord's Day, meant only for rest and concentration on the Lord.

A high proportion of the missionaries, Bible college students, pastors, and seminarians we have counseled at the Minirth-Meier Clinic have had a number of obsessive-compulsive personality traits. Many of these individuals were willing to sacrifice lucrative careers to go into the Lord's work. A recent survey of the faculty of a large Christian college also indicated that 80 percent of the teachers considered themselves to be primarily obsessive-compulsive.

Obsessive-compulsives have a strong passion for truth. They tend to be well organized and to handle facts carefully. When they research biblical information they are likely to be careful and accurate—important traits when one is dealing with doctrine and theology.

When taken alone, the obsessive-compulsive traits described above give the impression that the obsessive-compulsive personality type is the most desirable one to have. We know, however, that God didn't make everyone alike. He made us equally important and interdependent on one another. We need, therefore, to recognize the importance of the personable hysteric (or histrionic), the sensitive paranoid, the servant-hearted passive, the highly energetic cyclothimic, and other personalities.

We must also recognize that some negative traits do overshadow the positive aspects of the obsessive-compulsive personality. Most obsessives are aware of those negative traits but tend to deny them, for denial is one of the chief defense mechanisms (reactive behaviors) people employ to cope with the anxiety they would feel if they were fully aware of their sinful or selfish emotions.

ADDITIONAL EXTREME TENDENCIES

The obsessive-compulsive personality is also likely to possess the following extreme characteristics.

PERFECTIONISTIC

A perfectionist has a tendency to expect himself to be perfect all the time. He becomes intensely angry with himself when he demonstrates such imperfections as losing his car keys, forgetting his checkbook, or even failing to keep his checkbook balanced. If an obsessive-compulsive homemaker fails to take care of all her children perfectly, she may become very depressed.

Furthermore, perfectionistic obsessive-compulsives have a tendency to expect perfection from others.

This can create chaos in marital and work relationships, and even may produce another generation of highly perfectionistic, workaholic, obsessive-compulsive children.

DETAIL-ORIENTED

Obsessive-compulsives have a tendency to develop a meticulous concern for detail. They frequently will labor far too hard over a given project. In fact, one obsessive author we know, writing a voluminous book, spent many months writing and rewriting the first three chapters, unable to go on to chapter four, because the first three "just aren't perfect yet." As perfectionists drive themselves to the limit, they are frequently unable or, more accurately, *unwilling* to relax. Obsessive-compulsives become overly concerned about every detail. They are strong in organization but may spend more time getting organized than they spend on just about anything else.

They have a tendency to focus on the future and have a great deal of difficulty relaxing and enjoying life in the present. Obsessives are the kind of individuals who, when eating a hot fudge sundae save what they consider the best part, the maraschino cherry on top of the whipped cream, for last. Or, after considering the amount of number-two red dye contained in that topping, they refuse to eat the cherry at all!

PROJECT-DIRECTED

Obsessive-compulsives tend to focus on projects rather than on people. This is undergirded by an orientation toward facts rather than feelings. Psychiatric research has long demonstrated that the left side of the human brain is used for processing factual or logical data. The right side is used for more creative thinking as well as emotional or relational thought. Obsessive-compulsives tend to rely primarily on the data-oriented part of their thinking. In fact, obsessives have a strong tendency to deny most emotional feelings or responses, even though they are frequently dominated by strong, underlying emotions. You might say that the obsessive *feels* with his mind.

Furthermore, obsessive-compulsives have a tendency to criticize themselves and others for being less than perfect. Coupled with that is a motivation toward control—of self, circumstances, personal environment, and others. All Christians tend to feel inferior at some time and try to compensate for those feelings of inferiority. On the part of the obsessive-compulsive, those inferiority feelings lead to power struggles because of their strong motivation to be in control. Both internal and interpersonal conflicts are often the result.

Members of a large division of a Fortune 500 company had a party in honor of their vice-president, not to celebrate his retirement or even his hiring, but his being fired. The vice-president was strongly control-oriented. Throughout his division, he insisted on personally supervising and approving even the simplest decisions, such as which office supplies the secretaries purchased and from which vendors they ordered them.

Many workaholic obsessive-compulsives have what might well be described as a "Martha complex." During Jesus' last week on earth, Martha opened her home to Jesus. Mary, Martha's sister, sat and listened to Jesus as Martha busied herself preparing a meal. Martha displayed numerous obsessive-compulsive traits in her first recorded utterance to Jesus, "Lord, don't you care that my sister has left me to do the work by myself? Tell her to help me!" (Luke 10:40).

The traits exposed in that one statement revealed that Martha:

- considered the *project* of having the Savior for dinner more important than acknowledging the *Person* of Jesus Christ.
- labored far too hard over the project.
- would not or could not relax and enjoy the Lord's presence.
- preferred working to anything else.
- was critical of her sister, Mary (for not helping her), and even of Jesus (for not having encouraged Mary to help her).
- was motivated to control Mary as well as Jesus (to help her control Mary).
- took action that would likely lead to interpersonal conflicts.

Jesus' reply to Martha put the differing outlooks of the two sisters into proper perspective, although what He said was something that an obsessive-compulsive would find disagreeable, even when the words were from Jesus Himself.

> Martha, Martha, . . . you are worried and upset [tied up in knots, distracted] about many things, but only one thing is needed. Mary has chosen what is better [relating personally with others, particularly with Jesus], and it will not be taken away from her. [Luke 10:41]

DIRT-OBSESSED

The obsessive-compulsive's concern with dirt gives us a candid look at perfectionism. The key question is, how clean is clean enough? As a young boy, one of the authors was taught by his mother how to wash dishes.

He never enjoyed the chore, partly because he never knew how clean was clean enough, and partly because his mother was somewhat obsessive-compulsive herself. She always insisted that the dishes be carefully scrubbed in scalding water, rinsed in hot water to remove all germs, then rinsed again in cold water to remove all traces and residue of soap (which might have caused diarrhea). Finally, the dishes needed to be carefully dried and put away.

While he did the dishes, this particular author wrestled with the question, how hot does the water have to be and for how long must the dishes be immersed in it to kill every single germ? In fact, can that be done? Is it worth the trouble? What if one germ slips through? The result of this kind of obsession is obvious: childhood training that spawns such fearful thoughts can cause children to develop obsessive-compulsive personality problems.

Dirt in other areas of life—personal hygiene, housekeeping, laundry—is often an obsession. "Cleanliness is next to godliness" is the maxim that spells disaster for some obsessive-compulsives. To them, perfect cleanliness can mean the next best thing to perfection itself. It becomes a substitute for washing one's sins or imperfections away so that one can be more perfect and acceptable.

MONEY-FOCUSED

The obsessive-compulsive tends to be conservative, which can be a positive trait; however, this particular characteristic is often taken to the extreme. Because of a strong need to feel secure and in control, obsessives tend to be strongly money-oriented. In fact, many obsessive-compulsive church treasurers will treat church funds like their own, rather than the

Lord's. They will not only exercise the conscientious stewardship demanded of a person serving in that position but will treat any expenditures, even those for benevolent purposes, as a personal affront, justifying such an attitude in the name of financial conservatism.

At times, an obsessive-compulsive husband may deeply resent the needs of his wife to spend money on their children, a new hairdo, a dress, or on other personal expenses because of his strong desire to save that money for the future.

TEMPTATIONS OF THE O-C

Like every other Christian, the obsessive-compulsive has an "old nature" that manifests itself in sinful or selfish behavior. With more than five billion people on planet earth, each of us feels insignificant and inferior to some extent. We try to compensate for those feelings through selfish, sinful, or inappropriate behavior patterns. Three such behavior patterns outlined for us in 1 John 2:13-15 are the lust of the flesh—*sexual and other physical enticements;* the lust of the eyes—*materialism,* or preoccupation with money and material things; and the pride of life—*power struggles,* or a desire to control, dominate, or be more prominent than other people.

Obsessives can fall into sexual temptation, especially because of their tendency to deny emotions, their own sexuality, or their need for emotional intimacy. However, they tend to be tempted primarily in two other areas—materialism and power struggles.

MATERIALISM

Because of their preoccupation with money, obsessives can become very materialistic. Frequently, their materialistic behaviors are hidden under the guise of "saving for the future." Sometimes obsessive-compulsives refuse to give to God or to others because of their strong drive to build up personal security by saving. That kind of behavior was demonstrated by the farmer who tore down his barns to build bigger ones, a pattern condemned as foolish by the Lord Jesus Christ. The possession of money is not wrong, but as Paul pointed out to Timothy, the *love* of money is the root of all kinds of evil. While the love of money is obvious and overt in other personalities, it may be more subtle in the obsessive-compulsive and therefore more difficult to deal with.

POWER STRUGGLES

A second major area of temptation, and perhaps the most crucial for Christian obsessive-compulsives, is the desire for power, or the "pride of life." Because they themselves usually have experienced a great deal of conditional love (a concept we will deal with later), obsessive-compulsives tend to approach others with the same attitude. As one obsessive-compulsive put it, "I love my fellow workers unconditionally, but they just don't measure up to my performance standards." That same person later acknowledged that these personal feelings were at the root of several intense, on-the-job conflicts in his Christian working environment.

The intensely competitive nature of obsessive-compulsives frequently makes them successful in their work. Yet the kind of success they achieve is often worldly success in contrast to the kind of success that Jesus commends in Luke 22:25-26:

> Jesus said to them, "The kings of the Gentiles lord it over them; and those who exercise authority over them call themselves Benefactors. But you are not to be like that. Instead, the greatest among you

should be like the youngest, and the one who rules like the one who serves."

It is important for the obsessive-compulsive to work at avoiding inappropriate obsessive behavior patterns, especially crucial ones such as workaholism, materialism, power struggles, and self-critical, perfectionistic behavior. How to do that will be explored later.

Now that we see how obsessive-compulsives behave, let's look at how they think and feel.

4

IS MY THINKING STRAIGHT?

Obsessive-compulsive personalities usually have strong mental capacities and seem to be fact-oriented. They are ideal for jobs that demand an ability to master a number of facts. Good researchers, accountants, computer programmers, airline pilots, air traffic controllers, nurses, doctors, pastors, theologians, business administrators, managers, and many other professional workers usually include numerous balanced obsessive-compulsive individuals who utilize factual, organizational, and work-ethic strengths.

However, although obsessives are thinkers, they do not always think accurately. The following are a sampling of some irrational beliefs held by Type A obsessive-compulsives.

TYPE A OBSESSIVE-COMPULSIVE THINKING

1. *Quantity of output is more important than quality of output.* The major emphasis of Type A obsessive-compulsives is to "churn out" a lot of work. For instance, three highly productive obsessive-compulsives decided to form a "book of the month" club. They weren't going to read a book each month, however; they intended to *write* a book each month, in addition to their already busy schedules and other demands.

Every day Joe makes lists of fifteen to twenty things to do. He feels motivated to check off his list daily, even if the items are poorly or sloppily done. It doesn't bother him if they're not done well, but it does bother him if they are not checked off. But for the Christian, excellence ought not to be simply a matter of checking off items on a list. It involves establishing a balance between quality and quantity, even as we recognize that we are not perfect in either category. Instead, success means giving our best in any given situation.

2. *Faster is always better.* Many obsessives' lives are like a treadmill moving faster and faster. And, somehow, the charge of adrenalin from life in the fast lane motivates them to work even more rapidly. Though the passive-aggressive O-C personality tends to become slower and slower under pressure, the Type A obsessive works faster, talks faster, and even tries to think faster. Unfortunately, working faster doesn't always produce a better product. In fact, faster can create disaster.

Consider Wayne. Wayne works in a factory that rebuilds spark plugs. Although he was already doing a fine job reaching his assigned quota, he wanted to turn out more rebuilt spark plugs than the other workers. But in the process of working faster, he ruined an entire batch of plugs and cost the company a large sum of money. As a result, he was reprimanded for working *too* fast. Life is like freeway driving. We shouldn't be moving so fast or so slow that we're out of sync with the rest of the traffic.

3. *Horrible disaster will occur if deadlines are not met.* A highly successful Christian radio professional became physically ill when through a number of unavoidable circumstances, including equipment failure, a documentary missed a preparation deadline.

Such feelings would have been perfectly understandable, except that in this case the deadline missed was seventy-two hours before the documentary was scheduled to be broadcast. In the October 19, 1976, *Family Health Magazine*, psychologist Leonard Cammer asks, "What about your punctuality? Mostly, it serves you in good stead, but can you allow yourself to be five or ten minutes late when it really would make no difference? Do you panic at the very thought?"

Here is one O-C who learned the benefits of procrastination. Horace, a pastor, learned of a conflict in his church. His initial reaction was to attempt to gather all the people involved in the conflict in his office that same day. Because of his schedule, however, he was unable to do that. In the meantime, those directly involved in the problem got together and resolved it, probably much more adequately than if the pastor had tried to wade into it. A lesson that many of us need to learn is that meeting deadlines is far less important than dealing with people, issues, or even taking time out. A good biblical example of that is Jesus' timing regarding the death of Lazarus and His arrival in Bethany. According to Lazarus' family, Jesus was several days late; yet in reality He was exactly on time. Another example is Mark 6:30 where we find Jesus and His disciples taking time out. (See the Minirth-Meier booklet *Taking Time Out*, published by Moody Press.)

Paul Meier likes to give this advice to obsessive-compulsives: Never do today what you can put off till tomorrow.

4. *Winning or losing a competition is a reflection of my worth as a human being.* In American society professional sports, business, and industry have produced a "win at all cost" mentality. Seminars are available to aid individuals in "winning" the game of life, which usually means successfully competing with oth-

ers. College football fans from various universities discuss the relative merits of their favorite team and which team will be crowned the national champion. In professional sports the Super Bowl, the World Series, and the NBA playoff finals settle the same question. However, in any competition there is always one winner—and many losers. Unfortunately, we have somehow developed a connection that links personal worth to winning. Thus, when we lose, we feel horrible. A magazine article describes a twenty-game-winning major league pitcher as unable to accept losing and feeling totally worthless whenever it happened.

For the Christian, the goal is to win God's approval in the race of life (1 Corinthians 9).

5. *I am only as good as my accomplishments.* This is closely linked with the previous belief. One way of spotting Type A obsessive-compulsive behavior, particularly the workaholic kind, is to check your conversation. Do you spend a lot of time talking about your accomplishments? (You may not be the best judge of this—so check with your wife or husband, your children, your business associates, or other professionals with whom you interact.) Frequently, we focus on our accomplishments because we feel we are *only as good as our achievements*. However, for Christians, personal worth is rooted in our *position* in Jesus Christ, not in our performance. It is irrational for the Christian to feel so competitive or achievement oriented that self-worth becomes linked to personal accomplishments. Nor will an endless string of achievements insure that we will like ourselves. Usually, a list of accomplishments simply produces either an appropriate response —thanking God for the positive things He allows me to achieve, while giving Him the glory—or an inappropriate response—feeling that I am really special because of what I achieve, or worthless because of my

inability to achieve. These feelings lead to another irrational belief.

6. *Nonachievement-oriented activities are a waste of time.* Why do the spouses of Type A obsessive-compulsive workaholics frequently complain that they are ignored when it comes to personal conversation? Why do their children often feel conditionally loved or, worse, neglected? Why do Type A's look for excuses to work overtime, bring work home from the office, and try to do three or four things at once? Because of the irrational conviction that nonachievement-oriented activities are just a waste of time. There is no question that wasting time is a sin, but it is probably not as great a sin as most Type A O-Cs assume. Furthermore, the list of activities considered time-wasters by Type A O-Cs is a lot longer than the lists other personality types would create. Even Jesus told His overworked disciples, "Come with me by yourselves to a quiet place and get some rest" (Mark 6:31). Although rest is an activity considered a time-waster by many Type A O-Cs, there is positive value to time away from the productive mind-set.

In fact, God places a premium on certain nonachievement-oriented activities such as relationships, rest, and even waiting. Some time ago a friend challenged one of the authors to study the concept of waiting in Scripture. After some procrastination, the study was completed. It proved to be an insightful study, as the author learned the value of waiting and discovered several benefits individuals in Scripture received by heeding instructions to wait.

7. *I can have complete control over my life if I only try hard enough.* The obsessive-compulsive is often convinced, without rational foundation, that just a little more effort will give him or her complete control

over circumstances, self, and even others. To the obsessive-compulsive, nothing seems worse than "losing control." Obsessive-compulsives have been known to become extremely angry and depressed when placed in emotional circumstances that bring tears. In traffic, Type A obsessives sometimes feel they can make all the traffic lights if they just drive hard and fast enough. Being put on hold on the telephone, being caught in a traffic jam, spending time circling a busy airport—those kinds of uncontrollable situations make life miserable for the Type A obsessive-compulsive. A frequent corollary to this for the Type A is the thought that speeding up the pace of his activities is the best way to keep or regain control.

The obsessive-compulsive needs constantly to remind himself that personal effort is always secondary to utilizing God's resources. The best example of that is the apostle Paul in 2 Corinthians 12. No amount of personal effort could remove his thorn in the flesh. In that situation God explained to Paul that His strength was being perfected in Paul's weakness. Read Isaiah 40, which is another classic example of those who renew their strength by waiting on the Lord. The truth is that God is the only One who really can or should be in control. So why should we worry about being in control in life? We can't be.

8. *Being perfectionistic is the best way to insure high quality achievements.* A successful, obsessive-compulsive medical doctor had always made straight A's throughout high school and college. When he reached medical school, suddenly he found himself to be just one of the average students, since all the rest of the medical students were also the "cream of the crop" in their high schools and colleges. To assure himself of quality achievements, this doctor became increasingly perfectionistic and, in the process, became highly crit-

ical of himself and others. His marriage relationship became strained, and his friends began to avoid him. He expected perfection of himself and of others. He had not reconciled himself to the fact that none of us is perfect. Only Jesus Christ reached sinless perfection. Not even the apostle Paul, who, prior to his conversion, probably was extremely obsessive-compulsive as a "Pharisee of the Pharisees," was perfect.

Often, relaxing perfectionistic standards leads to greater excellence and more successful results than perfectionism does. On one of our radio programs Texas Rangers catcher Jeff Sundberg told of pushing himself and trying harder but being less successful at the plate. But his batting average improved dramatically after his batting coach encouraged him to relax and have fun at the plate.

The bumper sticker on one reformed obsessive-compulsive's car reads, "Christians aren't perfect, just forgiven." Being perfectionistic only underscores how far we can fall. We all fall short of perfection, which leads to feelings of anger and depression in the Type A obsessive.

9. *Openly expressing my anger and hostility makes other people pay for getting in my way.* Although many Christian Type A obsessives would not admit to such thoughts, they tend to couch them in terms of "appropriate" confrontation. "I believe in taking a strong stand for my convictions." "I believe in confronting people when they need to be confronted." One young obsessive-compulsive pastor was involved in three church splits before somebody finally communicated to him that it wasn't his "biblical confrontation" of sin in the lives of others or their personal shortcomings that was causing the problems. Rather, it was his own underlying anger and hostility that created the series of tragic rifts.

The proper alternative to expressing anger is to acknowledge and confront it. The next step is to turn the
issue of vengeance over to God, particularly because
Scripture teaches us to do so. Three times in the New
Testament we are instructed that God is to be in charge
of vengeance (Romans 12; 1 Thessalonians 5; 1 Peter 3).
We must place it in His hands.

What we discover as we consider this facet of the
Type A obsessive-compulsive is that, although he generally has superior thinking capabilities, he is susceptible to numerous irrational thoughts. Those thoughts
are related to some very strong underlying emotions,
ones the obsessive-compulsive refuses to acknowledge
but which nonetheless play a key role in his or her life.
They will be discussed in the next chapter.

5

FACING MY FEELINGS

This chapter is being written while seated in a DC-9 aircraft on a Monday morning against the beautiful mountain backdrop of Colorado Springs. However, I shouldn't be here. This aircraft was scheduled to leave nearly two hours earlier than it did. First, we experienced a fog delay. A half hour later, while we were taxiing into position for takeoff, the pilot ran the aircraft off the edge of the runway. We were stuck in the mud for almost two hours. Finally, the plane was pulled from the mud, restored to the runway, and readied for takeoff. During the delay the pilot consoled us over the intercom, "I feel terrible about this. It is an awful way to begin a Monday morning. I know most of you have tight schedules and connecting flights to make."

How did the passengers feel? Most were fairly good-natured, but several voiced anger over fouled-up flight schedules and connections. Others were fearful of missing important meetings or appointments. And underlying several of the conversations with flight attendants were feelings of guilt for expressing those emotions of anger and fear. It was obvious that many of those passengers had a number of obsessive-compulsive traits.

Although most obsessive-compulsives have strong feelings, they do not like to feel. They would much rather think. They keep their emotions hidden from others and, if possible, from themselves. As a result, obsessive-compulsives may seem cold and indifferent.

Rick, a highly successful senior pastor of a large evangelical church, was known to his congregation as a gifted communicator and a capable administrator. Yet many people considered him to be cold in his personal relationships, unfeeling, and unable to relate to the emotional expressions of others. Speaking to a member of our counseling staff, he conceded that he was more interested in facts than in feelings. And even though he recognized the need for hospital visitation, counseling, and other people-oriented aspects of ministry, he strongly preferred to study in his office with the door closed while his secretary screened personal calls and visits.

EMOTIONS

What emotions do most obsessive-compulsives actually feel? Let's examine some typical O-C emotions and how they deal with them.

ANGER

According to a number of authorities, a primary emotion of obsessives is anger. Many obsessive-compulsives had strong, dominant parents who demanded unquestioning obedience and forbade their children to express anger, classifying such as tantamount to rebellion. Thus, in early life the obsessive-compulsive developed a struggle between obedience and defiance.

Outwardly, obsessives are usually extremely compliant, so we know that the pull of obedience usually wins. Occasionally, however, defiance wins. When obsessives submit or comply, that obedience usually creates feelings of strong anger, sometimes even rage.

As one obsessive-compulsive housewife put it, "Both my parents expected me always to do exactly what they said. I usually did, but underneath I seethed."

When asked, "Did you ever decide not to comply with their wishes?" her reply was, "Seldom. I was scared to death whenever I didn't do what they said."

FEAR

On the rare occasions when obsessives allow defiance to win out over their inclination toward obedience, the act of defiance will later lead to even stronger feelings of fear of authority. Actually that defiance is fear of parental authority left over from childhood. Although obsessive-compulsives do not like to admit it, they are frequently dominated by powerful emotions of intense anger or fear. Their fears tend to lead to perfectionistic traits and to future compliance, whereas their feelings of anger or rage often lead to nonperfectionistic traits and a present refusal to comply.

Thus, while obsessive-compulsives tend to be conscientious in most areas of their lives, they usually have a few areas in which they tend to be extremely negligent. For example, one obsessive-compulsive who was always punctual, orderly, and neat, frequently misplaced his keys. An obsessive-compulsive housewife who managed two children, a husband's ministry career, and a college-level computer course successfully, nonetheless found it extremely difficult to maintain any semblance of neatness in her home. Obsessive-compulsives often tend to be characterized by opposing traits that arise from their mixed feelings.

Just what does the obsessive-compulsive fear? He fears:

Dependency. He prefers relationships in which he is in control and others are dependent on him.

Close relationships. Close relationships demand emotional vulnerability or dependency, feelings that are unthinkable and highly undesirable to the obsessive-compulsive.

Loss of control. Being in control of himself and having control over his circumstances is of extreme importance to the O-C. He feels helpless and fears those feelings of helplessness whenever he loses control. The more he experiences feelings of powerlessness, the more an obsessive under stress wants to "do something about it," even when the appropriate course of action may be to "wait on the Lord."

GUILT

Related to anger and fear are the feelings of guilt experienced by most obsessive-compulsives. While guilt is a valid emotion created by the Holy Spirit to warn us when we are wrong, we fallen human beings tend to experience one of two extremes of this emotion. Self-centered, sociopathic personalities (aspects of which all of us are born with to some degree) tend to minimize or ignore feelings of guilt while persisting in selfish or sociopathic behavior that fulfills the biblical description of having "consciences seared with a hot iron." They seldom feel guilty, even when they should.

On the other hand, some Christians, because of strict upbringings and exposure to legalistic teaching, feel guilty about almost anything. For example, one of the authors was raised in a strict home where reading a newspaper was not allowed on Sunday. It took years for him to feel comfortable when sitting down to scan the front page, the sports section, or even the comics, not because any Scripture says, "Thou shalt not peruse the Sunday paper," but because of a combination of parental upbringing and inappropriate guilt.

Many obsessive-compulsives are plagued by an overly strict conscience, one that causes continued feelings of guilt and lack of forgiveness long after a failure. For example, a conscientious college student was cheating in school primarily because of years of being unsuccessful and parental disapproval. When he was caught and confronted with his misconduct, he confessed, both to God and to the school authorities. During the balance of his college career, he maintained a "clean slate." However, feelings of guilt and even depression over the incident continued to plague him years later, hampering his efforts to minister to others. The problem was not with God's forgiveness or with the student's refusal to acknowledge his sin. Like many of his obsessive-compulsive colleagues, the student had admitted his failure to live up to God's absolute standard of perfection and had accepted God's forgiveness, yet he could not forgive himself or quiet his hyperactive conscience.

Because of the tendency to deny feelings or to turn them inward, O-C's tend to experience a greater degree of depression than almost any other personality type.

Another kind of obsessive-compulsive, however, has a tendency to hold in feelings of anger and then occasionally ventilate them, often in hostile, aggressive, or inappropriate ways. In fact, as one obsessive-compulsive businessman put it, "It is much easier for me to express myself when I am feeling angry with my wife than when I want to express warmth." Through intensive counseling he discovered the reason for that. He was extremely fearful of becoming emotionally close or dependent and used anger to maintain what he considered to be a safe distance in his relationships.

Obsessive-compulsives become angry with others who affect or limit their ability to be "perfect," with themselves for their own imperfections, and perhaps even angry at their own feelings. They may be angry with God for allowing circumstances to prove their imperfections.

A classic biblical example of an obsessive outburst of sinful and inappropriate behavior is the incident in Numbers 20:2-13, where Moses struck the rock against God's instructions. Although God had provided water for Israel through a similar incident in the past (in which Moses followed God's instructions to the letter by smiting the rock once), under the stress of Israel's constant carping and complaining, Moses exhibited the underlying anger of a normally obedient O-C that came boiling to the top. God said to Moses, "Speak to the rock." But Moses' anger was overflowing. "Listen, you rebels, must we bring you water out of this rock?" (v. 10) He then *struck* (but did not speak to) the rock—twice.

In this incident Moses exhibited all three primary emotions of an obsessive-compulsive:

- *anger*—with the Israelites, with God, with himself, and with the circumstances
- *fear*—of loss of control or of being unable to "produce" (seen in the statement "Must we bring you water?")
- *guilt*—when God confronted him (God disciplined Moses by forbidding him to enter the Promised Land)

DEFENSE MECHANISMS

Frequently, the obsessive-compulsive copes with his feelings by using defense mechanisms. Defense mechanisms are the automatic and subconscious ways we respond to conflict or frustration. In essence, they are ways in which we deceive ourselves to avoid facing our true desires, emotions, and motives.

Two verses of Scripture illustrate this point. The first is Proverbs 21:2, "All a man's ways seem right to him, but the Lord weighs the heart." That shows how commonly we exercise self-righteousness to justify things we do, even when our motives are improper.

The second verse is Jeremiah 17:9, "The heart is deceitful above all things, and desperately wicked" (KJV*). We consider this verse to be the cornerstone of Christian counseling. Obviously, the more we become aware of the truth about ourselves, the better we will be able to engage in Christlike, or biblical, thinking, feeling, and behavior. Although every individual practices defense mechanisms many times each day, certain defenses are most common to obsessive-compulsives. Let's examine these mechanisms.

DENIAL

An individual using this defense mechanism denies access to consciousness of thoughts, feelings, or motives. Although denial is most commonly seen in histrionic or hysteric (outwardly emotional, attention-seeking) personalities, obsessives frequently practice denial regarding emotions such as anger or fear. For example, one obsessive-compulsive pastor was experiencing marital conflict, yet insisted that he had never been angry with his wife. What he meant was that he had never allowed himself to get in touch with his feelings of anger—feelings that in many instances were already evident to his wife.

* King James Version.

INTELLECTUALIZATION

Individuals who intellectualize frequently develop strong inferiority feelings. Yet they cover those feelings by attempting to impress others, using extensive philosophical discussion, technical jargon, and intellectual vocabulary. We knew a seminary student who spent hours in the coffee shop discussing philosophical and theological issues and debating obscure concepts. But in spite of all that discussion, he never got in touch with his feelings.

ISOLATION

The individual who practices isolation separates or isolates unacceptable feelings from his conscious awareness. This is one of the more common ways obsessives deal with anger, particularly those who have been taught that all anger is sin. At times, individuals who believe feelings of greed or lust are totally unacceptable isolate those emotions in spite of the fact that most normal people do experience them from time to time.

REACTION FORMATION

Often found with isolation, reaction formation is adopting attitudes or actions that are the exact opposite of those conscious or unconscious impulses we experience. An example would be a television evangelist who preaches long sermons against materialism but secretly holds large bank accounts. Or a youth pastor who has strict and complex rules forbidding the young people in his church to have any physical contact with the opposite sex, but who secretly reads pornographic magazines and views sexually explicit movies.

PHARISEEISM

Those who practice phariseeism become increasingly self-righteous. The Pharisee (in Luke 18) thanked God that he was not as others—robbers, evildoers, adulterers—and carefully maintained a list of dos and don'ts, tailor-made to his personal preferences and designed to maintain his own personal selfishness, hostility, and anger. Those who practice phariseeism frequently regard anyone less legalistic than themselves as worldly or even diabolical. They make a great show of religious ritual to cover up their inappropriate emotions. One pharisaical preacher was exhorting his flock not to engage in the evils of drinking. "I am the temple of the Holy Spirit," he admonished with a sweeping gesture of his arm, which caused a hidden package of cigarettes to fall from his pocket in full view of his astonished congregation.

MAGICAL THINKING

Magical thinking is a defense mechanism by which individuals compensate for feelings of inferiority by fooling themselves into thinking they have subtle supernatural powers. This tends to be present to a greater degree in obsessive-compulsive adults and young children than in other groups of people. It is extreme in those suffering from schizophrenia but manifests itself more mildly in obsessives.

One immature Christian obsessive was trying to decide whether to marry the girl he was dating or begin dating another girl. Deciding to seek "God's will" by using a form of magical thinking, he opened his Bible and came across a verse that read, "He taketh away the first, that he may establish the second" (Hebrews 10:9). Convinced that he had found God's clear direction, he broke off his relationship with the first young lady and married the second. Whatever God's will regarding the marriage, the young man had clearly violated the rules for biblical interpretation in his use of that verse.

Magical thinking frequently leads to guilt in obsessives who become angry at friends or relatives but later experience some tragedy. One young obsessive housewife had shouted over the telephone at her mother the day before her mother suffered an automobile accident. Her mother later died of the resulting injuries. It took months of intensive therapy to help that obsessive-compulsive individual recover from her magical thinking that left her believing that she had in some way caused the mishap.

UNDOING

Undoing is the unhealthy side of appropriate restitution, that is, offering an apology or attempting to right specific wrongs we have done to others. Obsessives and others who practice undoing try to perform positive verbal communication or benevolent acts, attempting to counter other negative acts. The problem is that they do that without acknowledging the wrong deeds, as if they had never made the errors.

One example of undoing was a Christian lady who frequently criticized the members of her women's Bible study group behind their backs. However, when she was with them, she was warm, effusive, and outgoing in her praise and encouragement—almost to excess. Because she considered herself to be a highly encouraging and positive individual, she managed to use that undoing as a means of escaping personal awareness of her sinful gossip and criticism. Whether with respect to inappropriate thinking or undesirable emotions, obsessive-compulsives find it extremely painful to face the truth.

Some secular psychologists encourage the use of defense mechanisms to "prevent insanity." However, a more biblical alternative for mental health is to experience the forgiveness from sin that results from the new birth in Christ, and to allow the Word of God to progressively conform us to Christ as we study, meditate, and apply it to our sinful thought patterns, emotions, and motives.

Jesus pointed out to a group of obsessives, "You will know the truth, and the truth will set you free" (John 8:32). Unfortunately, the response of those highly obsessive Pharisees was denial. "We are Abraham's descendants and have never been slaves of anyone" (v. 33).

Though it may be painful to discover the truth about our emotions, such as guilt, fear, and anger, as well as about our dualistic and inappropriate thinking, it is important for us to progressively give up our defense mechanisms in order to become emotionally and spiritually healthy.

6
HOW DID I GET THIS WAY?

Recently one of us was speaking at a conference in a Western state. During the conference this author stayed in the home of a staff member of a parachurch organization. Following the service one evening his hostess stated rather strongly, "I am really not sure I agree with all of what you said about obsessive-compulsive behavior or workaholism. In fact, I don't like it."

"Really?" the author replied. "Tell me why."

"I just think those things don't apply to me."

"Tell me a little about yourself," the speaker replied.

"Well, I am certainly not obsessive-compulsive or a workaholic," she said. "However, my dad certainly was. He was an extremely critical, highly demanding, hardworking businessman, and he expected a lot out of us. In fact, I decided early in life that I would make it a point not to be at all like my father."

It's not hard to imagine the direction the conversation took. Within half an hour the housewife reluctantly began to admit that she had a number of obsessive-compulsive personality traits—characteristics she had sought to suppress or deny for years. Finally, she threw up her hands. "The reason I didn't like what you were saying is that it described me to a 'T.' I must have caught my father's obsessive-compulsive behavior after all."

However, being an obsessive-compulsive is not a "caught" behavior. And there is no evidence that O-C traits are hereditary. Psychological studies indicate that the primary factor is one's early environment. Many of those studies indicate that the majority of our personality traits are formed prior to our sixth birthday and certainly by the time one becomes a teenager.

Most individuals with a large number of obsessive-compulsive traits have parents who were also obsessive. A person is especially likely to become O-C if the parent of the opposite sex was extremely strict, demanded complete devotion and total obedience, and gave a minimal amount of attention—love, affection, hugs, or positive strokes. To such a parent, everything was either black or white. The child was either a success or a failure. So the child felt accepted on a conditional basis. That conditional love led to the child's need to achieve or to perform to get the parent's approval.

As one highly motivated obsessive-compulsive told her counselor, "Dad was very successful in his business, but he wasn't very good at relating to my mother or to us children. He always expected us to be the best, but he never seemed to think that we could do anything. Whether it was chores around the house, helping him with his business, or doing things at school, we had to be perfect." When asked if her father had ever told her that he loved her, her quick reply was, "No, never. Not until I was grown and out of the house."

"Did he give you lots of hugs when you were growing up?"

"No, he wasn't affectionate at all."

This daughter, like many obsessive-compulsives, attempted superhuman achievements to try to overcome her feelings of uncertainty that conditional love had produced.

Describing the workaholic, obsessive-compulsive father in the *Wall Street Journal* (April 6, 1981), Sanford L. Jacobs writes, "He gets home long after the children have eaten. She used to eat with them but now she waits for her husband. Usually the children have gone to bed by then. One child asked recently, 'Isn't daddy going to be home again tonight?'" Two possible consequences of obsessive-compulsive, workaholic behavior in parents are: (1) a child acts out and tells the parent to "buzz off," and (2) the oldest child develops an intense motivation to strive after achievements to try to win the workaholic or obsessive-compulsive parent's approval.

The great majority of obsessive-compulsives are workaholics, and most workaholics have a large number of obsessive-compulsive personality traits.

Type A behavior patterns also fit many obsessive-compulsive workaholics. They exhibit the following characteristics:

1. *High competitiveness*. Everything Type A's do becomes competition, even in relationships. That sometimes causes them to encourage competitiveness in their children. As a result, a Type A workaholic usually encourages his children to strive after achievements, rather than accepting them for who they are. Frequently, spouses compete with each other, sabotaging meaningful communication and peaceful coexistence in the home. Their competitiveness also affects their job circumstances and even their recreational activities.

2. *Excessive striving for achievement.* Involve a Type A obsessive-compulsive in conversation, and soon the subject becomes his or her latest project or list of achievements—either those already accomplished or those he is about to perform. He or she usually experiences an inability to say no. Thus, as time passes, the list of things to do generally grows longer rather than shorter.

3. *Impatience or hurry sickness.* Type A obsessive-compulsives despise waiting for elevators. They would much rather take the stairs, even if there are twenty flights. They can't stand being placed on hold on the telephone, and traffic tie-ups sometimes leave them feeling physically ill. As one Type A person described it, "For me and others like me, life probably consists of three words: *hurry, worry,* and *bury.*" A consequence of this trait is that because of his schedule, the Type A workaholic generally finds it hard to spend more than a few minutes in passing with his children. Also time spent with children is generally relational rather than task-oriented, so it is even more difficult for him to make the effort to be with them. Since Type A workaholics frequently can't say no to anyone, they usually end up saying no to their family by default. Such behavior patterns led to the writing of the book *When I Relax I Feel Guilty.*

4. *Aroused anger and hostility.* When asked whether their fathers gave them more positive or negative verbal feedback and reinforcement, a group of pastors responded almost unanimously that they received 75 to 90 percent negative feedback. As one of them put it, "My dad was always blowing his stack at me. He came home with all this anger from work and took it out on us kids, especially me, since I was the oldest."

Another common characteristic of the obsessive-compulsive is that he gives himself and others a highly disproportionate number of "should," "ought," or "must" messages. Although clear parental direction is extremely important, constantly communicating "shoulds," "oughts," or "musts" to our children leads them to believe that if they don't perform, they aren't worthy. That message, reinforced throughout childhood, produces many second-generation obsessive-compulsives. A number of psychological studies reveal the following list of traits found in parents of obsessive-compulsives:

- *They spend a great amount of time talking to their children but very little time listening.* Most of their talk centers on commands, instructions, criticisms, and the previously discussed "should" messages.
- *Obsessive-compulsive parents have a tendency to expect perfect manners, even at an early age.* One particularly obsessive-compulsive couple pushed their children into church each Sunday and seated them in descending order from the oldest to the youngest and wouldn't allow even a wiggle out of the two-year-old. Obsessive-compulsive parents don't tolerate mistakes, not even a small amount of spilled milk.
- *Obsessive-compulsives tend to be extremely critical of other people, especially in front of their children.* Many of them practice snobbery, and even Christian O-Cs tend to put down others with whom they come in contact. By the same token, friends of obsessive-compulsives are often introverts and seldom allow their children to interact openly with other people.
- *Obsessive-compulsive parents have a tendency to emphasize the letter of the law, to the extent of practicing phariseeism.* Emphasizing the Victorian ethic, they tend to communicate to their children the view that high moral standards demonstrate personal superiority and can even contribute toward

earning one's way to heaven, a notion obviously contrary to the gospel of God's grace. Such an emphasis frequently results in obsessive Christians who feel insecure in their relationship with Christ. However, despite personal rigidity and "no exception" rules, obsessive-compulsive parents frequently avoid any serious personal commitment to God. Their commitment is on the surface.

- *Obsessive-compulsive parents are usually extremely critical of the material convictions of the child's grandparents, which frequently they characterize as miserly.* The grandparents may have resented even normal childhood expenses—school fees, allowances, new shoes and clothes for rapidly growing children. As a result, the second generation of O-Cs often develops a personal preoccupation with money and communicates a materialistic mind-set to their own children, the third generation.

  Surprisingly, materialistic thinking cuts across economic levels. It can be seen in children of multimillionaires and missionaries alike. In fact, we have observed that some of the most materialistic people are obsessive-compulsive missionaries, pastors, and Christian college professors. In the case of one missionary family whose income was well under the poverty level, the parents constantly communicated a resentment about the things they didn't have and how the family was being unjustly called on to "suffer for Jesus."

  Not surprisingly, several of the children dedicated themselves to earning large sums of money and, in the process, became obsessive-compulsive workaholics themselves.

- *Obsessive-compulsive parents outwardly communicate that the father is the boss; however, the chil-*

dren soon learn that he is just a figurehead. The mother is actually the dominating force in the family. One obsessive-compulsive observed rather caustically, "My dad was sort of a cross between Archie Bunker and Jackie Gleason's Ralph of 'The Honeymooners.' He went around thumping his chest saying, 'I am the king of this castle.' But in reality we knew that mother was in charge."

Those are just a few of the traits we've observed in the parents of obsessive-compulsive workaholics. We have also observed that it is most common for a first-born child, regardless of his parents' personality types, to become obsessive-compulsive. Perhaps the reason is that new parents tend to expect a lot from themselves as parents and a lot from their children. As a result, they tend to be harder on their firstborn. Because they are more uptight about the process of parenting, they don't allow themselves room for error. Consequently, they cannot handle mistakes in their children because they see those mistakes as reflections on their own parental abilities. In most instances, by the time the second child arrives on the scene, the parents have mellowed in their approach to parenting. Thus, second children tend to have more problems with competing for attention than with striving for perfection. They tend to develop histrionic (or hysteric) personalities, which are emotional, excitable, overly dramatic, self-centered, manipulative, and naive. By the time the final child arrives, the parents hate to give up their controlling influence in the child's life. They tend to pamper and baby the youngest, turning that child into a passive-dependent or passive-aggressive personality who expects other people (first parents and later others) to fight all his or her battles in life.

Obviously these general principles have exceptions. However, if you are aware of the ways in which your obsessive-compulsive personality was produced, then you may be able to avoid pushing your own children too far down that same road.

7

PERFECT OR PERFECTIONIST?
A Theological Perspective

Evangelical churches today are populated with a significant number of people with obsessive-compulsive traits. These people tend to make good church workers and church leaders. Many are found in the pastorate or other forms of vocational ministry. They tend to be punctual, reliable, able to cope with responsibility, and concerned about doctrinal integrity and theological accuracy. However, from our experience in the pastorate and in counseling, we are convinced that obsessive-compulsive personality traits can often have a negative effect on a person's theological perspective.

AN EMPHASIS ON THEORY

Because of their emphasis on facts and their opposition to feelings, obsessive-compulsives tend to stress the importance of knowing theology in great detail but spend little time getting to know people—God's creation—in detail. They stress studying and understanding Scripture and theology but see little value in reading fiction or biographies, both of which contain insights into the nature of people—their needs, reactions, ambitions, and views of life. Though it is true that the apostle Paul emphasized accurate doctrine, many modern obsessive-compulsives tend to go beyond Paul to "split hairs," sometimes over questionable issues.

Paul's writings in Romans 14 and 1 Corinthians 8 demonstrate how the obsessive characteristic of black-and-white thinking creates theological difficulties. A recent survey in the largest evangelical seminary in America noted that approximately 75 percent of the students were firstborns. The overwhelming majority of those students indicated that they enrolled in the seminary because of their agreement with its doctrinal position and their concern for proper interpretation of Scripture.

This obsessiveness in theology can be both a strength and a weakness. It is important to fulfill the mandate expressed in Jude 3 to "contend for the faith," and Paul's instruction to Timothy to correctly handle the word of truth (2 Timothy 2:15). Obsessive-compulsive personality traits can certainly motivate us toward doctrinal integrity and appropriate exercise of separation from the world. However, when taken to the extreme, obsessive thinking can lead to doctrinal hair-splitting while ignoring the weightier matters of the Law. Obsessives may develop a tendency toward oppositional thinking and debate, practices for which Jesus condemned the Pharisees:

> Woe to you, teachers of the law and Pharisees, you hypocrites! You give a tenth of your spices—mint, dill and cummin. But you have neglected the more important matters of the law—justice, mercy and faithfulness. You should have practiced the latter, without neglecting the former. [Matthew 23:23]

A Sunday school teacher at an evangelical church is an excellent case in point. When he relocated from one Midwestern city to another, it took him almost a year to find a church with which he was comfortable and a pastor whose teaching he could respect. Yet, almost immediately he began tearing apart the church's constitution and doctrinal statement, pointing out what he perceived to be inaccuracies that needed modifications.

At the end of each service, he made a beeline to the pastor, eager to point out statements he had "caught" during the service or to clarify issues he felt the pastor had not sufficiently resolved in the message. Given a Sunday school class to teach, he became bogged down in such intensive detail that many of the class members left in frustration. Those people he promptly condemned as being unspiritual, disinterested in the truth, and of a lesser commitment than he. On a regular basis, he threatened to quit the church, and finally, after several sessions with the board of elders, he fulfilled his threats. Finding another church, he soon began to repeat the same obsessive cycle. Although he had many positive obsessive traits, including his concern for doctrinal accuracy, his obsessive overkill actually produced more spiritual harm than good.

Another obsessive-compulsive church member strongly encouraged his church to drop what he called "preliminary trappings" such as music. The pastor and elders refused, citing numerous scriptural exhortations to sing and examples of the proper place of music and other worship activities in the service. Then he began criticizing the *content* of the music, looking for anything he considered to be "doctrinally inaccurate." A major conflict developed between this individual and the minister of music in the church. Most of the congregation were polarized around the resulting schism.

HIDDEN PERSONAL DOUBTS

Ironically, obsessive-compulsives tend to come across as having a theological handle on every doctrinal issue, yet frequently they are privately plagued with personal doubts. In fact, they are one of the most likely groups of people to experience doubts of salvation, even after trusting Christ as Savior. In a sense, those doubts can take the form of a "theological panic attack." They are not rooted in any objective reality but seem to stem from the conditional love the obsessive received as a child from his father. Because a great deal of our thinking about our heavenly Father is formed by our earthly father, it makes sense that if our earthly father loved us conditionally and rejected us when we failed to perform, we attribute the same responses to our heavenly Father when we fail Him. Thus, when obsessive-compulsives rebel against God, disobey, fall into sin, or even when they are rationally working out their salvation, they often begin to experience doubts about their salvation.

INABILITY TO TRUST

This is also related to another trait of obsessives —difficulty in trusting. A rather interesting observation regarding the theology of obsessive-compulsives is that they tend to gravitate toward a rather strong Calvinistic position with an emphasis on the sovereignty of God.

People who have predominantly hysterical traits tend to take a more emotionally involved approach to their faith. Those who have a high degree of obsessive-compulsive traits, on the other hand, have a tendency to take an intellectual approach to faith and are more doctrinally oriented.

We are strongly committed to the sovereignty of God, but we believe in a balanced approach that also includes personal responsibility.

One of the reasons people hold to the all-encompassing sovereignty of God is to give themselves a sense of control in a seemingly uncertain world. Many people who are classified as "hypercalvinistic" have taken that position for a very interesting reason. Each would probably stress that he or she took that position because of a personal study of the Scriptures and related literature. However, in our counseling experience we have seen many of these individuals made aware that they emphasize the sovereignty of God so completely in order to develop a sense of control in an uncertain world and at times even to try to avoid personal responsibility for certain areas of misconduct. Sometimes an obsessive-compulsive struggles with the presence of evil in the world when he or she really has trouble with the evil in his or her own heart. One of the ways in which many obsessives cope with that is by adopting an extreme hypercalvinistic position—"whatever happens was meant to be."

We are convinced that obsessive-compulsives tend to make excellent theologians, gifted pastors, biblical expositors, and highly competent teachers. However, it is important for obsessives to gain insight into the relationship between the theological positions they adopt and their personality traits. Because they are such perfectionists, they have trouble accepting the fact that they are imperfect. An inability to handle their own imperfection causes them to doubt the reality of the commitment they made in trusting Christ. Then, when they do sin or even err with the best of intentions, they may feel that somehow they have lost their salvation. This occurs on a feeling level in spite of the fact that most of them profess to believe in the Christian's "eternal security."

8

AT THE END OF MY ROPE

John was a dedicated, hard-working student who graduated from college with superior marks. During seminary he was highly motivated and anticipated a successful ministry. Following seminary he entered a pastorate, where he began implementing his goals for what he called a "biblical, New Testament church." Within a year, the church was wracked by conflict. John resigned, disillusioned. Compounding his frustration were conflicts in his marriage, conflicts that could be traced largely to his perfectionistic tendencies. John was experiencing two important consequences of extreme obsessive behavior—personal burnout and marital conflict.

PERSONAL BURNOUT

Within the last decade, psychologists such as Herbert Freudenberger have popularized the term *burnout*, a term defined by Christiana Maslach as "a cluster of symptoms, including emotional and physical exhaustion, depersonalization or a tendency to withdraw from people, and decreased personal and professional performance" (*Burnout: The Cost of Caring* [Englewood, N.J.: Prentice-Hall, 1982], p. 3). In our counseling ministries, we are seeing more and more people suffering from burnout. These include not only perfectionistic homemakers, factory workers, and farmers but also hardcharging executives and people involved in such caring professions as medicine, Christian ministry, and counseling.

What are the factors that cause a large number of people with obsessive-compulsive traits to suffer burnout? Let's look at the major ones.

IDEALISM

Obsessive-compulsives tend to have a high number of idealistic expectations. Obsessive-compulsive pastors like John anticipate that people will come to hear all their sermons, integrate the messages into their experience, and noticeably grow as Christians. An obsessive-compulsive expects an enthusiastic response to new programs, a willingness to become involved in work projects, and faithful attendance at committee and activity meetings.

However, when people prove themselves to be people—indifferent to many of the Bible study programs and church services, unwilling or unable to attend the multiple church meetings and functions, and simply too tired or too indifferent to become involved in work projects—the obsessive-compulsive pastor's idealism is shattered, and that frequently leads to burnout.

BITTERNESS

Closely related to idealism and unfulfilled expectations is bitterness, the most significant factor in burnout. Bitterness, which involves prolonging anger with a vengeance motive, is the result of holding grudges. It is an even greater factor in burnout than current stresses or perfectionistic personality traits. (For a more detailed treatment of this factor, see our book *How to Beat Burnout.*)

When our idealistic expectations about marriage, work relationships, material gains, or other factors in life are not met, the natural result is for us to feel angry toward someone or something. We may be angry at our spouse for not being the "perfect marriage partner" (even though we ourselves are imperfect), angry at our supervisor or fellow workers for failing to appreciate our efforts to improve the quality of work in the workplace, or even angry with God for failing to recognize our efforts or for allowing us to suffer adversity.

Such anger is expressed in two statements by the prophet Isaiah: "Why do you say, O Jacob, and complain, O Israel, 'My way is hidden from the Lord; my cause is disregarded by my God'?" (40:27). Here Isaiah articulates on behalf of Israel the two statements commonly heard from people today who suffer from burnout:

1. "Nobody sees or appreciates the adversity I am experiencing—not even God!"

The second is similar to it, but subtly different.

2. "Life isn't fair. I'm getting a raw deal."

When our idealism is shattered, we start to feel that life isn't fair, and we naturally look around for someone or something to blame. The anger produced by blame confronts us with a choice. We must either choose immediately to forgive, as God instructs us in Ephesians 4:26, "Do not let the sun go down while you are still angry"—or by default we will choose to harbor anger and resentment, which ultimately leads to bitterness and easily infects those around us (Hebrews 12:15). Bitterness can affect marriage relationships (Colossians 3:19), as well as other relationships. As we have seen, bitterness can quickly lead to burnout.

William, a young Bible college graduate, was invited to join the staff of a rapidly growing church in the Southeast. At first he functioned well in his assistant pastor's role, although, as he shared with his senior pastor, "I consider every situation an ideal one." Within a matter of weeks, his idealism began to be shattered by the realization of the harsh facts of life—husbands lose their jobs or are just unwilling to work; wives are caught up in materialism and gossip; parents demand appropriate behavior from children without showing a willingness to relate to them or show them love; children are indifferent to parents or spiritual issues; and church people just don't seem to care.

Within a year, William was invited to serve as pastor of a small nearby church. He told his wife that he was thrilled with the opportunity to finally be able to motivate people himself. "Up until now I've felt that part of our problem has been our senior pastor. If he only had the right commitment and vision, our church would be moving by now."

When he settled into his own small church, however, William once again collided with the harsh realities of life. His new congregation met in a building that desperately needed improvements and repairs. When he pointed out the need for a renovation project in what he considered to be a tactful way, the response ranged from, "We were satisfied with this building before you came," to, "Who do you think you are, you young whippersnapper?" It wasn't long before William began preaching a series of scathing sermons designed to invoke the wrath of God on what he called "my carnal, indifferent people."

Soon things went from bad to worse. Within a year, William resigned, relocated his family a thousand miles away, and decided to have no further contact with Christians. All that occurred within two years of graduating at the top of his Bible college class, where he had been recognized as one of the graduates with the potential for a long-term ministry for Christ.

What had happened? William had clung to his idealism, which resulted in unfulfilled expectations. That led to holding grudges and anger, which resulted in burnout.

MEASURING BURNOUT

How can you tell if you are burning out?

Burnout is approaching:

- if you find yourself griping more and more and enjoying it less and less;
- if you can't stand people;
- if you want to withdraw;
- if you feel like the school bus driver who said, "I love my bus; I like my route, but I hate every single student who rides my bus";
- if you have trouble separating people from their performance, especially if no one's performance matches up to your rigorous standards;
- if you are experiencing drug or alcohol abuse;
- if you have had a major blowup—yelling at people or collapsing in tears;
- if you have felt "paralyzed" when you needed to take action.

Burnout is probably acute:

- if you have experienced a coronary or other serious physical problem;

- if you are experiencing an emotional breakdown or suicidal feelings;
- if you are involved in "acting-out" behavior—an affair, an arrest for driving while intoxicated (burnout doesn't excuse sinful behavior but may explain why it occurs);
- if you are completely overcome by exhaustion or uncontrollable anger.

Burnout has become chronic:

- if you continually find yourself withdrawing physically from your job;
- if you have trouble maintaining contact with people—even eye contact or verbal communication;
- if you quit your job without good reason;
- if you lack the emotional energy to handle the daily hassles of family life;
- if you refuse to discuss your problems or acknowledge a need for help.

BEATING BURNOUT

How can the perfectionistic obsessive-compulsive suffering from burnout deal with it? For an individual to beat burnout, we are convinced that a comprehensive approach is absolutely necessary. To be successful, the individual must take a number of steps.

First, he must deal with current causes of stress, including his frantic schedule of "burning the candle at both ends and in the middle." Many people have found it necessary to quit one of the two full-time jobs they were trying to sustain, or to take a less demanding position, even at lower pay.

Second, he must correct physical stress by taking needed steps, including proper exercise, rest, and diet.

Third, he must realistically assess his goals and schedules.

Fourth, he must pay attention to the effects of his personality type and deal with his early environment factors (those unmet, idealistic expectations left over from childhood). As Mark Twain once pointed out, "It's not what you eat that destroys you; it's what eats you."

Fifth, he must learn to give up grudges and bitterness, choosing to forgive those with whom he is bitter, even if they don't deserve forgiveness. The emotional energy used to harbor those unresolved grudges and feelings of anger can often be redirected to useful pursuits surprisingly quickly when burnout victims *choose* to make peace with their emotions by forgiving those people who have let them down, including themselves.

Ultimately, forgiving others and ourselves is possible only when we have experienced God's forgiveness by placing our faith in the Lord Jesus Christ as our Savior from sin and its consequences. He died on the cross and rose again so that we might experience God's forgiveness from all our sins. Once we come to trust in Him and experience His forgiveness, we are in a position to forgive others who have offended us. We then can appropriate God's strength to face the pressures of life.

Two passages of Scripture give us a clue as to how this is done in the context of living the Christian life. Isaiah 40:31 points out that those who "*wait* upon the Lord shall renew their strength; they shall mount up with wings as eagles; they shall run, and not be weary; and they shall walk, and not faint" (KJV, italics added). The word Isaiah uses for *wait* does not imply a passive resignation but an active anticipation that God will provide the energy and will work within circumstances. A key New Testament principle can be seen in Matthew 6:33-34, where Jesus instructs His followers to seek first His kingdom and righteousness. Once God's kingdom and His righteousness have been made a priority, everything else falls into its rightful place. Furthermore, the Savior adds that it is inappropriate to be anxious or distracted about tomorrow, for "tomorrow will worry about itself. Each day has enough trouble of its own" (v. 34). The principle is obvious. One of the keys to beating burnout is to live life one day at a time, trusting God for grace for each experience we encounter, and not dwelling on our past mistakes or on harmful actions that were initiated against us. Neither are we to focus on the future, wondering what is going to happen to us next. Rather, we are to claim God's grace for the here and now.

MARITAL CONFLICT

The second major consequence of extreme obsessive-compulsive behavior involves the marriage relationship. In Frank Minirth's research on the obsessive-compulsive personality type, a number of characteristics are isolated that weaken the marriage relationship when they are present in the extreme. Even in courtship, the obsessive-compulsive tends to be characterized by caution or restraint. In some respects, this is a positive trait, preventing premarital sexual involvement or making a commitment to the wrong person. However, some obsessives can be so perfectionistic in their courtship that they never find the "perfect" mate.

Making a marriage commitment is extremely difficult for the perfectionist since he tends to live in the future a great deal of the time, working for a tomorrow that never arrives. A marriage commitment in the here and now can be a risky venture.

Once married, O-Cs have other problems. For example, Jerry, a successful businessman with many O-C traits, demanded that his wife, Julie, be totally loyal to him. In fact, he often became infuriated with her when she gave time to the church or to other people, demanding that she "fulfill her God-given role" to meet his needs. Despite his demands on his wife, Jerry had trouble recognizing that he himself was far from totally committed to his wife. Instead, he was a workaholic who was committed to his job "110 percent." He often worked overtime and weekends, frequently forgetting to call his wife to let her know that he would not be home in time to enjoy the meal that he still expected her to prepare so carefully.

Jerry's attitude illustrates several other difficulties O-Cs encounter in their marriage relationships.

1. *They give minimal commitment but demand maximal commitment.* Obsessives seem to have a tendency to think of themselves as being more committed than they really are. They often give themselves credit for not being involved in sexual affairs, counting that restraint as true loyalty to their partners. They fail to see the disloyalty in their workaholism or in their unwillingness to share themselves, that is, to communicate their basic, inner feelings.

2. *They limit intimacy.* Obsessives have an intense fear of vulnerability or lack of control, which includes emotional vulnerability. To express feelings is to give up a measure of control and to admit weakness, something the obsessive dares not do.

3. *They need to control both themselves and those around them.* That need frequently results in power struggles within a marriage, especially if both spouses are strong O-Cs. In such cases, control can ex-

tend from such petty issues as whether the toothpaste tube is squeezed from the end or the middle to such major issues as vocation or the number of children desired.

4. *They do only (what they consider to be) their share in the marriage.* This leads to a kind of "50-50" marriage relationship, one we have seen to be less than ideal or successful. Our conviction is that a marriage can be successful only when both partners give 100 percent to the relationship. When one, or both of them, looks to do only his share, resentments and conflict will naturally build.

5. *They experience unspontaneous and routine sexual function.* Female obsessives may have difficulty with orgasms. Males may encounter difficulty with premature ejaculation, caused by anxiety or a fear of loss of control. Frequently, over a period of time, obsessives will have a tendency to ignore the physical dimension of communication in marriage, replacing sexual harmony and spontaneity and emotional and verbal communication with an increased commitment to work or to acquiring and enjoying material things.

We have seen marriages in which both partners pursued their individual interests for years. Although they lived under the same roof, they were like ships passing in the night. The husband had his work, his golf, his fishing, and his interest in football; the wife had her tennis and her social club or church activities. In some marriages the only commonalities were the children and the problems. It's no wonder that such marriages die on the vine. Since obsessive-compulsives have a great capacity to work and to exhibit commitment, it's sad that they fear commitment in interpersonal relationships and therefore fail to work on the area that God considers a high priority—marital harmony.

We encourage obsessives to give up perfectionism in marriage, to avoid bitterness, to work on sharing personal communication verbally, not just physically, and to learn to enjoy their partner as a good friend as well as a fellow heir "of the grace of life."

We have examined two consequences of O-C behavior: personal burnout and marital conflict. However, those consequences need not come to pass. In the next chapter, we will consider some ways to cure excessive obsessive-compulsive behavior.

9
REACHING BALANCE OR BURNOUT?

A pastor/counselor was invited to address the annual meeting of a large mental health facility in northern Illinois. The subject was the relationship between stress and obsessive behavior. As the speaker walked into the facility where the meeting was being held, he was met by the mental health administrator who said, "Do I need to hear what you have to say! I hope you have some practical suggestions for getting a handle on my own stress and obsessiveness."

That same desire has been voiced to us by individuals from all walks of life. Many obsessives suffer periodic obsessive-compulsive disorders, receive counseling, and are aware of their unbalanced obsessive behavior. But they realize that simply understanding it, or even tracing it to its early childhood origin, doesn't do anything to reverse it.

Put another way, most perfectionists find that insight into the nature of their difficulties is not sufficient to effect change. We have found a total revamping of *attitudes* to be necessary, including (1) gaining insight into thought processes, (2) developing interpersonal relational skills, and (3) acquiring the motivation to change.

Some counselors say the way to overcome extreme obsessive-compulsive behavior is to remove all structure from counseling. Instead of giving specific direction, the counselor should simply provide support and encouragement.

The problem with that approach is that O-Cs have difficulty expressing their feelings, and they tend to be more comfortable with a high degree of structure. Often a counselor will simply try to get an obsessive-compulsive to remove all structure and organization from his or her life; however, the real issue is not structure or lack of it but an inability to get in touch with personal feelings. Removing all structure from one's life can actually hinder the process of balancing obsessive behavior.

STEPS TO OVERCOME O-C BEHAVIOR

We suggest the following practical steps, based on a survey of effective programs and on our own experience in dealing with obsessive behavior.

MAKE AN ADVANTAGE/DISADVANTAGE LIST

The first step is to make a list of the advantages and disadvantages of perfectionism. Then weigh the benefits against the costs. In this way obsessives can call into play familiar and often-used skills to help assess their perfectionism.

This process will hopefully bring about an awareness, perhaps for the first time, that perfectionism or obsessive-compulsive behaviors do not always produce positive results. This awareness, in turn, can provide a motivation to give up the imbalances in obsessiveness.

One obsessive, Julie, came up with the following interesting lists.

Advantages:

1. Obsessive behavior helps me produce quality work.

2. It also helps me produce a greater quantity of work.

Disadvantages:

1. I'm often so uptight I sometimes have trouble producing quality work.

2. My rigidity and perfectionism tend to stifle my creativity and my willingness to try novel approaches.

3. I constantly find myself criticizing myself and others. This takes all the fun out of relationships and the rest of my life.

4. I have trouble walking away from my responsibility. In fact, I sometimes have trouble relaxing.

Her conclusion: To be an imbalanced perfectionist is counterproductive.

DISCOVER NEW WAYS TO HANDLE STRESS

The second step is to discover less obsessive ways to handle the stress factors in your life. Again, a list or form of written evaluation can be helpful. Write down various stress factors, both major and minor, and then decide which ones you can influence and which ones you have no control over. Many obsessives have found help from the prayer of St. Francis of Assisi: "God grant me the serenity to accept those things that cannot be changed, the courage to change those which can, and the wisdom to know the difference."

Three keys can help us manage those stress factors that often add to the misery of imbalanced obsessive behavior.

First, learn to be assertive. Frequently, an O-Cs problem is either the inability to say no or the inability to say no graciously. Obsessives tend to adopt extreme "either-or" thinking; therefore, they are either passive, allowing others to run them over, or they become aggressive after just "taking it" for a long time and lash out at the people and circumstances producing the stress. A balanced approach to handling stress involves some assertiveness.

Assertiveness is the ability to stand up for one's rights, to express one's true feelings when appropriate—without fear of reprisal, to be able to say no to unreasonable demands, and to request the things we need and deserve.

Foundational to appropriate assertiveness is the basic underlying message "I count, and you count." If we refuse to be assertive, we are either saying, "I count, and you don't count" (which is aggressiveness), or, "You count, but I don't count" (which is nonassertiveness or passivity). The following list of suggested assertive statements can help obsessive-compulsives and others who need to become more balanced in this area.

"No, I won't do that."
"That makes me angry."
"I disagree with you."
"This really bothers me."
"Please stop doing that."
"Will you help me?"
"I really like that about you."

"I think you're not being fair."
"I need something from you."
"Thank you, but I don't care to."
"It hurts my feelings when you say things like that."
"There are some things I think we need to get straightened out."

Second, learn proper time management. Although many obsessives tend to overdo time management, they sometimes ignore good time management principles, including preparing for future events. Because they are so successful at being achievement-oriented, they frequently leave unfinished tasks for the last minute, assuming they have the ability to accomplish in minutes what takes other people hours and days. Type A O-Cs often see themselves as almost superhuman. Unfortunately, unforeseen snags are likely to trip them up. We have discovered through personal experience the wisdom of the old proverb "An ounce of prevention is worth a pound of cure."

Third, delegate to others when possible. One of the obsessive's favorite sayings is, "Thanks, but I'd rather do it myself." That's not usually an appropriate assertive response (although it can be under certain circumstances). Usually it indicates an unwillingness to relinquish control.

CORRECT FAULTY THINKING

Balancing obsessive behavior also involves correcting the flaws in our thinking. According to Chris Thurman in *The Lies We Believe*, a good place to start is to notice carefully our "self-talk," comparing it with inaccurate things or lies we tell ourselves ([Nashville: Thomas Nelson, 1989], pp. 35-57).

We sometimes suggest that obsessives keep a daily written record of self-critical thoughts and statements or that they ask a spouse or close friend to hold them accountable for their self-talk. Sometimes self-talk habits become automatic thoughts. As obsessives write them down, they are able to pinpoint inaccuracies and develop more objective and appropriate ways to talk to themselves.

Four of the more common unhealthy messages we give ourselves are:
"I must be perfect."
"I should please others."
"I must try harder."
"Life must be fair."

For example, Jeanne, a graduate student, faced a Monday deadline on a paper, in addition to an exam. However, family and work responsibilities caused her to have an extremely busy weekend with very little time for preparation. On Monday Jeanne hit the panic button.

Under those circumstances, hitting the panic button was not necessarily a bad thing to do. However, undergirding Jeanne's thinking was the feeling, *I've failed miserably. I didn't get my studying done this weekend. I allowed my schedule to get out of control. I'm a failure as a person. I'm a failure as a student. I will fail in the future.*

Furthermore, while she typed her paper Jeanne made several mistakes. Again, in her personal self-assessment, this was an unpardonable sin. Her thoughts: *The professor will certainly notice all these errors. He will think the paper is poorly thought out. He'll consider me an irresponsible student. He'll be sure I don't really care about doing well. I'll probably wind up with an F, or a D at best.*

Although we might be quick to recognize the "all or nothing" inaccuracy in Jeanne's thinking (she had some of the highest marks in the class), we ourselves have a tendency to fall into the same trap of irrational thinking.

Albert Ellis in his book *A New Guide to Rational Living* (Wilshire, 1975, p. 82), has identified a number of common irrational beliefs that are found frequently among obsessive-compulsive Christians. Here are some of those beliefs.

I must be perfect in order to feel worthwhile. However, the Scriptures tell us, "All have sinned and fall short of the glory of God" (Romans 3:23).

I must have everyone's love and/or approval. Again, the truth from Scripture is that no one will feel total approval at any time. Many people certainly didn't approve of Jesus Christ. He Himself said, "No servant is greater than his master. If they persecuted me, they will persecute you also" (John 15:20).

It is horrible or catastrophic when things don't go the way I want them to. A classic refutation of this is the prayer of Christ in the Garden of Gethsemane, "Father, if you are willing, take this cup from me; yet not my will, but yours be done" (Luke 22:42; cf. Mark 14:36; Matthew 26:39).

It is easier to avoid problems than to face them. Again, in the Garden of Gethsemane, Jesus told His disciples, "Arise, let us be going," and told them with full knowledge of His impending crucifixion.

Human unhappiness is caused externally. This idea is in clear contradiction to Paul's assertion in Philippians 4:11, "I have learned, in *whatsoever state I am*, therewith to be content" (KJV, italics added).

Life should be fair. One of the most obvious victims of injustice in human history was Job, yet he was able to assert, "He knows the way that I take; when he has tested me, I will come forth as gold" (Job 23:10).

Life should be easy. From his personal experience Paul wrote to the Philippians, "It has been granted to you on behalf of Christ not only to believe on him, but also to suffer for him" (Philippians 1:29). Also, 2 Timothy 3:12 says, "In fact, everyone who wants to live a godly life in Christ Jesus will be persecuted."

Correcting the flaws in our thinking involves an awareness, even though it may be painful, of the defense mechanisms we use to deceive ourselves. As we discussed earlier, some common defense mechanisms we use are: *intellectualization*, to avoid facing our emotions; *magical thinking*, to fool ourselves into trying to do more than we can accomplish; *reaction formation*, to develop acceptable attitudes and behavior to hide our lustful, greedy, or power-hungry thoughts from ourselves and from others; *undoing*, to compensate for the unacknowledged anger we feel toward others; *isolation*, to separate sinful areas of our lives from the reality we perceive about ourselves. It is imperative that we come to grips with these flaws in our thinking, confess them as sin (1 John 1:9), and allow God to deal with them.

Facing distorted thinking is difficult for practicing obsessives. The following checklist by Aaron Beck can help an obsessive recognize the distorted way he looks at reality:

Magnification—making a mountain out of a molehill

Personalization—relating everything that happens to yourself

Polarization—seeing everything in black or white, including nonabsolutes

Overgeneralization—making blanket judgments or predictions on the basis of a single incident

Selective abstraction—focusing on a single detail out of context

Emotional reasoning—treating facts as feelings

One of the most important keys to overcoming imbalanced obsessive *behavior* is to correct imbalanced obsessive *thinking*. As Jesus Christ so clearly pointed out, "As [a man] thinketh in his heart, so is he" (Proverbs 23:7, KJV). Balanced thinking will lead to balanced living.

IMPROVE YOUR ABILITY TO RELATE TO OTHERS

Unbalanced obsessives tend to take a "lone ranger" approach to life. Yet, even the Lone Ranger found it important to depend upon his faithful sidekick, Tonto, when facing adversity.

We see two aspects of this "people factor."

First, develop a network of significant people for support. Proverbs 18:24 says "there is a friend who sticks closer than a brother." Clearly developing friendships is an active, not a passive, matter. Because imbalanced obsessives tend to be more task-oriented than people-oriented, this is an area to which they need to devote themselves. Look for people with whom you are like-minded, people with whom you share values, interests, and goals. Work at accepting them unconditionally, that is, "giving them some slack," when they don't live up to your expectations. Treat them with the time-worn Golden Rule, as you would like them to treat you—*not* in the way you feel they have actually treated you. Loyalty and love, extended even in times of adversity, are the soil in which friendships grow (cf. Proverbs 17:17). And Proverbs 27 is replete with the benefits of having good friends in our lives (Proverbs 27:6, 9, 10, 17).

One of us has adopted a personal goal of developing one good friendship every two to three years. Frank Minirth says, "I find that I cannot develop really close friendships any more quickly than this. Developing good friends is hard work. But I've also discovered that having good friends with whom I can share my feelings is essential to my own mental and spiritual well-being."

Sometimes it can be helpful for O-Cs to develop or become part of support groups designed for the purpose of sharing friendships. One of us has been involved for some years with a group of obsessive-compulsives known as OCWA—the "Obsessive-Compulsive Workaholics Anonymous" group. Started informally, it has provided both mutual support and a number of mental health-producing laughs as well. Perhaps OCWA chapters will now spring up in other places around the country.

Second, learn to communicate feelings. For the obsessive, communicating facts is easier than expressing emotions. "I feel" messages are almost like a foreign language to many O-Cs. We suggest that obsessives develop a specific time to share feelings with their spouse and have an agreement with a few good friends, in the context of unconditional love, to feel free to express feelings whenever they need to do so.

Scripture commands that we get together to encourage one another. Hebrews 10:25, the passage often used by obsessive pastors and church leaders to produce guilt over laxity in church attendance, is in reality an exhortation to all believers to practice mutual encouragement and exhortation or, in more simple terms, to learn to communicate with other Christians.

GET TO KNOW AND ACCEPT YOURSELF

Get to know yourself, accept yourself, and become all God wants you to be in Christ. Thousands of Christians have memorized Romans 12:1-2, but few can quote verse 3. It is one of the most important verses in Scripture in terms of Christian living: "For by the grace given to me I say to every one of you: Do not think of yourself more highly than you ought, but rather think of yourself with sober judgment, in accordance with the measure of faith God has given you."

The point is that we need to come to a realistic appraisal of our personality, abilities, and unique God-given design. The clearest and most obvious danger is to think of ourselves more highly than we should, and Paul warns against that. But many of us react to the other extreme and spend a lot of time putting ourselves down. The authors have developed a motto to help implement Romans 12:3 in our personal lives. It is: *Strengthen your strengths while working on your weaknesses.*

Here is a practical suggestion: take a sizable chunk of time, sit down, reflect on yourself, and make a list of your strengths and abilities. Perhaps you are highly organized. Maybe you are a self-starter. Perhaps you have an ability to grasp intellectual material. You may be an excellent communicator. Write down those strengths. Then begin listing ways you can improve them.

When U.S. Congressman Bill Bradley was in high school, he worked one summer on Capitol Hill. Each evening he stopped by a high school gym. He picked out six or eight spots on the court from which to shoot baskets, and he wouldn't leave until he had made fifty shots from each. Bradley became an excellent shot because his hard work and patience paid off. He ultimately became an All-American at Princeton University and a highly successful professional basketball player for the New York Knicks before he ran for Congress.

Although spending time in strengthening your strengths is a worthy investment, make sure you don't overdo this to the detriment of other important areas of life. To do so will only weaken the base of your strengths.

Rachel grew up in a home in which relationships were primarily characterized by conditional love. Love was shown only when a family member did something that especially pleased another family member. Rachel's father loved her mother conditionally, and both parents practiced conditional love toward the children.

Because Rachel was the oldest and her parents had particularly high expectations for her, she was most affected by their conditional love. Thus taught, she found herself developing conditional love toward other people around her.

After trusting Christ as her Savior in high school, Rachel came into contact with Christians who had strong convictions about how to live the Christian life but who also practiced conditional love. Thus, conditional love was reinforced in her life even after she became a Christian.

Not until she moved away from home and met Christians at college and in a collegiate church that reached out to her with unconditional love did she begin to develop the ability to love and accept others, despite their failures and weaknesses. Through counseling, she was directed to use her obsessive-compulsive traits to work at practicing unconditional love instead of accepting others only on the basis of her own high standards of performance. It was a struggle; yet it ultimately paid off. Eventually, Rachel became known in her church family, among a wide circle of friends at college, and later at work as a person who could be counted on for unconditional love and encouragement.

One of the obsessive-compulsive's greatest strengths is a willingness to work. We suggest that obsessives pay attention not only to strengthening strengths, but also to working hard on their weaknesses—even harder than they do on their strengths, that is, on handling emotions, accepting and loving people unconditionally, or organizing areas of their lives that tend to escape order altogether. Whatever the weakness, the obsessive must work on it diligently.

LEARN TO LIVE IN THE PRESENT

Learn to live life in the present—one day at a time. Because obsessives tend to be people of extremes, they frequently find themselves living in the past, plagued with guilt. Sometimes it is *true guilt* over unconfessed sin, which their defense mechanisms have fooled them into sinfully denying. But sometimes it is *false guilt* over sins they have confessed and know God has forgiven, but for which they have failed to forgive themselves. Because Christ has forgiven us for every sin we have committed, we can confess them, then forget about them—refuse to dwell on them (Philippians 3:14).

For other obsessives a major problem involves their living in the future. They are anxious about what tomorrow may bring, and that intense anxiety distracts them. In fact, distraction is the basic concept behind the Greek word used for anxiety in the New Testament. Such distraction keeps them from enjoying life. Remember that Jesus said, "I have come that they may have life, and have it to the full" (John 10:10).

Because Christ holds the future securely in His hands, we can stop being anxious about tomorrow, for tomorrow will take care of itself (Matthew 6:34). The realistic obsessive-compulsive is an individual who learns to live one day at a time, without being haunted by the past or being overly concerned about the future. In other words, if life gives you a hot fudge sundae, eat it without feeling guilty but at the same time without gluttony.

An obsessive can become a truly balanced, highly productive individual—one who serves God and relates effectively both with God and other people. He can do so by establishing daily priorities consistent with his life goals, by learning to distinguish the important from the urgent, by obeying Jesus' instruction to wholeheartedly love God and unconditionally love people (Mark 12:30-31).

10
HUMAN ABILITY AND DIVINE ENABLEMENT

Occasionally an individual walks across the pages of history and leaves footprints that later generations interpret to be larger than life. Such an individual was Moses. It didn't really take the brush of Hollywood cinematographers to paint this man in grand and glowing terms. In fact, a first-century church leader named Stephen, in the sermon that cost him his life, described Moses as an incredibly gifted individual (Acts 7:20-22). Apparently, Stephen was familiar with the biblical evidence, the traditions, and the historical information passed down about Moses, the man who played such a critical role in his nation's history.

Stephen described Moses as physically beautiful. In fact, according to the historian Josephus, Moses was a man of such exceptional strength and beauty that the Egyptians would crowd around just to get a look at him.

Yet Moses' physical assets did not overshadow his intellectual accomplishments, which Stephen describes in Acts 7:22. From his infancy to the time he became a young man, Moses received an excellent education in the royal palace of Egypt. The Egypt of Moses' day was the most progressive and productive country in the world. Moses was exposed to the kind of training that led to the building of the pyramids—mathematics, engineering, art, and architecture. As the chosen heir to the king, he received a tailored course of study designed to equip him for political leadership and warfare.

This leads to a third key quality that Stephen describes: Moses' leadership abilities. In the simple phrase "powerful in speech and action," Stephen captures the essence of what made Moses such a great leader of men. Other incidents from Josephus's records illustrate Moses' leadership ability. When the Ethiopians attacked Egypt, Egypt was on the verge of defeat. Moses was appointed general in charge of the army, and under his leadership the tide turned and the Ethiopians were driven back. Certainly, if any individual had the ability to serve and please God on his own, Moses was that man.

Yet one incident in Moses' life demonstrates the difference between human ability and divine enablement. It is recorded in Exodus 3 and took place not in the palaces of Egypt but on the backside of a desert, in the arid land near Mount Sinai. At that time Moses was eighty. To understand this occurrence we must examine another incident that happened forty years earlier, when Moses was, humanly speaking, in the prime of his life. That event is recorded in Exodus 2:11-15:

> One day, after Moses had grown up, he went out to where his own people were and watched them at their hard labor. He saw an Egyptian beating a Hebrew, one of his own people. Glancing this way and that and seeing no one, he killed the Egyptian and hid him in the sand. The next day he went out and saw two Hebrews fighting. He asked the one in the wrong, "Why are you hitting your fellow Hebrew?"
>
> The man said, "Who made you ruler and judge over us? Are you thinking of killing me as you killed

the Egyptian?" Then Moses was afraid and thought, "What I did must have become known."

When Pharaoh heard of this, he tried to kill Moses, but Moses fled from Pharaoh and went to live in Midian, where he sat down by a well.

Moses was a gifted man, keenly aware of his mission in life. He was trained with the wisdom of the Egyptians and possessed strong leadership skills. Furthermore, he decided to become involved with the servant race from which he came, Israel. He took the life of a man who was persecuting one of his Hebrew kinsmen, perhaps expecting that action to prompt support and ultimately lead to Israel's liberation. After all, according to Hebrews 11:26, "he regarded disgrace for the sake of Christ as of greater value than the treasures of Egypt."

We might say that Moses burned brightly for a day; but because he depended on his own enablement "in the flesh," or "in his own strength," he became as burned out as a heap of ashes.

We're struck with a remarkable contrast of what happened when Moses returned to Egypt at twice the age he was when he had left and at a time when most people would already have found an opportunity to retire. Moses was able not only to successfully challenge Pharaoh but also to lead the Israelites out of Egypt, tolerate their complaints and rebellion, provide them with the written material of the Law as revealed by Jehovah God, and shepherd them over a tortuous route for forty years of desert wandering.

THE BURNING BUSH

How could Moses accomplish all of that? The answer seems to lie in the incident of the burning bush. Undoubtedly Moses had seen burning bushes before, yet there was a remarkable difference in this bush, because the fire did not consume it. The flame was the presence of the preincarnate Christ, which turned that desert shrub into a remarkable tool of God's personal revelation to Moses.

Through the bush Moses learned of God's holiness and uniqueness, and he learned that God was special, quite different from the gods of Egypt. Through the bush Moses verbally heard of the faithfulness of the God of Abraham, Isaac, and Jacob. At this point Moses began to adjust to God's compassion and purpose to deliver Israel from Egypt and to bring His people into the Promised Land. It was also through the burning bush that God clarified the role Moses was to play: "I am sending you to Pharaoh to bring my people the Israelites out of Egypt" (Exodus 3:10).

THE PRESENCE OF GOD

What made the difference in Moses' life? How did he endure at the age of eighty what he failed to endure at forty? Hebrews 11:27 states, "He persevered because he saw him who is invisible." The major difference that enabled Moses to avoid burning out while living an extremely active and significant life is that *he lived each day with the reality of the presence of God.*

A number of years ago a Bible college student was struck by the number of books written on the subject of the spiritual life. Many people had written seemingly profound books, giving formulas and equations that would guarantee spirituality. Yet it was easy to see that writing a book on the subject did not guarantee continued spirituality. Many who had written such books ultimately experienced significant spiritual failure.

On the other hand, many who had never written or taught on the subject obviously experienced a measure of spiritual endurance that could only be called successful. After talking with such people from all walks of life—pastors and missionaries, mechanics, housewives, factory workers, businessmen, architects, engineers, and students—the common denominator became evident to the Bible college student. Those who lived each day with the *reality of the presence of God* in their lives endured. Those who lost sight of the reality of God's presence were those who became "practicing atheists."

The Greek word for "endure," *ekarterēsē*, used by the author of Hebrews, is an unusual verb appearing only in Hebrews 11:27 in the New Testament.[1] The word is used in Greek literature (Sophocles and Josephus) and means "to be strong, steadfast, to hold out." According to one respected eminent Greek *scholar*, *ekarterēsē* comes from a term that means to be strong.[2] Although the term is not used elsewhere in the New Testament, its two uses in the Septuagint (the Greek version of the Old Testament) are illuminating. The first use is somewhat negative and is found in Job 2:9. Job's wife bitterly said to the patriarch, "Are you still holding on to your integrity? Curse God and die!" Many individuals today who face the adversities of a Job or a Moses opt to become bitter and lose sight of the presence of God. Job, however, continued to endure. In fact, he considered his wife's suggestion to be foolish. In response, he offered the perspective that en-

1. William F. Arndt and F. Wilbur Gingrich, *A Greek English Lexicon of the Greek New Testament and Other Early Christian Literature* (Chicago: U. of Chicago, 1957), p. 406.
2. James H. Moulton and George Milligan, *The Vocabulary of the Greek New Testament* (Grand Rapids: Eerdmans, 1930), p. 322.

abled him to endure. "Shall we accept good from God, and not trouble?" (v. 10). As with Moses or Job, endurance involves an ability to put things into perspective and to see the hand of God at work in our lives on days of cloudiness, rain, and even storm as well as on days of sunshine and blessing.

A second use of *endure* in the Old Testament is suggested in Isaiah 42:14. Here Yahweh is speaking to Israel, declaring His coming intervention in the affairs of His people. He says, "For a long time I have kept silent, I have been quiet and held myself back. But now, like a woman in childbirth, I cry out, I gasp and pant. I will lay waste the mountains and hills and dry up all their vegetation." We can see that endurance is a matter of personal choice. Just as God chose when to withhold His wrath and when to exercise it, so we can choose when we will persevere and when we will give up. Moses, when faced with such a choice, chose to endure.

The essence of Moses' choice to persevere involved a commitment of faith, because Moses saw Him who was invisible. In fact, the statement of Hebrews 11:27*b*, "He persevered because he saw him who is invisible," describes the essence of what faith is all about. It is acting not on the basis of what we perceive with our five senses, but on what we know to be true from God's revelation. It is saying, "God is with me, therefore, I will not give up."

That was the perspective that allowed Moses to persevere through the exhausting years of tramping through the wilderness while listening to the complaints of his followers and suffering incredible hardship. Tugging at the back of his mind certainly were the memories of his luxurious life in Egypt. But Moses maintained the perspective that ultimately spurred him to write Psalm 90:12, "Teach us to number our days aright, that we may gain a heart of wisdom." That verse was a reflection of his commitment not to give up, even after he knew that his personal failure would prevent his entering the Promised Land.

Because of his commitment to faith in God, Moses never quit. His strength came not from his abilities, intellect, or even leadership skills, but from practicing the presence of the Lord God. That was the divine difference. Like the bush indwelt by the presence of the preincarnate Christ, Moses never used up his resources.

GOD'S RESOURCES

Some may say, "But we don't have the opportunity Moses had to speak with the Lord face to face." And Exodus 33:11 and Numbers 12:7-8 do indicate that there were times in Moses' life when he was permitted that privilege. Yet the average believer today has far more in the way of God's resources than Moses had.

THE WORD OF GOD

We have the completed written revelation of God's perspective—everything we need and all things that pertain to life and godliness (2 Peter 1:3). The Word of God gives us clear and objective guidance (2 Timothy 3:16-17). It tells us what to believe (doctrine), and when we're wrong (reproof); it gets us "back on track" (correction); and it gives us positive principles that enable us to "stay on track" in our relationship with God and others (instruction in right living).

THE HOLY SPIRIT

We also have the resource of God the Holy Spirit living within us (Romans 8:9), which was not true for Old Testament saints. He is the ultimate Counselor, the one Jesus described in John 16 as the comforter, the *paraclete* ("called along side to help"). He is the One who provides our enablement, as we walk in His power, to keep us from fulfilling the evil desires of our old nature (Galatians 5:16). Are you sensitive daily to His presence? When you are involved in work situations, do you realize that God sees the ins and outs? When you're with other people socially, do you recognize that God knows if you're harboring feelings of envy, greed, or lust? Do you realize that God knows the very thoughts and intents of your innermost being?

PRAYER

Furthermore, we have a direct and instant access line for communication with God through prayer. We may be distressed over the past or anxious over the future, yet we are instructed: "In everything, by prayer [general contact with God] and petition [specific voicing of needs], with thanksgiving [acknowledging appreciation in advance for what God will do] present your requests to God" (Philippians 4:6). When we utilize this incredible resource, the apostle Paul promises not only peace of mind (v. 7) but the presence of God in our lives (v. 9), personal enablement for trying circumstances (v. 13), and provision for every genuine need (v. 19).

Do you utilize the communication line of prayer? As you face difficult circumstances and confront temptation, do you call on God? His part is to provide the resources. Our part is to exercise responsibility, making choices that will implement those inner resources.

OUR RESPONSIBILITY

Many of us know about God's resources—the Word of God, the Spirit of God, and prayer—but we still fail to endure because we do not claim and use those resources by faith. Our responsibility, quite simply, is to make the right choices. When confronted with overwhelming circumstances, difficult challenges, or impossible tasks, we must choose. The essence of God's method of dealing with mankind throughout history is that He gives individuals opportunities to choose to obey Him and to trust Him. It is our responsibility.

The essence of our responsibility to choose can be seen in the initial failure of mankind. In Genesis 2 man was given two responsibilities in his perfect environment. The positive one was to care for his surroundings (v. 15). The negative one was to abstain from eating fruit from the tree of the knowledge of good and evil (vv. 16-17). One chapter later, man was confronted with a choice. Satan, disguised as a serpent, presented an alternative to God's instruction. Like a large-mouth bass swallowing a brass hook hidden by a plastic worm, Adam and Eve bit. The results, according to Romans 5:12, were devastating.

Like Adam and Eve, we are affected by our choices. We are tempted to quit, or to keep going when we ought to quit, in order to prove our own significance. This may lead to such sinful behavior as the lust of the flesh (sexual or other physical temptation), the lust of the eyes (material temptations), or the pride of life (power struggles). We forget that God provides the resources that enable us to make the right choices. But we must utilize those resources. Often we fail to choose appropriately because we don't trust God or obey Him. Then, like Adam, we blame others—perhaps spouse, friends, environment, or even God. Or like Eve we may claim, "The devil made me do it." Genesis 3:13*b* says, "The woman said, 'The serpent deceived me, and I ate.'" Or we may use the excuse that we didn't really understand what was happening when we made the choices.

Regardless of what excuse we use, God makes clear that we are responsible for our choices.

We can implement God's resources by meditating on and memorizing Scripture, by praying, by walking in the Spirit, by investing daily time in devotions, by developing accountability to others in the Body of Christ, and by depending on "Him who is invisible," thereby gaining strength from a day-to-day relationship with Him. The bottom line is that we are responsible for our choices. However, it is important for us to understand that although our choices are our responsibility, on our own we are *not* able.

THE CONCEPT OF WEAKNESS

It is fascinating to study the concepts of weakness and strength in Scripture. The Old Testament has a half dozen words for "weak." The most common is the term *rafeh*, which means to be feeble physically, intellectually, or morally. It is interesting that a strong individual such as David occasionally described himself as weak (2 Samuel 3:39; Psalms 6:2, 109:24).

In the New Testament the primary word translated "weak," used in several forms, is *asthenōs*. It carries the idea of stumbling or being without strength. It can indicate physical weakness or material poverty (Acts 20:35), religious or moral weakness (Romans 14:1), or physical sickness (James 5:14, 16).

One of the best ways to gain insight into the New Testament concept of weakness is to examine Paul's use of the term in his two letters to the church at Corinth. Paul experienced controversy at Corinth, partially because the Corinthians viewed Paul as being weak. Paul even admitted that some described him as appearing weak in bodily presence (2 Corinthians 10:10). Yet he explained that the weakness of God is stronger than men's strength (1 Corinthians 1:25). God has chosen to use weak things, including weak individuals (1 Corinthians 1:27).

Furthermore, God can perfect or complete strength in weakness (2 Corinthians 12:9). This is precisely what Paul experienced as he relied upon God. It is for that reason that he was able to write those inspiring words in 2 Corinthians 4:16, "Therefore we do not lose heart. Though outwardly we are wasting away, yet inwardly we are being renewed day by day." Certainly the Corinthians were a difficult group to minister to. But Paul's ministry to the church there demonstrated the same reality as did Moses' ministry to Israel. Paul, like Moses, never quit. He ran the race, he finished the course, he kept the faith (2 Timothy 4).

TEMPTATION

Many people strive to be strong, capable, and successful. Often Christians get caught up in this mindset, but it's an impossible trap. The temptations of life are real. Many succumb to sexual temptations in the lust of the flesh. In fact, the warning of 1 Corinthians 10:12 has never been more relevant than in this day in which even well-known political and religious leaders are trapped in moral sin: "So, if you think you are standing firm, be careful that you don't fall!"

Several principles, found in Paul's words to the church at Corinth (1 Corinthians 10:13), enable us to overcome temptation. First, temptation is common to all of us. No one is immune. There is no vaccine that will prevent our succumbing to it. Psychological studies have indicated that individuals with predominantly hysteric or histrionic (openly emotional and attention-seeking) traits may be more susceptible to sexual temptation. Obsessive-compulsives (habitually hard workers) may be more susceptible to materialism, and those with paranoid or fearful traits may be more susceptible to power struggles. Yet, no matter what your personality type, you can be tempted in various ways, and you might fall.

Second, God is faithful. We cannot be counted upon except when we rely upon God. Only when we endure by faith, as did Moses and Paul, can we receive the promised resources of a faithful God, who will never let us down. In fact, Paul went on to explain that God will not permit us to be tempted beyond what we are able. Keep in mind that those words were written to believers who lived in a society as permeated with sexual temptation as ours is. Opportunities for sexual misconduct, homosexual and heterosexual, abounded in Corinth. Yet Paul promises that God will, with the temptation, make a way of escape that we may be able to bear it.

SEXUAL TEMPTATION

Recently, a young man, John, came to see one of our counselors. John was miserable. While walking in downtown Dallas en route to a business appointment he noticed a lady stepping out of a department store into a wind-blown street. The wind lifted her skirt above her head. The man immediately averted his eyes, but soon became absolutely miserable, plagued with feelings of guilt.

The counselor, on the basis of James 1 and 1 Corinthians 10:13 asked, "What did you do at that moment? Did you continue to look or did you turn away?"

The young man replied, "I immediately turned away."

"Did you continue to think about the woman?"

"No, once or twice the picture of her came into my mind. When it did, I asked God to help me think about something else, and I quoted Scripture to myself."

"Well, John," the counselor replied, "I have good news for you. On the basis of James 1 it seems that you handled this matter wisely."

For temptation to conceive (become sin), two ingredients are necessary, just as two ingredients are necessary for the conception of a human baby. Essential are the contributions of both the father and mother—the egg and the sperm. Similarly, James uses the idea of conception, consisting of two parts, to show us how temptation works. We have the external event, which provides the source of temptation—perhaps a television program, a picture in a magazine, or the sight of an actual person. We also have the internal response, which, according to James, originates "out of our own lusts." We choose either to dismiss the temptation or to give in to it. Frequently and tragically, we do the latter.

A classic example of this struggle is the account of David and Bathsheba. Although David could have come down from the housetop when he first saw Bathsheba bathing in her courtyard below, he continued to linger, looking and lusting after her. He ultimately acted on those sinful desires.

As we face similar kinds of temptations, we need to remind ourselves that God not only provides us with a way to escape but He also enables us to endure, to bear the temptation.

MATERIAL TEMPTATION

God likewise makes provision for overcoming temptation in the material realm. Paul, in writing to Timothy, explains that there are those who are particularly susceptible to the love of money, which is "a root of all kinds of evil" (1 Timothy 6:10). In our day, even in the Christian community, the attainment of materialistic success is a supposed evidence of godliness. Yet Paul reminds us to withdraw from those who suppose that gain is godliness. Would Paul have been comfortable with those who preach a "prosperity gospel" today? Even casual examination of Paul's warning to Timothy (1 Timothy 6) shows us where the apostle would stand on such an issue. Paul's equation for true success is, "But godliness with contentment is great gain" (v. 6). We are to be content with the provision of our basic needs (v. 8).

However, it is important to distinguish between those "who want to *get* rich" (1 Timothy 6:9, emphasis added), and those "who *are* rich" (v. 17, emphasis added). In the case of the latter, Paul gives instructions for avoiding temptations. Those who are blessed with a great deal of God's resources are not to be high-minded. In the Dallas area we often encounter people, even Christians, who hold to the fairly widespread mentality that if you live in north Dallas or certain suburbs, drive the latest model foreign sedan, carry a certain kind of credit card, and purchase your clothes at a ritzy department store, you are superior to those who live in other parts of the city, drive anything with four wheels, and shop at less prestigious stores.

Paul warns us not to trust in uncertain riches. We may be tempted to place confidence in material resources rather than in God. Many individuals in Texas believed that the booms in oil and real estate, which produced a show of wealth in the city of Dallas second to none, would keep growing forever. When the price of oil crashed and the economy in oil-based Houston collapsed, many Dallasites said, "It can never happen here. Our economy is more diversified." And for a couple of years it didn't happen in Dallas. But eventually the people of Dallas began to realize that their economy was indirectly tied to oil, which meant that though it took longer for the Dallas business climate to be affected, it was eventually affected. Several years after oil collapsed, when Houston was beginning to climb out of its financial depression, many Dallas citizens began declaring bankruptcy. Thousands of construction projects remained unfinished or sat idle. The economic slide shattered fortunes and lives, even in "diversified" Dallas.

The positive side of Paul's warning to Timothy concerning material things would have been good advice for Dallas, too. "Put your hope in God, who richly provides us with everything for our enjoyment" (1 Timothy 6:17). God is not opposed to our enjoying good things. It's not a sin to drive a nice car or live in a comfortable home or wear new clothing. Neither is it a sin to drive a vehicle with more than one hundred thousand miles or to purchase clothing from a "nearly new shop." In fact, Paul goes on to say that those who have material things are to do good, to be rich in good works and to be ready and eager to share and give, thus laying up treasure in heaven rather than on earth.

POWER-STRUGGLE TEMPTATION

The third area of temptation—the desire to have the preeminence (1 John 2)—may be even more subtle than the temptations we encounter in the sexual or the material realms. A classic example of a man who succumbed to such temptation is Diotrephes, whom the apostle John described in 3 John 9 as "[loving] to be *first.*" That word is used in only one other passage in the New Testament, Colossians 1:18, where it describes Jesus Christ, who is, of course, the only individual who deserves to have the preeminence and who has it in all things. The truth is that there is an element of Diotrephes in each of us. We, too, can be fond of the preeminence, whether it comes from recognition on the job, the ability to influence others, or having our personal kingdoms in the local church.

Unfortunately, many church boards and committees have been infiltrated with descendants of Diotrephes, individuals who are fond of being personally recognized and who rule their little fiefdoms. They enjoy getting their own way in areas ranging from music to missions to church buildings, all the while heading toward burnout or contributing to the burnout of others. Like Diotrephes, they are often guilty of malicious words. Sometimes they cover their power struggles under the guise of church discipline and kick those who disagree with them out of the church. That was the course of action Diotrephes followed (3 John 10). The apostle John makes it clear two verses later that our course of action is not to mimic that which is evil, such as Diotrephes, but rather that which is good. In language similar to 2 Peter 1:9 John implies that the individual who acts like Diotrephes is spiritually nearsighted and does not see God accurately.

Perhaps it would be helpful at this point to examine which of the three areas—lust of the flesh (sexual or other physical temptation), lust of the eyes (material temptation), or pride of life (power struggle temptation)—is your most persistent struggle. If you are an obsessive-compulsive, it is likely that you are vulnerable to material temptation or power struggles, although you are susceptible to all three.

Take time to develop a plan of action to overcome these temptations. This plan may involve a daily time spent in prayer and in the Word. We have found in our personal experience that the discipline of a daily quiet time spent with God can be extremely crucial. Some find it helpful to have this quiet time either immediately before or immediately after a period of physical exercise, combining physical exercise and spiritual devotions on a regular basis.

THE INNER LIFE

The palm tree is one of the most resourceful and durable of plants. Unlike ordinary trees, which have dead centers and thinning roots, the palm's survival depends on a thick, strong root and living heart rather than on the condition of its leaves and bark. That is why the palm can withstand much external abuse. It endures violent desert storms by bending its resilient trunk until the rains and winds pass, after which the palm springs back. Its thick, strong root taps nearby streams or ponds for nourishment. Even if those resources dry up, the palm can still survive because the root, which is the same size as the trunk, stores a great surplus of water. In time (up to fifty years) the palm begins to bear fruit, which becomes sweeter as the palm tree ages and as its bark is scarred by the elements.

Like the palm tree, we endure when we tap into the resources of God's Spirit and His Word to develop the inner rather than the outer part of us. Psalm 1:2-4 tells us that the man is "blessed" whose "delight is in the law of the Lord, and [who meditates] on his law . . . day and night. He is like a tree planted by streams of water, which yields its fruit in season and whose leaf does not wither. Whatever he does prospers." We will bear fruit, all kinds of good deeds, and will grow spiritually as we get to know God better and better. God's power will strengthen us so that we can endure life's hardships joyfully (Colossians 1:11). Furthermore, we bear fruit also as we constantly give thanks for the eternal inheritance toward which we are advancing (vv. 10-12). When that happens, our daily lives will begin to demonstrate the divine difference. And, like Moses, we will constantly endure by seeing Him who is invisible.

11
SOLVING OUR
RELATIONAL PROBLEMS

Living a balanced, healthy life is not something that can be achieved in isolation. No less an authority than Dr. Karl Menninger, who has been described as knowing more about the subject of mental health than any other living person, offers the following perspective on a mentally healthy individual:

> Indeed, when we wish to find out how well Mr. X is integrated, we do not check his performance randomly at any odd level and leave it at that, but we try to formulate an organized statement about his overall functioning with an ultimate emphasis on his topmost performances: how he gets along with other people, how "whole" he is, how well he can adapt himself to the demands of the day, how well he can master his inner and outer environment to the benefit of himself and society.[1]

Many centuries before, Jesus Christ offered a perspective that provided His hearers with a way to evaluate overall human functioning; one that encompassed certain aspects of Menninger's perspective, but that,

1. Karl Menninger, *The Vital Balance* (New York: Viking Press, 1963), p. 94.

significantly, included another element—the vertical relationship with man's Creator.

Near the end of His ministry, after successfully responding to the Pharisees' and Sadducees' hostile questions, Jesus was confronted by a scribe who asked the question that many have wrestled with philosophically and theologically through the ages: "Of all the commandments, which is the most important?" (Mark 12:28). In other words, divinely speaking, what is our ultimate responsibility?

Without hesitation the Savior replied, "The most important one . . . is this: 'Hear, O Israel, the Lord our God, the Lord is one. Love the Lord your God with all your heart and with all your soul and with all your mind and with all your strength.' The second is this: 'Love your neighbor as yourself'" (Mark 12:29-31).

In essence, the Savior was saying that our ultimate responsibility is to love—to wholeheartedly love God and unconditionally love people. And He classified this responsibility as of overwhelming importance: "There is no commandment greater than these" (Mark 12:31b).

Sadly, however, twenty centuries later an endorsed definition of mental health conspicuously omits the relevance of those commandments. Menninger, a popular expert of our time, doesn't acknowledge that having a wholehearted love for God and for people is the key to developing lasting relationships and maintaining mental health.

Relating to others is often a difficult area for the burnout-prone obsessive-compulsive. However, before focusing on human relationships, it is necessary to be able to relate appropriately to God.

WHOLEHEARTED LOVE FOR GOD

The Pharisees of Jesus' day catalogued the law into 248 positive commandments and 365 prohibitions. They engaged in frequent debate about which laws took precedence over others in cases of apparent conflict.

In contrast, Jesus explained that the total responsibility of man can be summed up in one word—love. This is the essence of Paul's assertion in Romans 13:10, "Love is the fulfillment of the law."

Examination of the term *agape*, the Greek word Jesus used for love, shows us that love is not simply an emotion but an act of the will. It involves a choice to make someone or something else a priority rather than ourselves. Agape love gives sacrificially and desires the very best for the one loved.

The initial direction of this love is toward God. Jesus prefaced His answer to the scribe's question by quoting the most familiar verse of the Old Testament, one quoted frequently in Hebrew religious practice, "Hear, O Israel: The Lord our God, the Lord is one" (Deuteronomy 6:4). That verse stresses the uniqueness of God—only He deserves our wholehearted love.

Furthermore, Jesus explained that every part of man's being is to be involved in this expression of wholehearted love toward God. We prefer the phrase *wholehearted* love, not only because it is accurate in terms of Jesus' original statement, but also because it contrasts sharply with the halfhearted commitment in our world today.

According to Proverbs 4:23, the heart was the hub and center of man's existence, the ultimate source of every thought, every word, and every deed. We are to use our *soul* (emotions and attitudes), our *mind* (intellect and thought processes), and our *strength* (physical energies and efforts) *to love God*. In short, Jesus was saying that our total being is to be committed in a relationship of loving submission to God.

Paul may well have had this foundation in mind as he approached the close of his letter to the Thessalonians: "May God himself, the God of peace, sanctify you through and through. May your *whole—spirit, soul and body*—be kept blameless at the coming of our Lord Jesus Christ" (1 Thessalonians 5:23, author's emphasis and punctuation). This love is also based clearly on God's initiative of love toward us (1 John 4:19): "We love because he first loved us."

Two implications for burnout-prone obsessive-compulsives are evident from this discussion. First, the ultimate foundation for proper relationships is an understanding and appreciation of God's unconditional love for us. When we respond with wholehearted love for God, we are doing so not in attempts to win His approval or love but in recognition that He loves us totally and unconditionally. We don't have to earn or merit His love, but can simply respond to it wholeheartedly.

Second, our commitment is to a Person, not to a series of projects. Rather than being committed to projects that we think will earn God's favor, we need to be committed to God as a Person.

As we saw earlier, Martha is the classic biblical example of an individual committed to projects instead of persons. She was apparently an oldest daughter, someone who wanted to get things done and someone who apparently found it difficult to sit still. Her motto may well have been "Do it now!" She wasn't afraid of becoming involved physically in serving others (John 11:30). She was a strong thinker, even theologically, compared to many women of her day (v. 24), but she seemed to relate to Jesus on a level of something less than that of Lord, even to the point of admonishing Him (v. 39). Positively, of course, she sought out the Lord (v. 20), demonstrated a strong faith (v. 22), and had an accurate doctrinal framework of belief (vv. 24, 27).

Like many obsessive-compulsives, Martha seemed to be preoccupied with dirt, time, and money. In Luke 10 she is concerned with getting the housework done; in John 11 she questions why the Lord delayed His coming; and later in the passage she even voices her concern over the degree of decomposition of her brother's body! (v. 39). She was probably concerned about money, too, since the home she, Mary, and Lazarus lived in was hers (Luke 10:38). In essence, Martha was a high-performance individual who operated on a performance basis, even with God's Son.

What does it take to get through to someone like Martha? How could she change her project orientation to a wholehearted love for God? Perhaps the most significant statement in the entire New Testament about this special individual is found in John 11:5: "Jesus loved Martha and her sister and Lazarus." Jesus' unconditional love for Martha prompted Him to communicate with her, even though she seemed to have trouble listening to Him (vv. 23-27).

In fact, both in this context and in Luke 10, Martha tried to give the Lord advice, something we ourselves tend to do from time to time. Patiently, our Lord called her name twice, "Martha, Martha" (Luke 10:41), graciously and lovingly pointing out to her the ultimate priority of loving fellowship with Him. The Savior did not take away her desire to serve, however. In fact, in our final scriptural snapshot of Martha (John 12:2), she is still serving.

The highlight of this passage in John takes place at the celebration of Lazarus's restoration to life, where

Mary pours costly perfume on Jesus' feet in an act of worship. It is significant that when Judas Iscariot voices criticism of the wastefulness of Mary's act (John 12:4), we read nothing of criticism from Martha. Perhaps in response to Christ's unconditional love for her, Martha had come into a place of such wholehearted love for Him that a costly sacrificial act of worship, such as the one initiated by her sister, no longer created a practical problem for her.

Many obsessive-compulsives can relate to Martha's attempts to obtain God's favor on a performance basis. Such individuals usually become irritated with other people who hamper their efforts to perform. Obsessive-compulsives can learn from Martha's example as one who did respond to the unconditional love of Christ.

UNCONDITIONAL LOVE FOR PEOPLE

The second half of our ultimate responsibility that Christ describes to the scribe in Mark 12 is that we show unconditional love for people (v. 31). It is in our interactions with people that we will ultimately succeed in the abundant life Christ came to give us or sink into the mire of unfulfilled expectations that lead to burnout.

Because God loves us unconditionally and, as the Savior explains, because unconditional love for people is the hallmark of discipleship (John 15:12), it stands to reason that a proper response to God will result in an appropriately loving response towards people. As John expressed it, "Anyone who does not love his brother, whom he has seen, cannot love God, whom he has not seen" (1 John 4:20). Obsessive-compulsives who think they are wholly devoted to God but who struggle to show wholehearted love for family members, neighbors, coworkers, and church members are in for a surprise when they realize that their love for God is expressed by their love for other people.

Jesus said that we are to love our neighbors—those with whom we come in contact—as we love ourselves. Note that we are not commanded to love ourselves. Such love is assumed, just as it was assumed by the apostle Paul (Ephesians 5:28) when he explained that husbands are to love and cherish their wives as they do their own bodies.

Throughout the New Testament the priority of love is clearly established (Colossians 3:14; 1 Peter 4:8; 1 John 3:14; 1 John 4:8). Furthermore, every appropriate interpersonal relationship can be summarized in the essence of love, as described by Paul in 1 Corinthians 13:4-7a:

> Love is very patient and kind, never jealous or envious, never boastful or proud, never haughty or selfish or rude. Love does not demand its own way. It is not irritable or touchy. It does not hold grudges and will hardly even notice when others do it wrong. It is never glad about injustice, but rejoices whenever truth wins out. If you love someone you will be loyal to him no matter what the cost. [TLB*]

That is how we are to relate to the people God allows to cross our path. That includes members of our family, people with whom we work, believers with whom we worship and fellowship, and neighbors with whom we come in contact. We're to unconditionally love people not on the basis of how well they measure up to our conditions or how likable they are or how kind they are to us, but as the ultimate, outward expression of our inward commitment to Christ.

* *The Living Bible.*

We have noticed that people who unconditionally love their neighbor are almost immune to burnout and its complications, in contrast to the school bus driver mentioned earlier who deeply loved his bus—his material "possession." He was extremely fond of his route and the drive each day, and yet hated each one of the children who rode his bus.

Love does not mean the absence of conflict or confrontation. When Martha inappropriately rebuked our Lord, He gently and lovingly confronted her, pointing out her misplaced priorities (Luke 10:41-42). On another occasion He redirected her misplaced focus regarding her brother's future. Love may involve confrontation, yet frequently we fail to solve interpersonal conflicts through loving confrontation. Instead we choose to dwell on unmet expectations. That only leads to bitterness and eventually to burnout.

Even the apostle Paul encountered difficulty as a result of unrealistic expectations. After the Jerusalem council, in which Paul and Barnabas determined to undertake a second missionary journey (Acts 15:36), a major contention arose over the question of whether to take John Mark. Although Luke's account does not place blame on either Barnabas or Paul, or defend or censure John Mark for his earlier defection in Pamphylia, we learn that Paul had evidently expected a greater measure of commitment from John Mark than the young man was able to give. Paul even broke fellowship with Barnabas over this issue. Later, however, in 2 Timothy 4, as Paul expresses his concern over others who have abandoned him, such as Demas, he exhorts Timothy, "Get Mark and bring him with you, because he is helpful to me in my ministry" (2 Timothy 4:11). Paul gave us an encouraging example by extending a second opportunity to John Mark, instead of writing him off because he failed once to fulfill expectations.

That is an important example for us to follow when it comes to our unconditional love for people. They may sometimes fail us, and when they do, we may be inclined to become embittered and not to trust them with important responsibilities. Yet it is crucial not to write off people. Our God is the God of the second chance.

Paul is a good example of balance. Even though in writing to Timothy (2 Timothy 4), he cited many potential reasons to become bitter—toward Demas for forsaking him, toward Alexander for doing him harm, and toward other friends for deserting him to become involved in other ministries—Paul refused to follow what might have been his obsessive-compulsive tendency. He looked out for others and developed proper relationships, taking time to greet his long-time friends Priscilla, Aquila, and Onesiphorus, and allowing Trophimus to rest when he became ill.

Paul was able to maintain balance because he held onto a perspective that looked beyond the temporal to the eternal. Even though he experienced loneliness (2 Timothy 4:11), he recognized that the Lord's presence was with him. He even asked Timothy to come and be with him "before winter" (v. 21). Furthermore, Paul didn't suppress his emotions. He verbalized to Timothy his feelings about the fact that no one defended him at his first hearing (v. 16). Yet he was willing to forgive those who had deserted him and prayed that they would experience God's forgiveness.

BITTERNESS AND FORGIVENESS

This brings us to the issue of forgiveness. When others have failed to meet our expectations, why do we so frequently become bitter toward them? Often it is because we do not practice or understand the concept of forgiveness. If bitterness is the hidden root of burn-out, then forgiveness is the antidote that enables us to move beyond burnout to abundant living. Often when we encounter individuals who are overwhelmed by burnout, it turns out that the source is primarily bitterness occasioned by a refusal to forgive others.

The meaning of the term *forgive* in both the Old Testament and the New Testament is "to release" or "send away." In fact, to forgive is to exercise a choice. In his excellent work on the subject *Let's Forgive and Be Free*, Richard Walters defines forgiving as "giving up all claim on one who has hurt you and letting go of the emotional consequences of the hurt" ([Grand Rapids: Zondervan, 1983] p. 18).

Several key New Testament passages articulate crucial principles we need to understand relative to forgiveness. Ephesians 4:32 explains the *degree* to which we are to forgive—"just as in Christ God forgave [us]." The *scope* of forgiveness is explained in Colossians 3:13: "Bear with each other and forgive *whatever* grievances you may have against one another" (emphasis added). Romans 12:17-21 expresses the *essence* of forgiveness: "Do not repay anyone evil for evil. Be careful to do what is right in the eyes of everybody. If it is possible, as far as it depends on you, live at peace with everyone. Do not take revenge, my friends, but leave room for God's wrath, for it is written: 'It is mine to avenge; I will repay,' says the Lord."

When we forgive, we are backing off and saying to God, "If vengeance is to be taken, if a score is to be settled, I'll let You take care of it. I give up the right to pay back anybody. I want to do what is right and use whatever power I have to get along with others."

The numerical *extent* of forgiveness is found in Jesus' statement to Peter—seventy times seven (Matthew 18:21-22). In other words, don't count or limit the number of times you forgive. The *priority* of forgiving is expressed in Matthew 6:14-15. When we who desperately need God's forgiveness claim it but are unwilling to extend forgiveness to those who have wronged us, we will not experience divine forgiveness. Furthermore, the *consequences* of not forgiving can be seen in Ephesians 4:31-32. When we refuse to forgive, we harbor bitterness.

Characteristic symptoms of bitterness include rage, outbursts of anger, brawling, shouting, clamoring, slander (speaking evil of people), and malice (feelings of ill will). Those characteristics are magnified when we refuse to forgive. Furthermore, refusal to forgive will hinder us from being kind or tenderhearted. We are to be kind, or *chrestoi*, which according to *The Bible Knowledge Commentary* means to provide what is suitable or fitting to a need (ed. John F. Walvoord and Roy B. Zuck, New Testament ed. [Wheaton, Ill.: Victor Books, 1983], p. 637).

The term translated "tenderhearted" (KJV) is used only here in Ephesians and in 1 Peter 3:8, although a similar term is used in several of Paul's other letters and in 1 John 3:17. The basic idea is that the individual who is forgiving will maintain emotional and spiritual tenderness, instead of developing what might be called a "hard edge." Just as calluses can develop on a person's hands, so individuals who refuse to forgive, and harbor feelings of ill will, resentment, and bitterness, can become "hard-hearted." Obsessive-compulsive individuals, who tend to avoid relating on an emotional level, often struggle in this area. Yet the consequences of refusing to forgive are far too grave to neglect.

Forgiveness is neither cheap nor easy. Yet we try to avoid that reality, falling at times into certain traps. One of those traps is to forgive without dealing with the issue. We counseled a pastor whose son had become involved in all kinds of problems, including drugs and stealing. The father was always willing to forgive, but he never really faced head-on the reality of his son's destructive behavior.

Similarly, a wife who sought our counsel claimed to forgive her husband, who had been unfaithful. But she forgave him conditionally. As long as her husband treated her perfectly and provided everything that she wanted materially, she "forgave" him his infidelity. But inside she still harbored smoldering resentment. For years that greatly affected her relationship with her husband.

Another forgiveness trap is suppressing anger rather than forgiving. One man had supposedly forgiven his business partner for making a mistake in a business deal that cost the company thousands of dollars. But the man found himself taking out his anger and frustrations on his partner in little ways. It took years before he realized that, rather than completely forgiving him, he had forgiven only to a degree and for the most part had simply suppressed the rest of his anger.

A third trap is when we allow people to continue to hurt us. Matthew 10:16 instructs us to be wise as serpents and as innocent as doves. When we forgive another person, we must not harm him, just as a dove never attacks. But we must also exercise the wisdom of a serpent, which never places its head on the path where somebody is about to stomp with his boot. Serpents are shy creatures who avoid confrontation. When they are cornered they may attack out of self-defense, yet the normal nature of the serpent is to simply stay away. The safest way to deal with snakes is to make enough noise as you approach so that they have an opportunity to leave the area before you get close to them.

Forgiveness doesn't mean condoning wrong. It presupposes that the issue has been dealt with, just as God forgives our sins because their price has been paid with the death of His Son. Does this mean we forget when we forgive? No. Our computerlike brains have an incredible capability for remembering, even though emotionally we sometimes block out painful things that have happened to us. The memory of painful experiences remains present, frequently existing in layer after layer.

So how do we forgive? Scripture clearly states that we are to forgive before sunset, which was bedtime in the first-century (Ephesians 4:26). However, sometimes we think we've thoroughly forgiven only to wake up the next day to persisting anger. Often, forgiveness involves a commitment to the process of dealing with bitterness over and over again, whenever it flares up. It's like peeling an onion. We peel back a layer only to discover another. We deal with that layer only to discover another. It's a painful process filled with tears and pain. We forgive at great cost to ourselves. Yet the goal is to continue to deal with the issues until the emotional pain no longer exists, and the onion is completely peeled away.

In some situations that will take intensive counseling and require that we will to make difficult choices. But if we are to appropriately, unconditionally love people, we have to forgive them.

Can we forgive? Yes. Why? Because God, for Christ's sake, has forgiven us. Think of all the ways God has forgiven us. He has blotted out like a thick cloud our transgressions (Isaiah 44:22); He has removed our sins "as far as the east is from the west" (Psalm

103:12); and He pardons sin and has hurled our iniquities into the depth of the sea (Micah 7:18-19).

Will we forgive? Ultimately we must make that choice. To choose to forgive whether we feel like it or not is an essential prerequisite for moving beyond burnout.

12

RELATING POSITIVELY
TO OTHERS

Recently a young man appeared in our office to interview for a job opening in a new clinic that was being established in a nearby city. During the course of the interview, he asserted, "Here's how I operate. Give me a job to do, and I'll do it. I'm the kind of person who likes to know what's expected of me, to whom I'm responsible, and how soon I need to get a job done. If there's one phrase that characterizes me it's, 'I am responsible.' "

The two of us present with the young man looked at each other and smiled as we thought the same thing, "Ah ha! Another obsessive-compulsive personality!"

Since this book is written about balancing obsessive-compulsive traits (which are not bad in themselves), it is important to recognize that one of the major strengths of the obsessive-compulsive is his conscientiousness about duty—a positive trait to have in the Christian life, for God has given us some important responsibilities to fulfill.

As we learn from Jesus in Mark 12:30-31, our ultimate duty is not a responsibility toward projects but toward persons. It is to love God wholeheartedly and to love people unconditionally. "Love the Lord your God with all your heart and with all your soul and with all your mind and with all your strength. The second is this: Love your neighbor as yourself. There is no commandment greater than these."

In the previous chapter, we examined some problem areas relating to our responsibility to love our neighbor. In this chapter, we shall seek to move beyond correcting the negative by addressing the positive. In addition, we will seek to present workable principles for building and maintaining positive relationships.

As we try to relate to others on the basis of unconditional love, we quickly find that forgiving isn't enough. We also have a strong need to develop positive relationships to which we can contribute and which will encourage and strengthen us. The book of Proverbs contains a great deal of wisdom about relationships. Much of that wisdom comes from Solomon, who learned it firsthand from his father, David.

Perhaps the classic example of a healthy interpersonal relationship can be seen in the friendship between David and Jonathan. A superficial examination of that unique and special relationship demonstrates that good friends don't have to come from the same social status. Jonathan was a prince and David only a poor shepherd, and Jonathan may have been fifteen to twenty years older than David. The biblical narrative in 1 Samuel tells us that this special relationship developed shortly after David's dramatic victory over Goliath. The record states: "The soul of Jonathan was knit to the soul of David, and Jonathan loved him as himself" (18:1, NASB*).

How could such a special relationship of love develop? The Hebrew word *aheb*, used for love, is one of two key words that describe relationships in the Old Testament. As a noun, it describes one who loves or one who is a friend. For example, it describes Abraham in

* *New American Standard Bible.*

2 Chronicles 20:7 and in Isaiah 41:8 as a friend of God. It denotes a choice, an attraction, and a camaraderie, which is seen in the process of "knitting of souls" between David and Jonathan.

From a human perspective, why did this friendship occur? It occurred because even though Jonathan and David came from different backgrounds, they had the same determination and spirit regarding God's purposes and victory over God's enemies. David had just demonstrated that attitude by his willingness to take on the giant Goliath, something the other warriors of Israel had been unable or unwilling to do. Somewhat earlier, Jonathan had demonstrated the same attitude, telling his armor-bearer, "Perhaps the Lord will act in our behalf. Nothing can hinder the Lord from saving, whether by many or by few" (1 Samuel 14:6). God used a courageous, responsive Jonathan and his armor-bearer to dispatch about twenty men across a half-acre of ground and to initiate an even greater victory as a result of a supernaturally timed earthquake, which terrorized the Philistines. "So the Lord rescued Israel that day" (v. 23).

The similarities between Jonathan's actions and attitude in 1 Samuel 14 and David's in 1 Samuel 17 are remarkable. Both realized they were facing tremendous odds, yet both recognized the power of God to overcome those odds. Each verbalized a personal faith and confidence in God, acted on that faith, and, as a result, each experienced victory. Their commitment to God and their attitudes toward life and struggles bonded them.

In seeking friendships we should look for people who realistically assess the difficulties of life but whose faith and confidence in God are genuine and strong; people who, rather than hindering or dragging down our faith, will encourage it or promote it; people who will stimulate our spiritual growth rather than retard it. We should look for people whose attitudes toward the things of God are positive rather than negative.

In addition to having similar attitudes toward God, David and Jonathan also exhibited a similar commitment to their friendship in the making of a covenant (1 Samuel 18:3). We're living in days when people are slack in making and keeping commitments to one another. In our culture of "least resistance" we often apply an attitude of convenience toward our relationships as well, expecting to start and stop a friendship whenever we feel like it. As a result, we lose out on the benefits of long-term commitments. Many marriages fail today because individuals base the marriage on short-term physical attraction or emotions and don't want to spend time and effort developing a substantial friendship and commitment within the marriage.

The Old Testament concept of commitment is fascinating. It signifies loyal love and refers to an important long-term relationship of the type exhibited by Jonathan and David. The concept of loyal love (referred to twice regarding their friendship) provided the basis for a covenant relationship between them (1 Samuel 20:14-15).

Even though Jonathan was next in line to the throne of Israel, and even though his father pressured him to turn against David and to pursue his own interests, Jonathan remained loyal to David—defending him to the point of risking his own life for his friend (1 Samuel 19:1-5, 20:30-34). The idea of loyalty is also mentioned in 20:15: "Do not ever cut off your kindness from my family." Jonathan even reaffirmed his oath to David, "because he loved him as he loved himself" (v. 17). The love and loyalty in this covenant were possible because the relationship was actually a three-sided one among David, Jonathan, and the Lord (v. 8). God blesses relationships that honor Him. Developing long-term, committed relationships that have the common priority of glorifying God helps us to grow closer to the Lord and prepares us to be an instrument He can use to care for and bless others.

Philip and Dick were college roommates who often played basketball together and double-dated together. After both graduated from college, they went their separate ways for five years without seeing one another. Yet each often thought of and even prayed for the other.

One spring, Philip's business took him to the Midwest where Dick was involved in a ministry. Certain about how he felt toward his old friend, but uncertain as to how he would be received, Philip decided to risk a phone call. Dick was ecstatic. The two men had lunch and Dick invited Philip to visit his family. As a result, both men verbalized their disappointment in themselves for allowing time and the pressures of life to erode their commitment to keep in contact.

Philip said, "Why don't you plan on bringing your family and spending some vacation time with us on the East Coast?" The two families spent a week together, and the ease with which the relationship was reestablished confirmed the genuine long-term commitment between Philip and Dick.

Have you ever been out of touch with old friends for years only to get back together and realize that the relationship is just as strong and solid as ever? If so, that friendship likely involved a long-term commitment. To verbalize such a commitment to a friend by saying, "I'm committed to you," "I care about you," or "I'm with you for the long haul" is appropriate and provides tremendous encouragement, support, and hope for friends who are experiencing adversity.

A committed relationship also involves a genuine delight and enjoyment in the success of the other. That was especially evident in Jonathan's attitude toward David. The scriptural record zeros in on Jonathan's delight in David's success, in contrast with Saul's extreme jealousy toward David (1 Samuel 18:8). Jonathan gave David a robe, kingly garments, sword, bow, and belt (v. 4); he defended David to his father (19:4-5); he communicated with David in order to restore him to Saul's household (v. 7); he encouraged David when David focused on the unfairness and the hopelessness of his deteriorating relationship with Saul (23:17), and even took personal risk to do so in the wilderness (vv. 16-18) where he reaffirmed his commitment to God's ultimate purpose, which was to establish David as king. Jonathan physically and verbally expressed appropriate affection toward his friend (20:41-42). Jonathan not only expressed his commitment to David (vv. 9-17) but even grieved for David because of the rift in the relationship between his father and his friend (v. 34).

Not everything in this friendship was praiseworthy, however. Jonathan lied on behalf of his friend (20:28), something clearly prohibited by the Scriptures, even when the falsehood grows out of a desire to be loyal to our friends. But overall the friendship was one we should emulate. There was no jealousy in the relationship but genuine, open communication and an unselfish, giving spirit. Possessiveness and self-seeking found no place, nor were the emotions of anger, bitterness, or envy allowed to pollute the positive qualities of the relationship.

As David experienced the benefits of developing a good friendship, he was able to communicate to his son Solomon the principles of friendship he had experienced in his dealings with Jonathan. Unfortunately,

Solomon did not practice everything he learned or even everything he taught in the book of Proverbs. Yet he established some important principles of relationships, which we need to apply.

One of those principles is found in Proverbs 13:20: "He who walks with the wise grows wise, but a companion of fools suffers harm." This principle relates to marriages, friendships, work relationships, and even relationships within the local church. Those who have allowed God to develop wisdom in them through His Word and their life experiences can help strengthen and enhance the wisdom of others. Yet our personal lives will be "broken down" (the literal meaning of the Hebrew word *yeroa*), harmed, and destroyed if we spend our time with and choose as friends those who have a foolish attitude toward life.

A classic biblical example of someone who chose the wrong kind of friends was Joash (2 Chronicles 24). Spurning the counsel of his wise guardian, Jehoiada, he chose foolish friends from among the princes of Judah—friends who instigated the murder of Jehoiada's son, Zechariah (2 Chronicles 24:21-22).

As has already been mentioned, the kind of relationships or friendships we develop can play a crucial role in determining whether we flourish in life or experience the bitterness that often leads to burnout. A key relationship principle is espoused in Proverbs 17:17, "A friend loves at all times, and a brother is born for adversity." Jonathan loved David even when he faced the loss of the privilege of becoming king, just as Joseph continued to love and care for his brothers, even after they had sold him into slavery.

Proverbs 18:24b tells us that "there is a friend who sticks closer than a brother." Some translations of the first part of Proverbs 18:24 suggest that a lot of friends can be destructive, but a few good, close, loyal friends can help. An authentic friend is one who knows you at your best and worst and still loves and accepts you.

Proverbs 27 contains a number of highly significant principles related to friendships. Proverbs 27:5-6 states that "open rebuke" is "better . . . than hidden love. Wounds from a friend can be trusted, but an enemy multiplies kisses." We need faithful friends—friends who can be trusted to tell us the truth. We may be tempted to surround ourselves with people who only flatter us, who only tell us what we want to hear. But a genuine friend is one who will tell us the truth even when it wounds us.

A pastor was investing far too much time in work and in ministry. Although many people said, "What you're doing is great. You must be really having an effect for Christ," a few close friends said, "What you're doing is destructive. It ultimately will cause you to lose your health and the ability to minister five or ten years down the road." Even though the words were painful, the pastor needed them.

The New Testament encourages us to admonish one another. Appropriate confrontation is far better than a "Judas kiss." A true friend tells it like it is in contrast to the flatterer, who may cause us to stumble. "Whoever flatters his neighbor is spreading a net for his feet" (Proverbs 29:5). A true friend faithfully comforts as well as confronts. "Ointment and perfume rejoice the heart; so doth the sweetness of a man's friend by hearty counsel" (Proverbs 27:9, KJV).

The Israelites lived in a hot, dry climate. So oil on the skin provided a soothing, refreshing balm, and perfume stimulated the senses and encouraged appreciation for the finer things of life. So it is with the encouragement and comfort of a good friend. None of us can be "up" all the time. We all need "counsel from the heart," the kind of encouragement a friend can give.

The book of Proverbs has a lot to say about the subject of counsel or direction. Many people are unwilling to ask for it. Others ask the wrong person or fail to heed good advice. Proverbs tells us we all need "hearty counsel" from time to time. The Hebrew word used for counsel here is *tahbuloth*, which carries the basic idea of seeking direction. We've all tried to find a place we've never been to before and have needed to stop and ask for directions. The concept of seeking counsel is the same. The word *tahbuloth* is used five times in Proverbs (1:5, 11:14, 12:5, 20:18, and 24:6). Its root is related to a nautical word for a rope that is pulled to steer a ship.

Proverbs 11:14 states, "For lack of guidance a nation falls, but many advisers make victory sure," pointing out that when counsel isn't present, a group of people is likely to fall. The context of this verse suggests people, relations, and activities possibly within a city or community (vv. 10-11), although the advice can apply also to individuals. Yet, security in each case comes from "a multitude of counselors." The idea is that ensuring safety or security requires skill in making decisions. The concept of utilizing many advisers, found in Proverbs 11:14, 15:22, and 24:6, carries the idea of our seeking a second opinion. We should not simply limit ourselves to the counsel of one friend or individual, just as we should not always depend on the opinion of one physician. One of the reasons God gave us two eyes is because perception and perspective are improved with two eyes rather than with only one. Similarly, it is far safer to utilize the perspective of two or more persons.

Proverbs 15:22 gives a similar perspective: "Plans fail for lack of counsel, but with many advisers they succeed." Here the issue is not simply safety but success and fulfillment in life. Earlier, the author of Proverbs contrasted a wise son who brings joy to his father with a foolish son who thinks little of his parents. Without counsel, purposes will come to naught. We may plan as we wish, but we may experience disappointment if they are made foolishly.

In the years following the oil bust in Texas, hundreds of new, empty office buildings in Dallas, Austin, and Houston lined the landscape. Each of those buildings represented plans and purposes that had been disappointed. Every week the newspapers carried column after column of new bankruptcy declarations, many of well-known, previously wealthy people.

However, there were individuals who were able to maintain fiscal stability and success during that time. Such a man was Jim, a banker who had been involved in oil and real estate investments. He was advised by two individuals to diversify and to exercise caution before going into projects during the years when the oil decline first affected the economy. Because he listened to his advisers, Jim experienced a personal and financial stability not experienced by many of his peers. Counsel heeded led to success. Jim was a living example of the truth of Proverbs 20:18, "Make plans by seeking advice; if you wage war, obtain guidance."

Proverbs 24:6 gives similar counsel. "For waging war you need guidance, and for victory many advisers." The context of the verse is strength and stability (see vv. 3-5), and the subject is an impending conflict or a developing war. Conflict is a common aspect of life; it often occurs among families, in business, and even in the church. The principle of Proverbs 24:6 applies not only to presidents, such as John F. Kennedy facing the Bay of Pigs, or Ronald Reagan dealing with Libyan leader Moammar Khadafy, but also to us when we face conflict at home, in church, and at work. Those are the times we need to seek counsel.

A church faced a major conflict over whether or not to build a new building. Even though the members had long agreed that a new building should be constructed, an offer for a different, free location for the new church building created controversy. Some members saw the new location as a great blessing and opportunity, but others remained loyal to the church's location of the past thirty years. The conflict threatened to split the church. The pastor sought counsel from the elders in the church, from other experienced pastors in the area, and from church leaders in other parts of the country. After seeking a multitude of counselors, the pastor and the elders devised a plan for harmony. Ultimately, the plan worked to pull together the congregation, and, although some members did leave the congregation, the number was far less than it could have been. Those who stayed worked together and saw the new facility constructed. And the church's growth and its outreach in the community continued in an even larger measure.

Everyone needs friends from whom they can seek open counsel—friends who will give them encouragement and friends they can mutually stimulate and sharpen. Proverbs 27:17 states, "As iron sharpens iron, so one man sharpens another." That verse gives a vivid image of mutual intellectual and spiritual interaction and growth among friends. Occasionally such interaction as "iron sharpening iron" will cause sparks to fly. One of the best definitions we know for "encouraging one another" (Greek *parakaleo*, Hebrews 10:25) is to comfort the afflicted or to afflict the comfortable. This process of encouraging one another can help all of us. Some people leave very little impact on our lives, whereas others who encourage us make indelible impressions on us.

Another important principle of friendship demonstrated in Proverbs 27 is loyalty. "Do not forsake your friend and the friend of your father, and do not go to your brother's house when disaster strikes you" (v. 10). When adversity strikes, it's time to demonstrate loyalty to friends and to anticipate their loyalty toward us.

Tim was a section leader in a medium-sized corporation. He and Harold, his department manager, had worked together for a number of years. They had started working for the company at the same time and had both worked their way up to management positions.

A new corporate vice-president was hired with whom Harold did not see eye to eye, and Tim was offered Harold's job without Harold's knowing it. Because of his loyalty to his friend, Tim turned down the offer. He knew Harold was a good manager and that the complaints of incompetence the new vice-president voiced about Harold had no basis. Turning down the position, however, almost cost Tim his job.

Ultimately, Harold quit the company and moved to another. He and Tim remained good friends. Tim was not promoted into Harold's old spot but, as he told a friend, "My friendship with Harold was a lot more important than the promotion, especially with what I would have had to do to get it. I believe Harold would have stuck with me if the shoe were on the other foot. I couldn't have faced myself in the mirror if I had done that to him."

Loyalty can include keeping issues between you and your friend without breaking confidences (Proverbs 25:9-10), or just saying the appropriate word of encouragement (v. 11) or a proper word of rebuke (v. 12). It includes verbally giving the right word of refreshment (v. 13) and not making promises that you cannot or will not fulfill (v. 14). Remember—loyalty and a close friendship don't mean we should presume on past times of intimacy. Proverbs 27:14 warns, "If a man loudly blesses his neighbor early in the morning, it will be taken as a curse." The principle in that verse is two-fold: (1) practice sincerity in verbal communication and be sensitive to a friend's feelings of the moment, and (2) know when to back off. Even close, loyal friends may need some distance at times.

We can see a classic example of appropriate friendship in the relationship we have with Jesus Christ and what He has done for us. The basis for our relationship with Him is His sacrificial love (John 15:13), which caused Him to lay down His life for us. The result of His love and friendship has changed us. We are transformed (v. 14), which leads to a close, personal intimacy with Him and to a fruitfulness in our lives (v. 16). We no longer relate to Him simply as servants but as friends, which was the highest title that could be bestowed by an oriental king.

Close examination of those verses gives us important principles to apply to friendships. For example: Do I have the kind of wholehearted commitment of love that Christ has for me? Am I willing to be open and to relate to others as friends rather than on a performance basis? Do I reach out to others as Christ did for me? Do I choose friends on the basis of my needs or on the basis of my willingness to give to them? Finally, are my friends becoming more like Christ and more effectively bearing fruit because of me?

We all need friends. Facing the most intense trial of His life—the cross—Jesus called out for Peter, James, and John in the Garden of Gethsemane and asked them to stay with Him (Mark 14:32-42). The apostle Paul, near the close of his life, wrote to Timothy about his loneliness and encouraged his friend to "come before winter" (2 Timothy 4:21, NASB). How are friends to treat each other? With encouragement, perhaps the most important principle in friendship.

The spiritual gift of exhortation or encouragement—the God-given ability to appropriately motivate another individual—is not the gift of manipulation, of arm-twisting, or of simply giving someone else "a piece of your mind." Exhortation or encouragement is described as a function of the Holy Spirit in John 14 and 16. Like the Holy Spirit, an encourager or exhorter is one who is called alongside another. The concept can include rebuking another, calling for a change of action (Philippians 4:2), giving positive encouragement and comfort (2 Corinthians 1:3-4, 2:6-8), or challenging an individual to take action (Romans 12:1, 15:30; Jude 3). Although encouragement can be either public or private, the private use of the function has particular significance for believers. For example, 1 Timothy 4:13 points out that church leaders are to practice encouragement, whether or not they have the gift, as are all believers (1 Thessalonians 4:18, 5:11; Hebrews 10:25).

Two individuals in the New Testament stand out as patterns for encouragement. One is Barnabas, who was given that name by the apostles. The term means "son of encouragement or exhortation." Several instances in his life, recorded in the book of Acts, show the ways Barnabas demonstrated himself to be an encourager. The first glimpse we have of this man shows him exercising generosity, using his financial resources to encourage fellow members of the Body of Christ (Acts 4:36-37). He generously and willingly gave of his personal resources in a sacrificial way, which starkly contrasted with Ananias and Sapphira, who made a show of complete giving but secretly held some back.

Later Barnabas encouraged young Saul of Tarsus, who had recently been converted to the Christian faith (9:27). When everybody else was afraid of Saul (because of his record of persecuting the church), Barnabas brought him to the apostles, declared his testimony, and attested to its truthfulness. Undoubtedly, Barnabas's loyalty, encouragement, and willingness to use his influence played a strategic role in shaping Saul's ministry. He was renamed Paul the apostle and became a champion of the faith.

The same personal loyalty in Barnabas led to a rift between Barnabas and Paul in Acts 15:37-39. Barnabas felt strongly inclined to give John Mark a second chance. As earlier observed, Scripture does not say who was right and who was wrong. The rift led to Paul and Barnabas going separate ways. In spite of their split, Scripture records that Barnabas and Paul were both used by God. Eventually, Paul extended a second chance to John Mark (2 Timothy 4:11). Perhaps that was a result of having recognized that attitude in Barnabas, who used forgiveness and a second chance as a tool for encouragement.

When the name of another biblical encourager is mentioned, it usually elicits the reaction, "Who's he?" Yet Paul recognized Onesiphorus as one of the most important encouragers in his life. Although he was probably dead by the time Paul wrote of him, Onesiphorus left a lasting legacy. Paul said, "He often refreshed me" (2 Timothy 1:16). The word he used for *refreshed* means "to lift up one's soul" and is used only here in the New Testament. It speaks of a striking act of encouragement.

Furthermore, when other people were embarrassed by Paul's incarceration for the cause of Christ, Onesiphorus was "not ashamed of [Paul's] chains" (v. 16b).

He sought Paul in Rome and found him. His efforts to find the apostle were not halfhearted attempts. He went the extra mile to make personal contact. And that was only a glimpse of his ministry of encouragement. Paul said to Timothy, "You know very well in how many ways he helped me in Ephesus" (v. 18). Onesiphorus had been like a personal servant to Paul, lifting his soul and bringing encouragement to him. In essence, he was the epitome of what relating to others should be. He left a lasting impact on Paul and provides a stellar example for us as well.

Onesiphorus illustrates a phrase seen on a greeting card: "Most smiles are started by another smile." How many smiles have you started? As obsessive-compulsives who have received conditional love, and as bitter victims of burnout, we may not be appropriately relating to others by initiating a chain of smiles. Yet, following the examples of Onesiphorus, Barnabas, David, Jonathan, Paul, Timothy, and others in the New Testament, we can choose to become the first link in an encouraging chain.

13

HANDLING THE CIRCUMSTANCES OF LIFE

Jesus Christ is our ultimate pattern. As we seek to learn from His example, several important characteristics stand out that we can emulate in His approach to life. Let's look more closely at these principles for living.

ESTABLISHING PURPOSE

First, every aspect of Jesus' life revolved around His purpose and mission. Throughout the gospels Jesus makes frequent reference to the will of "him who sent me" (cf. John 5:30). We see this early in His ministry, such as in His contact with the woman at the well and His subsequent explanation of that incident to the disciples, and in the discourse that followed His healing of the invalid at the pool of Bethesda.

When Jesus presented Himself to the multitudes as the true bread of life (John 6:35-40), He exhibited the same commitment to doing the will of God. In those verses John portrays Jesus as both human and divine in His personal relationship to God. Jesus explains that His reason for existing is to fulfill the will of the Father (v. 38). It is the will of God that drives Him to complete the work of salvation (v. 39). It is the will of

God that Jesus present Himself as Savior and pay the price for sin so that those who trust Him might have everlasting life (v. 40). Throughout John's gospel Jesus relates our doing God's will to assurance of salvation (7:17), genuine worship, and answer to prayer (9:31).

Jesus is our example in obeying God's will (Matthew 26:42). For Him, life was based on one consuming purpose—to obey His Father's wishes.

Yet His life revolved around that purpose in a balanced way. He took time to sleep, to eat meals, and to fellowship with friends (Luke 10:38). He found time to visit those who had personal needs (Luke 18). He encouraged His disciples to take time to rest and joined them in doing so (Mark 6:31). Still, whatever He did and planned centered on the purpose He Himself stated in Luke 19:10: "The Son of Man came to seek and to save what was lost" (NASB).

Just as Jesus did, we need to recognize that we are called of God, whether to vocational ministry or to personal service, and we need to gear our lives toward fulfilling that call and exercising balance in daily living.

ESTABLISHING PRIORITIES

The second principle, rooted in the first, is that Jesus demonstrated priority. The major focus of His time, as we observe in the gospels, was to train twelve men to carry on His work after He left. Perhaps we can best observe this focus in Jesus' conversation with His Father the night before the crucifixion. The conversation, recorded in John 17, is what may be called the "real" Lord's Prayer. In that passage Jesus gives perhaps the clearest outline of the process of discipleship. Although many books have been written about discipleship during the last half century, no one has improved on the manual for discipleship outlined in John 17. There Jesus tells us precisely how He invested His time in discipling others to carry on His work when His time on earth was completed.

In that prayer Jesus made several statements regarding His disciples, and each statement represented a component of discipleship. He considered those components of such high priority that He invested more time in training the twelve than He did in reaching the multitudes. Let's examine those six statements and the components they represent.

1. *Example*—"I have revealed you to those whom you gave me" (v. 6). Many Christians fail in discipleship because they forget that what they do speaks louder than what they say. Because Jesus was perfect, He didn't have that problem; we might, but we need to give evidence of spiritual maturity to those lives we would impact.

2. *Evangelism*—"I gave them the words you gave me" (v. 8). Jesus, extending the call to His disciples, offered them the gift of everlasting life. He personally drew each of them into faith in Him. Many mature Christians see evangelism as too basic, something in which only young, exuberant Christians should engage. Nothing could be further from the truth. Evangelism is the duty of *every* believer and is an intrinsic part of the process of discipleship.

3. *Endurance and encouragement*—"I protected them and kept them safe by that name you gave me" (v. 12). Clearly, we do not have the same ability today to keep people in Jesus' name that He had as a supernatural Savior. Yet, through endurance (not giving up) and encouragement (motivating those we disciple not

to give up), we can play a key role in keeping others from becoming spiritual casualties.

4. *Edification*—"I have given them your word" (v. 14). Here the consequent growth Jesus describes progresses to such an extent that the world sees the difference in those who are disciples of Jesus Christ. Later, in verse 17, Jesus adds, "Sanctify them by the truth; your word is truth." Teaching spiritual truth to disciples is commonly considered a key role of discipleship. We cannot have discipleship without the teaching-learning process, for it is inherent to discipleship. The gospels show that Jesus invested a great deal of His time teaching His disciples. We, too, need to be involved in teaching God's truth to those we disciple.

5. *Extension*—"I have sent them into the world" (v. 18). Ideally, the person who is discipling another should be training him to disciple others. As Jesus uttered this statement, He was less than twenty-four hours away from a dramatic separation from His disciples. In less than two months He would return to heaven and no longer be with them physically. We, also, need to prepare those we disciple for the time when they will be on their own—training them not to simply survive but to disciple others.

Today we see highly visible leaders drawing disciples after themselves. In his letter to the first-century church in Corinth, Paul pointed out the same tendency (1 Corinthians 1:12). Our priority in discipleship should be making disciples of Jesus Christ, not of ourselves or of other leaders. To the extent that we make disciples who follow Christ, we succeed; to the extent that we make disciples of other men, we fail. That is the standard that guided the apostle Paul: "Follow my example, as I follow the example of Christ" (1 Corinthians 11:1).

DEALING WITH INTERRUPTIONS

Jesus was able to handle interruptions, which provides us a third principle. Most of us are interrupted on many occasions, and frequently we do not handle those interruptions well. We may become distracted and lose sight of our purpose, or we may be so purposeful as to ignore the priorities of the persons who interrupt us. Our children, for example, frequently demand attention when we are busy with things we consider to be more important. Sometimes our immediate concerns *are* more important, but not always. When we see ourselves placing a newspaper article or the nightly television news above spending time with our children, we need to rethink our priorities.

The gospel of Mark provides many examples of Jesus handling interruptions well. After He healed a man with an unclean spirit (Mark 1:21-26), Jesus was suddenly interrupted by an entire city who demanded His attention (1:33). He was then interrupted in the midst of His teaching by four men carrying a paralyzed man (2:1-5); they let the man down through a hole in the flat roof of the building in which Jesus was teaching. Later Jesus was pursued and interrupted by a large multitude (3:7-9). At one point, after being interrupted by Jairus, a synagogue ruler whose daughter was at the point of death (5:22), Christ was almost immediately interrupted again by a woman with a long-term physical problem, an issue of blood (v. 25-29). The Savior compassionately handled all of those interruptions well. Later, en route to Jerusalem to die for the sins of the world, Christ responded to the insistent interruption of Bartimaeus, a blind beggar (10:46-52).

In examining these and other instances in which the Savior was interrupted, several important principles stand out that we can apply to our own lives. First,

Christ always responded graciously. He never conveyed the attitude that people did not have a right to interrupt Him. He was available. Second, He made people a priority. For the most part, those who interrupted Christ were not prominent individuals. Yet Christ treated them as important individuals, those for whom He had time and about whom He cared. Third, although He was frequently interrupted, Christ did not allow those interruptions to deflect Him from His ultimate purpose. For example, after dealing with the woman with the issue of blood, Christ immediately went on to raise Jairus's daughter from the dead. And after restoring Bartimaeus's sight, He immediately resumed His journey to Jerusalem. Fourth, on occasion the Savior actually initiated an interruption Himself. He interrupted His healing of the paralytic to point out the hardened unbelief in the hearts of some of His observers (Mark 2:8). Later, He interrupted His teaching of the multitude to call Levi the tax collector to follow Him (2:14). Fifth, when important priorities made it necessary, Christ isolated Himself from interruptions, for example, in the period immediately before His selection of the twelve disciples (3:13).

Learning to handle interruptions in a Christlike fashion will take us a significant distance down the road of handling life's circumstances.

PUTTING COMPETITION INTO PERSPECTIVE

Jesus never felt competitive. The Pharisees led obviously competitive lives, competing among themselves and with the Sadducees. Both of those groups competed with the Herodians and sought to compete with Jesus. Even Jesus' disciples competed with each other to see who would be the greatest in His kingdom (Matthew 18:1). The mother of Zebedee's sons asked Jesus to grant them the honor of sitting on either side of Him in the kingdom (Matthew 20:20-23). But our Savior was not interested in competing with anyone. For Him life was simply a matter of fulfilling the purpose and calling for which He had come.

ENSURING OUR CONTINUED GROWTH

Even though Jesus was the perfect Son of God, the Scriptures say He grew physically (stature), intellectually (wisdom), and socially (in favor with God and man). This is an extremely important principle for living. We must experience growth as well. According to Gail Sheehy, development is needed in three basic frontiers—our work, our relationships, and ourselves.

Perhaps it is this failure of continued growth that leads to spiritual bankruptcy and what we have come to call a mid-life crisis. Psychologist Daniel Levenson, in *U.S. News and World Report*, describes a mid-life crisis as a time when people question seriously their life patterns and goals. If we have invested time toward balanced growth, we are far less likely to experience a mid-life crisis than those individuals who fail to make those investments.

One of King David's life goals was to build a grand temple for worshiping God. Although he completed preparations for the project, he was not allowed to achieve his goal. Rather the task was completed by his son Solomon.

Many years later, while Israel was in captivity, Nehemiah learned of the destitution of Jerusalem and committed himself to rebuilding the walls and city. He invested prayer, courage, careful planning, and hard work. And he completed his goal.

The apostle Paul was motivated by the goal of proclaiming the gospel of Christ where others had never preached (Romans 15:14-22). That goal drove him from one end of the Roman Empire to the other and ultimately led to his imprisonment. Paul also had the goal of achieving spiritual maturity. Paul had both goals in mind when he wrote, "I press on toward the goal to win the prize for which God has called me heavenward in Christ Jesus" (Philippians 3:14).

Our goals and objectives need to be broken down into specific subgoals. Physical goals may involve exercise. The overarching goal of being physically fit may include specific targets concerning weight control and proper eating habits. The overarching goal of maintaining thriving interpersonal relationships may include a specific checklist having to do with developing friendships and spending time with one's spouse, children, and friends. The overarching goal of developing intellectual sharpness may include the subgoal of enrolling in academic courses and embarking on a personal reading program. The goal of developing spiritual maturity may include subgoals having to do with Bible reading, Scripture memorization, or participation in an advanced Bible study course.

Our goals need to be *attainable*. Unfortunately we tend to set our standards too high, particularly if we are perfectionists. Recently, a staff counselor at our clinic lost nearly fifty pounds within a year. For most of us, such a goal probably would not be attainable. We are often faced with a dilemma: what price are we willing to pay to achieve a specific goal and will the achievement of our goal create imbalance in other areas of our lives?

Our goals need to be *measurable*. It is of little value simply to plan to "pray more." Rather, you need to have a specific measure of both quantity and time. If you plan to pray ten minutes daily throughout the next year, you will know whether or not you are fulfilling your goal.

Our goals need to be *flexible*. This is particularly true for the obsessive-compulsive. It is easy for us to become so enmeshed in a specific goal that we feel like a total failure if we fail to reach that goal. Even worse, in the process of trying to meet one goal we may neglect other basic needs or the needs of those around us. Occasional mid-course corrections have been necessary of every manned venture into space; such should be incorporated into our lives as well.

We need to remember that growth is *not instant*. A few years ago one of the authors and his family moved into a house in a suburban community north of Dallas. In that subdivision houses were stacked row upon row. Each house had two "instant trees" planted in the front yard. Within the first three months his instant trees had to be replaced twice. However, in the backyard was a massive pecan tree that obviously had been around long before the subdivision. Many years before, a pecan had fallen to the ground and taken root, and from it sprouted a small, fragile tree that grew and withstood the elements. It drew nutrients from the soil, carbon dioxide from the air, and energy from the sunshine. Today it furnishes shelter, shade, beauty, and even the makings of an occasional pecan pie—all because it was allowed time to grow.

The author of Hebrews 5 expresses sorrow over the lack of growth in those to whom he is writing. Second Peter 3:18 exhorts us to "grow in the grace and knowledge of our Lord and Savior Jesus Christ." To grow in grace is the continuous expansion of the enablement He gives us through His indwelling Spirit. To grow in knowledge is the continued development of both the understanding and application of the truth of His Word. Both are essential to spiritual progress.

OUR IMMEDIATE PRIORITIES

What are some priorities of growth that we need to recognize as immediate needs?

CHARACTER DEVELOPMENT

Many people today emphasize only excellence in what they do. Scripture focuses more on character—what we *are*—for that is where God's concern lies. Over an extended period of time former Dallas Cowboys head coach Tom Landry has exhibited excellence of character. For most of that time his Dallas Cowboys succeeded, but there were times they did not. In an article in *Sports Illustrated*, one of Landry's coaching adversaries said, "All I can say is if Tom Landry is a Christian, then the Lord help the Lions." It was evident that to the person who uttered that statement, Tom Landry was a man who exhibited excellence, not simply in achievement but also in character.

OUR STEWARDSHIP OF TIME

In the New Testament we find two references to time using the Greek word *kairos* (Ephesians 5:16; Colossians 4:5, KJV). In both of those passages the apostle Paul exhorts us to "redeem the time." The idea seems to be that we should utilize our opportunities. Jesus did that, even in the process of handling interruptions. Those verses do not simply tell us to do more, now and faster. In each reference the context has to do with dealing with unbelievers, who live under the influence of a pagan world. The word translated "time" is the same term translated "season" in Paul's exhortation to Timothy to be "instant" in season and out of season (2 Timothy 4:2, KJV). To be "instant" means to be prepared. The idea of redeeming the time, a phrase that literally means "to buy back," is the idea of freeing our time. It is not simply packing life with more activity, even in ministry. Rather, it involves developing balance in our lives so that we can utilize opportunities that come our way.

There is so much we want to do, so much that needs to be done, and so much that society insists we must do. As one O-C housewife put it, "We must not have ring around the collar. We must have floors that gleam until we can see our faces in them. We must have furniture that reflects an arranged bouquet in living color. We must be gourmet cooks, publicly aware, socially active, and academically and intellectually current."

Our obsessive minds can easily operate on a strictly scheduled basis, but we need to allow ourselves to incorporate opportunity. In *How to Have All the Time You Need Every Day*, Pat King says of interruptions, "When we drop our list and change our plans for His work . . . He more than makes up for the time given." She goes on to observe that from her experience almost miraculously everything on her list winds up being accomplished anyway [(Wheaton, Ill.: Tyndale, 1980] p. 49).

Jesus invested significant time in solitude. On one of the busiest days in His life, He dealt with the multitudes, taught with authority, cast out demons, and faced an entire village of people with incredible needs (Mark 1:32-33). The following morning the Savior made it a priority to arise before daylight and depart to a solitary place to pray. He did not neglect His mission in life (v. 38). But He did make prayer—time alone with His Father—a priority. Jesus spells out what is a genuinely important priority: "Seek first his kingdom and his righteousness, and all these things will be given to you as well" (Matthew 6:33).

THE ETERNAL PERSPECTIVE

To move beyond burnout an individual must develop the ability to live life in light of eternity rather than within the constraints of time. No one has captured that concept quite as well as Moses. Moses' life was marked by many significant events. He was born with great disadvantages but under supernatural circumstances; he was raised with a "silver spoon" in his mouth. But he chose to suffer affliction with the people of God rather than to enjoy the pleasures of sin for a short time (Hebrews 11:25).

Following an easy life in Egypt as the son of Pharaoh's daughter, Moses spent forty years caring for a small herd of sheep on the backside of the desert. Yet God called him from tending sheep to lead a flock of more than two million Israelites from Egypt to the land He had promised them.

Moses' final thoughts summarizing his life are found in Psalm 90. Here he makes two significant observations. First, *God is eternal, though man is finite.* For every generation, God has served as the *ma'on,* the "refuge" or "dwelling place." Every human being is a transient, a pilgrim; yet God predates the mountains and the inhabited world. He is the God who is "from everlasting to everlasting" (v. 2). Just as the Israelites were pilgrims, so we who live in the closing decade of the twentieth century will only be here for a short time.

Second, Moses observes that *because man is sinful, God is a God of wrath.* Utilizing vivid language to describe man's finiteness, Moses further notes that the all-knowing God is fully aware of our perverseness and even knows the secret imperfections that are part of the "tale" of our lives. It is the result of sin that we become slaves to the clock and the calendar. Whether we live seven years or seventy, ultimately we will all experience death (v. 10).

Moses articulated a principle that we need to remember when we face discouraging circumstances: "Teach us to number our days aright, that we may gain a heart of wisdom" (v. 12). When Moses wrote those words, the number of his days had grown exceedingly short. He knew his time was at hand. In the time he had left he wanted to make the most of each day of life.

As we follow the example for living Jesus provided us, we can better order our priorities and align our lives to those things that matter most. Jesus' life exhibited an eternal quality because He lived with eternal values in view. As we set our life's goals, we need to adopt His perspective and thereby find skill in handling the unpredictable circumstances of life.

14
BEYOND DEATH—
THE LAST ENEMY

After years of successfully managing the New York Yankees, Dick Howser reached the pinnacle of his managerial career in 1985 when he led the Kansas City Royals to a dramatic seventh-game World Series victory over the St. Louis Cardinals. A man of small stature yet boundless energy, Howser had seemingly reached the top.

The following year he led the American League All Stars to a 3 to 2 victory over the National League squad. Although no one knew it at the time, that was to be Dick Howser's last appearance as a major league manager. Shortly afterward he complained of serious pain and was hospitalized. Surgery revealed a malignant brain tumor. Although Howser attempted a comeback, he eventually announced his resignation just before the start of the 1987 season.

Less than eleven months after reaching the pinnacle of his career, Dick Howser died on June 17, 1987.

During the long months of struggling against his debilitating illness, he did not allow the prospect of death to defeat him. The day after Howser's death, *Kansas City Star* sports writer Gib Twyman described him as a man who focused "on the positive, the upbeat, a high note as high as heaven itself." Twyman quoted Howser as saying, "God has already told me I'm going to heaven. I know I'm going to be happy." In fact, three weeks before he died, Howser turned to his best friend, Trevor Grubbs, and said, "Jesus wants me to come home. It would be fine if He took me today."

NUMBERING OUR DAYS

What gave Dick Howser victory over death? He had learned to number his days and apply his heart to wisdom. All of us will eventually face death. If we, like Dick Howser, are to have victory over death, we also must learn to number our days and apply our hearts to wisdom. Why is it important to "number our days"? Several reasons are given in Psalm 90. Moses prays in verse 14, "Satisfy us in the morning with your unfailing love, that we may sing for joy and be glad all our days." We need to number our days, to be satisfied with God's unfailing loyal love, so that our joy in life each day will be the more complete. When we "number our days" we will also be able to balance the sorrow of affliction with gladness from God. Moses experienced many difficult times in his life, but God balanced those difficulties with blessings. As Christians we can expect lasting, genuine gladness in our relationship with Him.

Finally, numbering our days will give us a legacy that outlives this present life. Our lives, properly invested, can produce lasting fruitfulness.

During the summer of 1987 a number of men met with Dr. James Dobson and other members of Focus on the Family at El Canyon Ranch in Montana for a week-long retreat of fellowship and mutual encouragement. After the retreat, four men from Dallas, Texas, boarded a twin-engine Cessna 421 to return home. They never made it.

Three days later rescue workers found the bodies in the wrecked aircraft in a treeless area of the Shoshone National Forest fifteen miles west of Kote, Wyoming. The impact of the deaths of those men jolted the Dallas-Fort Worth area. Local media provided extensive coverage. Thousands gathered to pay tribute at a joint memorial service at which Dr. Dobson gave an eternal perspective:

> Would you not have enjoyed being there when these men made the transition to the other side? The Lord greeted them and wrapped His arms around them. Creath was laughing. I know he was. And Hugo was talking in that Texas accent that most of us couldn't understand very well. Knowing them as I did, I can hear them saying, "But Lord, what about our families?" And I know the Lord gave them the assurance that He is going to be with you all —and He will. . . . Your fathers are alive, and we will see them again some day. [*Focus on the Family,* September 1987]

They were men whose lives had made incredible impacts; yet their deaths made equally great impacts.

So it was in 1956 when Jim Elliot and four other men were martyred by Auca Indians in South America. Willing to invest their lives in service far from home, they were ultimately called, as the apostle Paul expressed it, to pour out their lives as sacrifice (Philippians 2:17). Some time before his death Jim Elliot had written his wife-to-be, Elisabeth, of his philosophy of life: "Wherever you are, be all there. Live to the hilt each day what you believe to be the will of God." That is how Jim Elliot and his colleagues lived, and that is how they died. Through the impact of their deaths, literally hundreds of young men and women responded to the call to serve Jesus Christ in foreign missions.

Like Jim Elliot and the other martyred men, we must live with eternity in view. Why? Because we never know when we will pass from this life into eternity.

ACCOMPLISHING GOD'S PURPOSES

Moses taught also that it is important to build meaning and beauty into the daily routine of life and to temper it with a lasting work consistent with the purpose of God. Moses left a legacy. The same perspective motivated a brilliant Benjaminite named Saul of Tarsus who became the apostle Paul of the New Testament, a man whose life ministry was wrapped up in the goal of serving Jesus Christ and telling others about Him.

In 2 Corinthians Paul captures the essence of his perspective on ministry. His observations were set in the context of his statement in 1 Corinthians 4:11 that we are "homeless," or as the King James Version puts it, we "have no certain dwelling-place." Paul, like Moses, considered himself a pilgrim, and he devoted his life to serving the Savior who had called him.

Second Corinthians 4:7-12 provides Paul's explanation for and defense of his ministry. It is an insightful passage that captures lessons about God's purposes in our lives. After describing the glory of the ministry to which he was called, Paul gave a threefold perspective as to why his life was meaningful.

PAUL DEPENDED ON GOD'S STRENGTH

Looking at his circumstances, Paul noted that ministry or service for God, though glorious, is accomplished in human bodies, which are essentially "jars of clay." Thus, instead of rejoicing in our abilities, we need to recognize "the excellence of the power [to] be of God and not of us" (v. 7, NKJV*).

* *New King James Version.*

Later, in the same book, Paul refers to a thorn in his flesh, a physical adversity about which he prayed three times for relief. He finally came to recognize the problem as God's way of telling him, "My grace is sufficient for you, for My strength is made perfect in weakness" (2 Corinthians 12:9, NKJV).

Furthermore, although Paul was surrounded by adversity he looked beyond the circumstances of this life. He had been troubled on every side—perplexed, persecuted, and cast down—yet he never entertained the idea of giving up. He felt pressured but not abandoned. He was down but never rendered inoperative. We find the reason in 2 Corinthians 4:10-11: Paul considered himself to have been given all of God's life, power, and resources to cope with his present distress. Ultimately, God's purpose was to use both good and bad circumstances to demonstrate the life of Jesus in Paul's mortal flesh (v. 11).

PAUL FOCUSED ON GOD'S PROVISION

Paul focused on God's provision. In 2 Corinthians 4:12-13 he speaks of faith, using a quote from Psalm 116:10. We have the same spirit of faith manifested by the psalmist who said, "I believed; therefore I said." We are to trust God today, one day at a time.

Paul directs us also to focus on hope. That is implied in verses 14-15. That hope is based specifically on the resurrection of the Savior. Paul points out in 1 Corinthians 15:23 that Jesus is the "firstfruits," which gives us not only the hope of resurrection beyond death, but also the anticipation of being presented together with other believers in the presence of God. Thus, not only can I trust God for today; I can trust Him for tomorrow as well.

PAUL HAD PERSPECTIVE ON GOD'S PURPOSE

Moving beyond faith and hope, Paul concludes his perspective on God's purpose in verses 16-18. Here we find three timely exhortations to help the obsessive-compulsive person live in light of eternity.

1. *Fight to the finish.* We must never give up. Paul says, "We do not lose heart. Though outwardly we are wasting away, yet inwardly we are being renewed day by day" (2 Corinthians 4:16). Note the emphasis on living life one day at a time. Every day brings with it another opportunity not to give up and to live life joyfully one day at a time. In the book of Acts we see Paul's resolve not to allow circumstances to shake him: "None of these things move me" (Acts 20:24*a*, KJV).

Such perspective is consistent with Jesus' purpose for His disciples: "that they should always pray and not give up" (Luke 18:1). During the darkest days of World War II, Sir Winston Churchill gave his countrymen a brief but poignant message: "We must never, never, never, never quit."

2. *Weigh your life.* We must evaluate the present in light of eternity. We often hear the phrases "weigh the difference" or "weigh the options." Paul encourages us to weigh the afflictions of life against the glory of eternity. Paul measured the intensity of suffering against the ultimate glory and the length of present suffering against the duration of eternity.

As a result he was able to look at his personal sufferings as "light" and "momentary" (cf. 2 Corinthians 11). For Paul, comparing the present with eternity was like comparing a pocketful of copper pennies with a large trunk of thousand-dollar bills. Centuries before Paul, the Hebrew prophet Jeremiah wrote about the reality of daily living, sharing words that sustained him through the darkest hours of Israel's history: "Yet this I call to mind and therefore I have hope: Because of the Lord's great love we are not consumed, for his compassions never fail. They are new every morning; great is your faithfulness" (Lamentations 3:21-23).

3. *Keep an eye on eternity.* We must look beyond the temporal to the eternal. The word Paul uses for "look" (2 Corinthians 4:18) is not the word generally used. Instead he uses the Greek word *scopos*, from which we derive the English word "scope," as in a telescope or the scope of a rifle. Paul uses this term to describe a sharply focused look that does not consider anything outside that focus. Picture a man on a bluff in Colorado focusing his rifle on a large bull elk several hundred yards down a slope. Other things are happening around the man—birds are chattering, wildlife is moving, sunlight is filtering through the trees. But the hunter is not deterred by those potential distractions. His eye, his trigger finger, his shoulder, and his very being concentrate only on the hunted game he observes through his scope.

In the same way Paul tells us we are to focus beyond our temporal circumstances onto that which is eternal. That is precisely what the author of Hebrews had in mind when he said, "Let us run with perseverance the race marked out for us. Let us fix our eyes on Jesus, the author and perfecter of our faith" (12:1b-2). Peter provided us with a vivid illustration of this truth when he requested of the Lord that he might walk on water (Matthew 14:28-29). Most of us long ago learned that walking on water isn't something the average person can do, even on a perfectly calm body of water. Yet, in the midst of a violent storm Peter said, "Lord, if it's you . . . tell me to come to you on the water" (v. 28). As long as Peter kept his eyes on the Lord, he was able to step across the waves as though they were pavement. But when he took his eyes off the Savior and noticed, as the King James Version puts it, that "the wind was boisterous," Peter began to sink.

The obvious lesson for us is that maintaining perspective involves keeping our eyes on the Savior. That is how Moses kept going: "He persevered because he saw him who is invisible" (Hebrews 11:27). That is how Paul endured the adversities he faced in life. And that is the perspective that can pull us through life's trials.

One test of how we handle adversity is what we do when we lose possessions. With many of us obsessive-compulsives, maintaining hold of possessions is an important factor in life. That is because we often have the wrong perspective on success. We frequently view success as determined by what car we drive or how we look. Many of us have a dress-for-success mentality. Webster defines success as "the attainment of wealth, favor, or eminence." Michael Corta, in his book *Power! How to Get It, How to Use It,* says, "All life is a game of power. The object of the game is simple enough—to know what you want and get it."

Our society places a strong emphasis on "getting." We become consumers geared toward the lust of the flesh, often overeating and harming the temple of the Holy Spirit. We also have become caught up in the lust of the eyes, going on shopping sprees, waving our plastic credit cards, grabbing far more than we ever need. We become caught up in the pride of life, proud of our designer clothes, our carefully manicured hands, and our landscaped lawns. Yet, according to 1 John 2, all those things are temporal.

Certainly it is appropriate for us to enjoy our possessions. First Timothy 6:17 tells us that we can enjoy the world without loving it. We are to be content to have our basic life needs met (v. 8), but at the same time we must avoid the temptation and harmful consequences of the overwhelming desire to be rich (v. 9). We are to flee from coveting material possessions but should pursue virtuous character (v. 11). Though the world has a "go for it" mentality regarding possessions, our focus should be on "the eternal life to which [we] were called" (v. 12).

An obsession for acquiring money can be a major problem for many obsessive-compulsives, who have a strong need for security and tend to be materialistic. Sadly, rather than bringing security, the love of money is likely instead to lead to burnout. The Bible teaches that we are not to trust in material possessions. Rather, we are to trust in the living God and be thankful for His provisions as we strive to live godly lives in light of eternity. God requires that we be good stewards of our resources. Moving beyond burnout involves having the right perspective on financial matters.

Stanley Marcus of Neiman-Marcus, in a *Dallas Morning News* column titled "Burnout: A Passing of the Buck," wrote, "Today psychological wiring on fire is everywhere." Marcus relates burnout to a "declaration of bankruptcy—something necessary but often irresponsible and undignified." He stated that the word *burnout* gained increased use in Texas during the current oil-induced recession of the late 1980s. According to Marcus, blaming burnout allows us to pass the buck to other people and circumstances rather than forcing us to learn to overcome life's obstacles. In short, Marcus says, we need to exercise responsibility before burnout occurs.

THE BOTTOM LINE

The bottom line in facing adversity is to understand that God has a gracious purpose for allowing us to experience suffering. Job saw that purpose and drew three important observations from his experience (Job 23:10).

1. *God knows what is happening to me.* I am not isolated from God. "He knows the way that I take" (v. 10). For many years the football field at the University of Alabama was dominated by a twenty-foot tower. Brian Newman, a therapist at our clinic and an Alabama alumnus, remembers that tower as the place where legendary coach Paul "Bear" Bryant spent the hours of football practice. While Bryant's assistants worked with the offense, defense, and special teams, Coach Bryant carefully observed from his tower. He always knew what was happening; he knew when the players were doing well and when they were not.

In similar fashion, God in heaven sees and knows every facet of our every experience. We can take comfort in the fact that nothing escapes His omniscient scrutiny.

2. *God uses circumstances to discipline us.* He is not an angry, punitive Father in heaven trying to bring us harm. But He may put us to the test. Job said of God, "He has tested me" (v. 10b). One of the authors played football in high school. His first two weeks of summer practice under the hot sun were an unforgiving introduction to the world of athletic conditioning. One session of leg lifts seemed especially brutal. The coach quietly encouraged the players, "Think of the good things in life." To which one of the players replied, "There aren't any." The coach said, "Sure there are. In a couple of weeks you'll be able to do this with no pain." Sure enough, two weeks later the coach's prediction proved to be correct.

3. *God uses a process to refine us and reflect His glory.* That is the ultimate purpose for this life. Job was reminded that he would "come forth as gold" (v. 10*c*). Some suffering is unnecessary. We do not need to fall into the trap of becoming victims. And there is suffering we bring upon ourselves as the consequences of our sins (1 Peter 4).

At other times adversity simply happens. And when it does, we need to have the appropriate attitude. Thankfulness should be a significant portion of that attitude. In Psalm 103 the psalmist reminds us to remember all of God's benefits. Throughout the book of Deuteronomy we find the words "remember" and "forget."

Thankfulness is therapeutic. Many times the authors of this book have recommended that individuals who feel overwhelmed by their problems make a list of the positive things for which they are thankful. We have also recommended that they maintain a "blessing" journal as a long-term project and that they regularly review the benefits catalogued in that journal.

We need to encourage and motivate thankfulness in others. Three references in the book of Proverbs indicate that others benefit when we adopt a positive, optimistic outlook on life (15:13, 15; 17:22). Our disposition affects both our own well-being and the well-being of those around us.

Another significant element of attitude is a positive spirit. Note that in Proverbs a "merry heart" is not the mirth of modern comedians or fools. The idea of *merry* means "joyful" or "good" in the sense of "pleasant" or "happy." The heart is one of the most important concepts in the Old Testament. This component of our personality can have a strong influence, for the condition of the heart leaves its stamp on the appearance and the activity of an individual.

A merry heart produces a pleasant countenance (Proverbs 15:13). This pleasant countenance in turn produces a festive outlook on life (v. 15). It is interesting to note that the contrast in this verse is not between the poor and the rich, but rather between the poor and the poor. A person may spend each evening eating at upscale restaurants, yet feel miserable. Another person, however, may be able to look at a trip to McDonald's as the ultimate eating experience.

In addition, a merry heart can actually produce good health (17:22). Psychiatric research has noted that more than 50 percent of all hospital beds have a significant emotional component in the diagnosis of the patients who occupy them. Why? Because the emotional affects the physical, and the spiritual can affect both. Yet so often we allow the circumstances of life to crush our spirits. It is interesting that in James 5 the concepts of a merry heart and good health both appear within the context of sickness. "Is anyone happy? Let him sing songs of praise. Is any one of you sick? He should call the elders of the church to pray over him and anoint him with oil in the name of the Lord" (vv. 13b-14). Developing a merry heart and encouraging it in others can lead to good health.

It is also important, especially for Type A's and perfectionists, to balance the long and short views of circumstances. One of the contrasts we have examined is between the quantity-oriented Type A and the quality-oriented perfectionist. The Type A often tends to jump into too many tasks and develop that as a style of relating. Often he does not think of the long-term consequences of that decision.

Mike, a typical obsessive-compulsive businessman, was offered a new position with his company, plus a substantial increase in pay. Without consulting anyone for advice or input—or even discussing the matter with his wife or family—Mike made his decision. Soon the moving van arrived and Mike's family and belongings were transported to a new home thousands of miles away.

Sadly, however, Mike hadn't considered the long-term consequences of his decision. His wife became depressed because she lacked friends. The children began acting out in school because of the trauma of being uprooted. Mike soon ran into conflicts in his new job responsibilities. The result was devastating. Mike needed to develop a long view to better visualize the long-term consequences of his decision, either through counseling or simply by working on it himself.

On the other hand, the perfectionistic obsessive-compulsive needs to develop the short view. These people will often refuse to make a short-term decision or to take action immediately because they are so fearful of being overwhelmed by the long-term consequences of present actions.

Janice had just graduated from college with a degree in teaching, and she had the opportunity to become a skilled teacher. She was given three or four opportunities, but she wound up letting deadlines pass on all of them, instead taking a job in a grocery store. Janice was afraid that whatever decision she made would unalterably commit her to that particular job, with its strengths and weaknesses.

The O-C somehow needs to achieve balance, and, as in these examples, balance can be observed in attitude. Type A tends to have a "go for it" mentality and sometimes tends to give up and become discouraged. The perfectionist will tend to fear "going for it" but will "keep on keeping on." There is a time to go for it, and there is a time to keep on keeping on. Both the fearful perfectionist and the gung-ho Type A compulsives need to recognize that they can learn from each other.

OVERCOMING THE LAST ENEMY

In our fast-paced society, an increasing number of people are being devastated by burnout. For some people, as Stanley Marcus pointed out, blaming burnout is a cop-out. Yet simply avoiding burnout is not enough. Life should not consist of mere existence or mediocrity. The scriptural standard is that we should be abounding. In 1 Corinthians 15:58 we read, "Therefore, my beloved brethren, be steadfast, immovable, always abounding in the work of the Lord, knowing that your labor is not in vain in the Lord" (NKJV). That exhortation from the apostle Paul is sometimes viewed as being for someone who works so hard that he just burns out. But that is not what the verse is saying. Nor is it describing "the abundant life" as some kind of nebulous state of being for people whose heads are in the clouds spiritually. Rather, Paul was writing to a group of very down-to-earth people who struggled with conflicts, personal holiness, proper exercise of spiritual gifts, and doctrinal truths. In other words, he was writing to real people.

The church at Corinth was a problem church. Yet Paul concluded his letter to the Corinthians with a chapter detailing the difference the resurrection of Jesus Christ made—the impact of the transforming power of the gospel. He described how the gospel and the resurrection pointed ahead to the ultimate return of Jesus Christ and how the Savior would destroy death, the last enemy. Then he gave that ultimate perspective by which to live in the meantime.

How are we to live? Paul told the Corinthians, whom he loved, three things he wanted them to be: steadfast, immovable, and abounding.

BE STEADFAST

The primary connotation of the word *steadfast* (Greek, *hedraios*) is regarding something seated or set in place. It is used in Colossians 1:2 of one who is doctrinally settled, grounded in the faith with a firm foundation. The steadfast individual has doctrinal, moral, and spiritual moorings and is solidly connected to God and His Word.

The ups and downs of the world often strike like waves rocking a boat. If the boat is firmly secured, even a storm cannot destroy it. Some time ago a storm struck a sheltered Caribbean bay in which a number of fishing boats had sought shelter. The clouds lowered, the winds kicked up, and the force of the waves was quite ferocious. However, the fishing boats were solidly tied with heavy rope to the dock; pilings had been driven deep into the ground, and the boats were firmly connected so that no action of the wind or waves could break the boats from their moorings.

BE IMMOVABLE

The next word takes our perspective a step further. "Immovable" (Greek, *ametakinetos*) carries the idea of "being firm" and is used only here in the New Testament. However, in Colossians 1:23, the positive form of the word is used along with the same term for "steadfast" to mean not moved away from the hope of the gospel. A related word is translated "the water is stirred" (John 5:7). This word has the idea of something being displaced or moved from one place to another. It was used in the Old Testament to prohibit transferring a landmark from one place to another (Deuteronomy 19:14, Septuagint). It was also used to mean "put . . . to flight" (Deuteronomy 32:30; Isaiah 22:3, Septuagint). When boats are not anchored and steadfast they can be moved from one place to another. So it is with people.

BE ABOUNDING

The prerequisite to abounding is to be steadfast and unmovable. However, it is not enough just to be firmly fixed in one place. God's goal for believers is that we may be always abounding. The implication of the term "always" seems to be "on every occasion." Paul brought this out several times in his writings to the Thessalonians:

"Be joyful *always*" (1 Thessalonians 5:16, emphasis added).

Paul gave thanks for them *always* (1 Thessalonians 1:2; 2 Thessalonians 1:3; emphasis added).

He *always* prayed for them (2 Thessalonians 1:11, emphasis added).

The significant term for moving beyond burnout is "abounding" (Greek, *perisseuo*). It was a common term in the vernacular of Paul's day. It meant something that was present in overabundance. Paul was fond of this term. At times he intensified it to "superabounding" as in Romans 5:20, 2 Corinthians 7:4, and Ephesians 3:20. In fact, an examination of Paul's writings reveals areas in which we are to be abounding.

- We are to abound in hope (Romans 15:13).
- We are to abound in unconditional love for others (1 Thessalonians 4:10). Yet this love is to abound within the parameters of knowledge and discernment (Philippians 1:9).

- We are to abound in thanksgiving (Colossians 2:7).
- We are to abound in the grace of giving, or generosity (2 Corinthians 8:7).

The Corinthians abounded in faith, in utterance, in knowledge, in diligence, and in love. Likewise, our lives are to be characterized by abundant growth and an abounding walk that continues to please God in increasing measure (1 Thessalonians 4:1).

In addition, we are to abound in the work of the Lord. Being thankful for what God has given us helps us to do that. First Thessalonians 5:18 talks about always giving thanks. Psalm 103:2 reads, "Praise the Lord, O my soul, and forget not all his benefits." Not only do we need to express thankfulness to God, but we must *maintain* this attitude as well. Our lists should include thanks for hope, the work of the Lord, unconditional love, generosity, and our walk.

For the individual who experiences burnout, all of life is fruitless and pointless. Labor is hard and frustrating. Solomon, the author of Ecclesiastes, poured himself into many areas of endeavor, but found each to be futile. "Yet when I surveyed all that my hands had done and what I had toiled to achieve, everything was meaningless, a chasing after the wind; nothing was gained under the sun" (Ecclesiastes 2:11). Yet the individual who has moved beyond burnout will acknowledge that a great deal of life involves work.

In fact, life actually is a sort of hard labor, the kind of toil that results in weariness. Yet it is labor with a purpose, not labor in vain. The phrase "in vain" is like an empty jar. Picture an individual who has worked very hard in a garden under the baking sun and is desperately thirsty. He returns to his house, opens the refrigerator door, and sees what appears to be a jar filled with water. He reaches for the jar and finds it is empty.

In Christ, life is neither empty nor in vain; it is meaningful and refreshing—even when circumstances seem exceedingly hard. Paul emphatically declares that the individual who is steadfast, immovable, and abounding will be firmly fixed, rooted, and planted in life.

FINISHING THE RACE

In light of the victory we have over death through Jesus Christ, we need to remain firmly fixed in our faith. Growing toward maturity requires that we do not quit. Rather, we need consistently to pursue excellence in our service for Jesus Christ and our relationship with Him, knowing that there is both present and eternal benefit, even though at times life may be hard. To avoid burnout it is imperative that we live one day at a time. That means we cannot approach life as a fifty-yard dash. Instead, we must view life as a ten-kilometer race, which we have our entire lives to run.

None of us knows how many days we will be given in this life. We are to live as though death could come any day while we focus on the long haul. That way we will grow old God's way—better, not bitter. Paul said we are to live life so as to "finish [our] course with joy" (Acts 20:24, KJV). When we have achieved our goal—moving beyond burnout toward healthy, abundant living—we will be able to say with the apostle Paul, "I have fought the good fight, I have finished the race" (2 Timothy 4:7). We can do that by being committed to a wholehearted love for God, an unconditional love for people, and a loose grip on our possessions.

As we seek to align our daily priorities and our life goals with God's eternal values, we will become more conditioned and better prepared for eternity. Death will lose its sting. Like Dick Howser, we can look ahead with anticipation to the day Jesus takes us home, yet continue to live life abundantly, one day at a time, with joy.

GLOSSARY

ACTING-OUT

This term describes how some individuals use action as a response to unconscious conflicts. Often instead of responding to insight, a person relieves the repressed emotions by undertaking some kind of behavior, which is usually aggressive, antisocial, or otherwise inappropriate. For example, a young lady who has repressed anger toward her father may act out that anger by becoming sexually promiscuous; or a man with unconscious hostility toward his father may become physically aggressive toward his boss.

BURNOUT

A cluster of symptoms, including emotional exhaustion, depersonalization, or a desire to withdraw from people, and reduced accomplishment (working harder and harder while accomplishing less and less). Although current stresses contribute to burnout, other significant factors include obsessive-compulsive or perfectionistic personality traits and bitterness or unresolved anger.

COMPULSION

A seemingly irresistible urge to carry out an action or ritual series of actions. Closely related to obsession, the anxiety that leads to the compulsion stems from ideas or obsessions that may be unacceptable to the individual but nonetheless force their way into conscious awareness. The compulsion displaces attention from the obsessions, thus relieving anxiety. Common compulsions include checking and rechecking locks, or repeated handwashing.

CONFLICT

The presence of divergent goals or aims within an individual, between two individuals, or within a group. Internal conflict may involve such competing feelings as the need for autonomy versus the need to be dependent on a partner, or a highly positive, idealistic view of self conflicting with a despising attitude toward self. One kind of conflict is termed approach-approach, when a person is attracted toward two desirable but mutually-exclusive goals. Also common is approach-avoidance conflict, where a strong attraction (purchasing a beautiful new home) may be balanced by a strong aversion (increased indebtedness). Conflict between individuals is frequently intensified when one individual wishes to cooperate while the other views the situation as competitive. The ability to function is usually improved as conflict is reduced.

CYCLOTHYMIC

The cyclothymic personality tends to experience intense ups and downs. Such individuals may feel highly elated for a period of time, then experience a period of deep depression. When high, a cyclothymic person is generally cheerful, humorous, and outgoing, though sometimes anger or sarcasm surface. In the depressed stage the same individual may appear sad, hopeless, helpless, despondent, or unable to perform.

Periods of highs and lows may fluctuate rapidly, or they may persist over an extended period of time. Some individuals may spend the majority of their time in a depressed state, whereas others may tend to remain in the energetic high. Some individuals exhibit high energy and high achievement most of their lives and may be referred to as having "hypomanic" personalities.

HYPER-CALVINISTIC

This term is frequently used in theological circles to describe individuals who take the teachings of John Calvin to an extreme, particularly their emphasis on the sovereign control of God over the universe. Such individuals see little use in exercising the human will, praying, or encouraging others to make decisions since, "after all, God controls everything." Usually strong psychological dependency underlies this theological perspective.

HYSTERIC OR HISTRIONIC

A cluster of personality traits including a tendency toward immaturity, feelings that are intensely expressed but shallow, difficulty with interpersonal relationships, and an inclination toward the overdramatic. The Diagnostic Manual DSM III-R uses the term *histrionic*, which is derived from the Latin term for actor, *histrio*. Individuals with such personality traits may be charming and socially active, yet they also have difficulty with deep or intimate relationships. They may be demanding and manipulative. Frequently internal sexual conflict, such as unresolved anger with the parent of the opposite sex, may be present. The terms *hysteric* and *histrionic* are often used interchangeably.

OBSESSION

A persistently recurring thought or feeling, usually involuntary and inconsistent with the individual's conscious character. Obsessions usually originate in conscious attempts to deny certain unconscious desires or anxieties. Often an obsession will lead to a consuming preoccupation with philosophical or theological questions such as whether the individual has committed the unpardonable sin. Obsessions generally lead to compulsions.

OBSESSIVE-COMPULSIVE

Individuals with this particular cluster of personality traits tend to be conscientious, self-sacrificing, organized, perfectionistic, and devout. Such individuals are driven by repetitive persistent ideas or obsessions that intrude into conscious thought. Frequently their content is the opposite of what the individual would think voluntarily. Such obsessions lead to compulsions, or repetitive behaviors that are often performed ritualistically.

Obsessive-compulsive personality types commonly experience a wide range of difficulties, including perfectionism, Type A behavior, burnout, clinical depression, anxiety attacks or phobias, and even suicidal thinking. Drinking, gambling, sexual disorders or overeating are often classed as obsessive-compulsive behaviors. Obsessive-compulsive tendencies can be present in degrees ranging from mild to such severity that the life of the individual is disrupted. Gaining and acting on insight into the origin of the obsessions and compulsions can help the obsessive-compulsive personality strengthen his strengths while working on his weaknesses.

Those with intense obsessive-compulsive traits may gain help through appropriate psychiatric medications, since obsessions and compulsions are currently seen as an expression of the brain's tendency to form repetitive or circular response patterns when certain alarm responses are inadequately dampened. Medication can frequently eliminate these "short circuits," bringing important relief.

PARANOID

Individuals with paranoid personality traits tend to be suspicious, argumentative, hypersensitive, and jealous. Frequently they blame others for shortcomings and conflicts. Often the paranoid person is unreasonably jealous and may have delusions of persecution or of grandeur. Some individuals with a paranoid disorder may have an intense, unshakable system of grandiose or persecutory delusions in one area, yet may be remarkably logical and functional in other areas. Usually the paranoid individual feels an intense lack of self-worth, which has grown out of long-term stress, abuse, or rejection. An important aspect of the paranoid personality is inability or difficulty with personal trust.

PASSIVE-AGGRESSIVE PERSONALITY

Individuals with this cluster of personality traits handle underlying emotions such as anger with passive action, which tends to disrupt both work and relationships. A typical passive-aggressive individual tends to procrastinate, obstruct, forget, and dawdle, while denying that such behavior is in any way intentionally oppositional. Often this individual may be negative, sullen, pessimistic, disinterested, or stubborn. While obstructing those around them, such individuals often seem unaware of the effects of their behavior. Passive-aggressive personality traits are often a hostile response to prolonged or intense dependency. In some cases the strong dependency needs of the passive-aggressive personality may leave such individuals susceptible to substance abuse.

PERFECTIONIST

This individual frequently has a large number of obsessive-compulsive personality traits that remind him: (1) of the concept of the ideal or perfect and (2) that he, himself, utterly fails to measure up to perfection. Often we see in perfectionists a combination of obsessive-compulsive and passive-aggressive personality traits, as seen in the example of the college student who discards a carefully researched and laboriously typed paper because of one small typographical error near the end of the document. Christian perfectionists frequently misunderstand or misinterpret the concept of perfection. In our Bibles such Greek words as *teleos* or *artios* are translated "perfect," but they actually refer to maturity or growth. For the believer, perfectionism can be dealt with by delving into its hidden roots, by restructuring of ideals so that they correspond more closely with reality, by persistence in spiritual and emotional growth, and by placing our expectations on Christ rather than on ourselves or others. Although those who are Christians will ultimately become perfect in Christ, perfection will never occur in present human experience.

PERSONALITY TRAITS

The term "personality" is one of the more abstract concepts in the English language. It originates from the classical Latin term *persona*, which described the mask an actor wore in a play. *Personality traits refer to specific characteristics in an individual which, when taken together, give substance to the personality and allow one to categorize generally the individual with others who have similar characteristics.* Personality traits are the concrete differences that make individuals unique but that also mark individuals as similar.

Personality reflects the image of God, whereas individual traits may represent strengths to be strengthened or weaknesses to be worked on.

SCHIZOPHRENIA

A clinical disorder marked by a thorough disturbance of feeling, mood, and thought involving psychotic breaks with reality. Classical symptoms have been described as involving "4 A's": flat or inappropriate facial affect, loose associations, autism, and ambivalent features. Other symptoms may include delusions—beliefs held to be true in the face of solid evidence to the contrary—and hallucinations—hearing, seeing, or feeling things that are not present.

Schizophrenia generally occurs in about 8 to 10 of every 1,000 people. Treatment involves medication, psychotherapy, community support, and stress management, which tends to exacerbate schizophrenic breaks.

SELF-TALK

The internal process by which we give ourselves feedback and messages on an ongoing basis. Self-talk can be either negative or positive, accurate or inaccurate. Many individuals become conditioned to give themselves inaccurate, negative, and debilitating messages that are destructive in nature. Such negative self-talk often incorporates such distorted thinking as:

> Magnification: "This is a terrible, horrible disaster!"
>
> Selective attention: "This single low test grade outweighs all my other positive scores put together."
>
> Personalization: "He's rejecting me. I must be a terrible failure."
>
> Polarized thinking: "I have to be either totally good, or I'm totally bad."
>
> Overgeneralization: "I can never do anything right. Locking my keys in the car today just proves it."

Insight into the underlying reasons for our negative self-talk (such as parental conditioning) coupled with cognitive restructuring can help turn self-talk into a positive tool rather than a negative habit.

SEPTUAGINT

A Greek translation of the Hebrew Old Testament. It represented the first attempt to translate the Hebrew Scriptures of the Old Testament into another language and was accomplished in the Egyptian city of Alexandria by seventy or seventy-two elders, according to tradition. LXX (meaning the Septuagint) is an abbreviation representing the numeral 70.) Ultimately the Christian church in Alexandria began using the Alexandrian Septuagint, and Christian scholars still utilize it as an important resource for studying the Old Testament today.

TYPE A

Commonly associated with the obsessive-compulsive personality, Type A generally refers to a cluster of traits representing a person of high energy and intense activity. Type A personalities are prone to cardiac and other health risks; sometimes they are described as having "hurry sickness."

Coupled with the tendency to rush through almost everything in life, Type A's frequently exhibit symptoms of underlying anger. The combination of those stress-inducing tendencies make Type A's a high risk for burnout.